GUARDING
DIANA

Inspector Ken Wharfe, MVO, was personal protection officer to the late Diana, Princess of Wales, in charge of round-the-clock security at home and abroad, from 1987 until 1993. He retired from the Metropolitan Police in 2002, after thirty-five years' service, nearly half of it in royalty protection, and on his retirement, was appointed a Member of the Royal Victorian Order, an honour in the Sovereign's personal gift. His memoir of his service with the late Princess, *Diana: Closely Guarded Secret*, co-written with Robert Jobson, was a bestseller on its first publication and again when it was reissued in a revised edition in 2016. He remains in demand both as a speaker and as a commentator on royal security.

Robert Jobson is a leading royal commentator and writer dubbed the 'Godfather of Royal Reporting' by the *Wall Street Journal*. He is Royal Editor of the *London Evening Standard*, Australia's Channel 7 shows *Sunrise* and *The Morning Show*, as well as royal commentator for ABC and *Good Morning America*. In the UK he is a regular on BBC, ITV and Sky News. A bestselling author and award-winning correspondent, he has been at the forefront of royal reporting for nearly twenty-five years.

'LIFE IS JUST A JOURNEY' –
DIANA, PRINCESS OF WALES, 1961–97

GUARDING
DIANA

PROTECTING THE PRINCESS
AROUND THE WORLD

KEN WHARFE, MVO
WITH ROBERT JOBSON

JOHN BLAKE

Published by John Blake Publishing,
3 Bramber Court, 2 Bramber Road,
London W14 9PB, England

www.johnblakebooks.com

www.facebook.com/johnblakebooks
twitter.com/jblakebooks

First published in hardback in 2017

Parts of this narrative were first published in the authors' earlier book,
Diana: Closely Guarded Secret (2002)

ISBN: 978-1-78606-388-5

The right of Ken Wharfe and Robert Jobson to be identified as the authors
of this work has been asserted by them in accordance with the Copyright, Designs
and Patents Act 1988.

Papers used by John Blake Publishing are natural, recyclable products made
from wood grown in sustainable forests. The manufacturing processes conform to
the environmental regulations of the country of origin.

Every attempt has been made to contact the relevant copyright-holders, but some
were unobtainable. We would be grateful if the appropriate people could contact us.

John Blake Publishing is an imprint of Bonnier Publishing

www.bonnierpublishing.com

For Deborah

CONTENTS

INTRODUCTION

'I don't envy you, Ken, looking after my two sons, they can be a bloody nuisance.' This was the first thing Diana, Princess of Wales, said to me – a typical icebreaker. She had a natural nobility and charm that immediately put you at your ease and there were certainly no airs and graces about her. It was November of 1986 at Sandringham House, Her Majesty Queen Elizabeth II's much-loved country retreat in the county of Norfolk, the private home of four generations of British monarchs. The Princess was staying there for a shooting weekend hosted by her then husband, His Royal Highness the Prince of Wales.

It was a courtesy call as I had already been appointed to the job. After all, she was not about to be my boss – that would still be the Commissioner of the Metropolitan Police Force, back then Sir Kenneth Newman. Whatever the outcome of our meeting, my appointment as a royalty protection officer was made by Scotland Yard, not by the Queen or the Royal Family. Our first meeting followed a series of training modules following my selection as an officer in the department initially encouraged by the Queen's policeman, Superintendent Jim Beaton, when he was my supervising officer at Kensington Police Station. My position was to be the personal protection officer (PPO) to Diana's young sons, Prince William and Prince Harry. (At this time I was appointed only to the young Princes – only six months later did I transfer to Diana.) Our meeting was my formal introduction to a member of the Royal Family and I knew it would certainly help our working relationship if we had chemistry or at least a rapport between us, so I was feeling a little apprehensive.

From that moment on there was never a dull day working alongside the Princess, her two sons and the Royal Family. I was in charge of her security, at home and abroad, during one of the most traumatic periods of her life until the end of 1993. Diana was not always easy, but to be fair, who is? Most of the time, however, she was a joy to work with – engaging, funny and someone who possessed a wicked sense of humour. It was my job as personal protection officer with Scotland Yard's elite SO14 Department (Specialist Operations) to look after her as she went about her daily life. I was effectively her security shadow, her eyes and ears, at her side to protect her, should anyone for whatever reason try to do her harm.

Royalty Protection was a special department of the Metropolitan Police Force that I would serve for a total of sixteen years, most of them in charge of the team of elite officers who watched over Diana and her two sons. The role heading up her security detail meant I had to deal with her more sensitive private engagements and public appearances, her official foreign trips and her private holidays. It was not only my job to keep her safe, but to facilitate her daily activities – both public and private – in what was to be an all-too-short but extraordinary life. We travelled the world together and over time I became one of her most trusted confidants. The nature of my job meant I was party to detailed information others in her team – even her most senior courtiers and domestic servants – did not have.

In 2002, five years after Diana's death, I penned a memoir about my time serving as the Princess's PPO, the international bestseller *Diana: Closely Guarded Secret*. It is fair to say the book created a global media sensation. The British Establishment, including some sections of the UK press egged on by key figures in the old order, vilified me for what it claimed was a breach of trust. It didn't seem to bother them that royals, prime ministers, ambassadors and even former commissioners of the Metropolitan Police Force have all published their books. Even the former Director General of MI5, Dame Stella Rimington, published her autobiography, *Open Secret*, a month after my tome hit the shelves. The reality was that the cronies surrounding the Royal Family didn't like me telling the truth because it didn't marry with their preferred version of history and what *they* wanted the public to believe. But I took the criticism on the chin because I knew what I had published was the truth and portrayed the Princess as she was and in a positive light, true to life. My account was not a sugar-coated portrait either, it was an honest portrayal.

At that time Palace spin doctors were busy rewriting their version of the Charles and Diana story in the aftermath of her life, with the Princess as the deranged villain of the piece and the Prince of Wales – the blood Royal, after all – as the wronged party. It was all part of a carefully crafted plan to ensure his long-term mistress, Camilla Parker Bowles, would be accepted by the public as his wife and later as Queen Consort. In the press, at the time, Diana was denigrated, dismissed as mad, bad or both. I took the flak as I felt I was right to put the record straight for the sake of historical accuracy, but more importantly for the memory of the woman I knew to be a profoundly good, honest and decent human being. She wasn't perfect. However, she did her best to be a good wife and mother and to serve the Queen and the institution she married into.

Ultimately, my original memoir, in the opinion of respected historians and royal commentators, helped change the view of Diana, Princess of Wales. Leading historian Dr David Starkey backed the book, saying, 'This is history, since Ken Wharfe was there.' Almost overnight it became a *New York Times* and *Sunday Times* runaway bestseller and has had four editions, and was often quoted as source material in books that followed. It stood the test of time because it was true and in so doing silenced the detractors.

This book, however, is different. It focuses on the exciting, colourful foreign visits Diana and I enjoyed when working together. In *Diana: Closely Guarded Secret* I have chronicled the circumstances of the Princess's untimely death in detail. For the record, in brief, it is my professional opinion, based on studying the subject in detail with a policeman's eye and with my inside knowledge of the woman, that Diana was not murdered. I believe all the evidence points to the fact that she died in a tragic accident – it is as plain and simple as that.

It seems wrong to me that after two exhaustive police investigations and a multi-million pound taxpayer-funded inquest that conspiracy theories still abound. So-called revelations that the SAS or rogue spooks were involved in the Princess's death will be categorically dismissed over time. To me it seems ridiculous that these theories are still given credence. Too many conspiracy theories have hijacked Diana's life achievements, and some of the claims have been downright tasteless, too. On Twitter I was even bizarrely accused of being part of some cover-up conspiracy for voicing this view. No, if there were a shred of evidence to show that Diana was murdered, then, like anyone, particularly a former policeman who served to protect her, I would absolutely want to expose it. But there is no evidence at all that she was. Her sons, whose views are surely the most important and telling, have said that they accept the findings of the inquest held in London in 2008. It is time we all did the same, or at least adhered to their wishes. Diana's death was due to the driver Henri Paul's grossly negligent driving under the influence of alcohol (he was not rolling drunk, but he had been drinking and was over the legal blood/alcohol limit), and the chasing foreign photographers who inflamed the situation. That is the truth.

So much has been written about the death of the Princess, twenty years ago in 2017, that the many achievements of her life are sometimes forgotten. So much has changed, too, in the Royal landscape. Her oldest son, HRH Prince William, Duke of Cambridge, has married his university sweetheart, Kate Middleton, and has a young family of his own. Sadly, Diana never lived to see Prince George and Princess Charlotte at play. Prince Harry has also made great strides in continuing the legacy of his late mother with his charity work. They are both a credit to her memory.

In January 2017 it was announced that the Duke of Cambridge and Prince Harry, twenty years after their mother's death, have commissioned a statue of her. The memorial will be erected in the public grounds of the Princess's former residence, Kensington Palace.

'It has been 20 years since our mother's death and the time is right to recognize her positive impact in the UK and around the world with a permanent statue. Our mother touched so many lives. We hope the statue will help all those who visit Kensington Palace to reflect on her life and her legacy,' the Princes said in a statement released by Kensington Palace.

The statue will be the fourth London-based monument dedicated to Diana and will be positioned close to the Diana, Princess of Wales Memorial Fountain in Hyde Park and the memorial garden close to Kensington Palace. In my view it is right and fitting that it will be erected as a positive tribute to her life. About time too – it seems incredible to me that it has taken so long. After all, Diana was named third Greatest Briton in the BBC's Top 100 in 2002 – yet there was no permanent memorial to her apart from the fountain in Hyde Park. The No. 1 entry, Sir Winston Churchill, has had a statue in the shadow of Parliament since 1973. William and Harry, for so long quiet in public about their mother, have begun opening up about the great personal loss and anger they felt. Indeed, William has said he felt 'very angry' and unable to talk about it for years.

William and Harry were just children back in the 1980s and 1990s when Diana was one of the world's most famous women. A giant force for good, she was the embodiment of compassion, glamour and duty and a great servant to the UK. Since then, I feel passionately that far too much has been made of the circumstances surrounding her death and not enough about what she actually did to change the lives of others for the better. Diana was a champion for those with HIV/AIDS, breaking down the stigma by holding the hand of a dying AIDS victim in an East London hospital as he called on the world not to be complacent about HIV. She comforted children in the Third World, victims of leprosy, poverty and those left homeless. She also made regular private visits to sick children in London's Great Ormond Street Hospital. Diana on a number of occasions took William to The Passage Day Centre in Victoria, a Roman Catholic charity for the homeless, privately with no media present. And towards the end of her short life she even courted controversy by becoming the anti-landmines activists' most visible advocate. Amid the conspiracy theories that surrounded her death, her achievements have often been lost; her real sense of public duty distorted.

Diana may still be a controversial figure who inspires a wide range of conflicting views, but as someone who knew her well, and was at her side as she tirelessly tried to change the lives of people for the better, it seems wrong that we have waited so long for a statue of her.

INTRODUCTION

Harry's work with the charity Sentebale, which supports orphans and vulnerable children, many of them affected by the HIV/AIDS epidemic, together with William's work with Centrepoint, an organisation that gives homeless young people a future, shows a determination on the Princes' part to continue Diana's legacy of compassion and kindness. And when her statue is unveiled twenty years after her death it will be not only a moment for reflection, but also a time for celebration of a great life.

In this, my second memoir, my aim was to develop the story of my time with Diana, I hope with all the humour, allowing me to share the fun-loving Royal that I knew and worked alongside. I hope the reader may be transported back in time to those cherished moments I shared with the Princess as we travelled the world, by new anecdotes and fresh stories.

Of course my remit as Diana's PPO was not just restricted to flying around the world. Together we undertook hundreds of engagements covering the length and breadth of Britain too. My role meant that Diana trusted me to carry out reconnaissance (known as recces) for private holidays as well as official visits on behalf of the Foreign and Commonwealth Office. Such visits were very distinct. On official visits I was her lead security detail, part of a large royal entourage that included private secretaries, equerries, personal assistants, press officers, hairdressers and even a chef. On private trips, however, it was often just my small team, the Princess, her two sons and me.

This book takes a new look at the official and unofficial visits, the amazing places we went to, and the extraordinary people Diana met. Twenty years after her tragic death in Paris I hope it will shed light on the picture of Diana, Princess of Wales. After all, the truth can so easily be, and is so often, blurred by myth and the haze of speculation by those who, unlike me, were not there to see what actually happened.

I would like to thank my publisher, the indomitable John Blake, who persuaded me at a convivial lunch at Langan's Brasserie in Mayfair that the twentieth anniversary of the death of the late Princess was a fitting time to publish a new and reflective account of my travels with her. He joked that every time we met up, I had a new story with which to regale the table and so I should put pen to paper again. My thanks too to my co-author and good friend Robert Jobson for using his considerable professional skills to help me expand upon my unique experiences and tell my story. I would also like to thank Toby Buchan, executive editor at John Blake Publishing, who along with Robert worked tirelessly on the original memoir, *Diana: Closely Guarded Secret*, as well as this, my latest work. I truly appreciate Toby's professionalism, friendship, generous support and belief in the project over the course of many years. Lastly, I would like to thank my partner, Deborah, for her love and unstinting support throughout this project, and much more beyond.

KEN WHARFE, MVO
August 2017

October 1990

She was a woman who simply oozed style. As she stepped
gracefully from a British Airways Concorde no one could
fail to notice that this woman was very, very special indeed. But
it wasn't her outfit, whether the finest haute couture or a casual
blouse and jeans, but the way she carried herself: she had real
presence. As a public figure she embodied glamour, intrigue, duty,
frailty and mystery in what proved an irresistible combination.
During our three-hour-thirty-minute transatlantic flight from
Washington Dulles International Airport to London's Heathrow
she had scarcely been able to keep still in her allocated seat (1A).
But it wasn't the fact that we were eleven miles up and flying at
the edge of space in the layers between the stratosphere and the
ionosphere that excited her. Her head was abuzz with new ideas; she
was exhilarated, childlike, about what was next in her life's journey.

'I'm going to spread my wings, Ken,' she told me. 'They won't
stop me, nobody will stop me.'

There was a steely determination in her voice, a renewed spirit.

Having listened to her hopes, fears and dreams in countless private conversations, I had no doubt about the identity of the 'they' she was referring to with such disdain. Her venom was directed in particular at her husband, the future King, His Royal Highness the Prince of Wales.

At that moment in time Diana, Princess of Wales was the most famous woman in the world, on first-name terms (at least in their eyes) with millions upon millions of people she had never even met. But that didn't matter to them because she was 'their princess', their 'Lady Di', their 'Princess of Wales'. Wherever she went in the world, she was adored. Complete strangers would tell her on first meeting how beautiful she was, or how soft her hands were, or what amazing eyes she had. They would share their deepest troubles, open up about their losses or afflictions. She was much more than a celebrity passing through. Indeed, many felt they shared a profound, almost spiritual connection with her. To those, like me, charged with keeping her safe, she was simply 'The Boss' – with the security code-name *Purple Five Two*.

I alighted from the aircraft just a few steps behind her, although no one noticed me. Why would they? I was simply her security detail, another suit in her shadow. We on her team didn't wear dark glasses or have a communication wire protruding conspicuously from one of our ears, unlike our American counterparts in the Secret Service charged with guarding the US President. Our firearms, a Glock 9mm semi-automatic pistol in my case, were discreetly out of sight – mine was holstered in the small of my back. But as she brushed past the crowds all eyes darted towards her athletic frame and beautifully coiffured hair almost in disbelief. Then would come the whispers, her name uttered in hushed tones. Accustomed to it, she dealt with the murmurings with a knowing, self-effacing smile, a little puff of the cheeks and tilting her head slightly, coyly, as she made eye contact. Her striking, piercing blue eyes could win almost anyone over.

I had sat next to her on the flight and she had talked non-stop about her AIDS charity mission to America. The Princess had opened her visit at Grandma's House – a home for children with HIV/AIDS, in DC. All those being cared for were expected to die before they were teenagers. Instinctively, she reached out to a three-year-old girl and held her in her arms. She was always a mother first, royalty second. A particularly moving visit, it had left a deep impact on Diana and those of us who were there. But that picture had been splashed across the front pages of newspapers around the world the next day.

The previous year Diana had dedicated herself to erasing the stigma surrounding HIV and AIDS and memorably held gloveless hands with patients. At the time many still believed the disease could be contracted through casual contact; in one moment of compassion she had changed the world's perception of AIDS. It is a legacy her son Prince Harry proudly champions to this day, never failing to acknowledge her groundbreaking and courageous works in this field.

On the same visit, 4 October 1990, the Princess had wowed the rich and powerful at a Royal Gala Evening to Benefit the London City Ballet at Washington's Department of Commerce, wearing a stunning full-length scarlet Victor Edelstein gown. Always more than a member of the British Royal Family, Diana was a solo performer, at ease and accepted as the star attraction among some of the most powerful people in the most powerful capital on the planet. As we left, the flashguns of photographers waiting outside startled her.

'They are too bright, I can't see where I'm going,' the Princess complained as we stood at the top of the sweeping staircase. Velvet ropes slung between stanchions controlled by two liveried footmen had been used to ease her passage through the packed reception, where the great and the good of America's capital had paid a small fortune just to be in the same room as her. Now she had to negotiate the grand staircase to reach street level – and she didn't want to do so in an ungainly tangle of scarlet silk and scattered diamonds.

'Ken, I'm serious! You're going to have to hold my arm. I'm sorry but I can't see a thing for those camera flashlights. I don't think I'm going to get down these stairs in one piece,' she said anxiously.

'Don't worry, Ma'am,' I told her as I slipped my hand under her arm.

My American colleague, Lanny Bernier of the US State Department security detail, rushed forward to whisper in her ear, 'Ma'am, can I hold your other arm?'

She turned to smile at me because no other security officer had ever asked her such a thing before, but clearly she was excited and thought it amusing that she should be almost lifted to her waiting limousine.

'Oh boys, that was fun,' she whispered when we reached the waiting vehicle. Then she turned to Bernier and said, 'Thank you so much,' the direct look and warm smile immediately gaining her another conquest. I then introduced them formally. Clearly smitten, Lanny turned to her and said, 'Ma'am, may I tell you something?'

'Yes, Lanny,' she replied.

'Can I say, don't let anyone say you don't look great – you're looking great,' he said in his American drawl.

Though a little taken aback at the compliment from this burly officer, Diana answered him with another winning smile.

'Oh, he's so sweet,' she murmured as we drove away.

The following day, I was in front of the White House with Lanny, arranging the departure for our next engagement. Stepping out from the White House doors, Diana smiled and beckoned him to her with almost a dance routine and Lanny was swiftly standing by her side. As they talked and laughed there was clearly chemistry between them and it was amusing to observe it. Then, out of the blue, Diana handed him a signed photograph of herself. He was bowled over and couldn't believe it.

Turning to me, Lanny said, 'This is just amazing, and thanks so much.'

I gave him a wry smile, somewhat irked at having worked with the Princess for years and not received a single thing.

'You turn up for less than a day, carry her down a flight of stairs and get a Royal present!' I teased.

White House staff assembled on the steps joined us in a frenzy of laughter – it was a great start to the day.

I should have guessed that Lanny would steal the show – he was quite a character. A few weeks earlier, I had arranged a recce visit to Washington ahead of Diana's trip to go through the visit with police and US State Department officials. I had been in touch with Lanny by phone during this process. Every time I had tried to pin him down as to where we should meet, and every time he simply said it wasn't a problem. Just before I set off, I tried one more time. 'It's not a problem, Ken – just have a safe flight and a good day,' he told me. The phone line then went dead.

I arrived at Dulles International Airport half-expecting him to meet me where the cab drivers gather as I came through customs. But there was no Lanny so I continued through the airport, passing several ornamental bay trees in huge terracotta pots, when suddenly, leaning against one of them, there was a man dressed in an ankle-length camel-coloured raincoat with upturned collar, and wearing a smart pair of designer shades. Out of his left ear and then hidden behind his upturned collar was a spiralling length of plastic. It was like a scene from a gangster movie. So, was he my contact? Was this Lanny?

I moved slowly towards him and in my polite English accent said, 'Excuse me, would you be Lanny Bernier, by any chance?' As his head turned and he removed what had now turned out to be a pair of expensive Versace sunglasses, our eyes met and he said, 'Hey Ken, I told you, you wouldn't have a problem.'

Lanny, like a figure from central casting, lived and played out this role as an agent of the US State Department with aplomb. It was a part he played to perfection when Diana arrived and it clearly amused her. That said, he was a top professional too.

During the visit Diana had been equally blown away by the way Barbara Bush, then First Lady and wife of George H.W. Bush, forty-first President of the United States, had been so generous in her support. They met at the White House for tea and really hit it off; she was for that moment at least Diana's new BF (best friend). 'We shared a genuine chemistry,' the Princess insisted. I nodded, not wishing to disabuse her, but I couldn't help but think that Mrs Bush, matriarch of a political dynasty, was perhaps the more accomplished political player, coming from a family that would boast two US presidents.

Mrs Bush had led us around the White House but during the tour the First Lady somehow lost her way and we emerged through a door to find a crowd of shocked tourists queuing for tickets on the other side. When we finally sat down for tea and cake the Princess seemed to know instantly that Mrs Bush would be a future ally in her fight against AIDS.

Indeed, the most powerful man on the planet at the time seemed on side too. He even delayed an official meeting so that he could join his wife and the Princess for fifteen minutes of the thirty-five-minute meeting before an aide interrupted to inform him that the Joint Chiefs were ready for him. Mr Bush stood up and drew a laugh from Diana when he said, 'Guess I'd better go and save the world!' The President's decision to interrupt his busy schedule to spend some time with Diana had clearly impressed her. Afterwards he praised her for her work with young AIDS victims. 'Tread carefully, Diana,' I said inside my head, though I said nothing aloud.

What would be the point in upsetting the Princess? If the President and his wife were happy to offer support, why should I express my doubts?

Back then Diana, who so often rolled with her highs and lows, was on top of the world again. Her marriage to His Royal Highness the Prince of Wales, direct heir to the British throne, might have been in meltdown, but the world didn't know that and the Princess, at that particular time, was determined to turn her personal crisis to her advantage. She knew she commanded great power – she had the media in her pocket and she was gaining confidence as a solo performer. Buoyed by her apparent success on the world stage as an independent or semi-detached Royal, she was now ready to use that power. At long last the Princess truly believed that she mattered and that she could make a significant difference in her own right.

In a tone that left no doubt about her intentions, she said of the Palace, 'They cannot stop me now, Ken,' each word a little louder as the supersonic jet whisked us and another ninety-eight passengers, all paying over £4,000 a seat, across the Atlantic Ocean at a speed greater than that of many rifle bullets.

'No, Ma'am,' I murmured. And then, turning to the Royals themselves, she added, 'That fucking family can just go to hell!' raising her voice just a little more. She could see I was increasingly uncomfortable with her indiscretion, concerned this instantly recognisable woman would be overheard, and it amused her. Without actually saying anything, I suggested she should lower her voice (using a raised eyebrow and a nod) – after all, Concorde's narrow tube interior was not exactly the height of sophistication, in fact it was decidedly cramped. But Diana was not overly concerned about the flapping ears of millionaire businessmen. She had a glass of vintage 'bubbles' – Krug Clos du Mesnil champagne – in her hand, which always made her more outspoken. (She was never a big drinker, it did not agree with her.) When she was in this kind of mood it was best to let her get on with it, I often thought. But I was saved by a tannoy announcement – even a princess shuts up when a Concorde captain speaks.

'Ladies and gentlemen, this is your captain speaking. Thank you for travelling aboard this British Airways Concorde. We will shortly be arriving at our destination, London Heathrow Airport. Could you please ensure your seat belts are fastened. Our flight time will have been three hours and twenty-five minutes of which two hours and fifty minutes was supersonic. I trust you had a very pleasant flight.'

At this I let out a gentle chuckle. This certainly wasn't a bad job, flying at twice the speed of sound with one of the most famous women on the planet. It was certainly better than directing traffic, as they say – although in my policing career I had done very little of that.

August 1988:
PALMA, MALLORCA

The year 1988 was certainly a year to remember. After eight years and 1.5 million dead, the Iran-Iraq War ended. An earthquake in Armenia claimed the lives of 60,000 souls. A Libyan terrorist bomb exploded on a Pan Am jet over Lockerbie in Scotland on 21 December, killing all 259 on board and 11 on the ground. The Special Air Service (SAS) caused a political storm when they shot dead three suspected IRA bombers in Gibraltar. The English pound note ceased to be legal tender and sprinter Ben Johnson won the coveted 100 metres gold at the Seoul Olympics, only to be declared a cheat and disqualified for taking the anabolic steroid Stanozolol. Yazz and the Plastic Population's hit 'The Only Way Is Up' was No. 1 in the UK hit parade, and Diana, Princess of Wales was at the peak of her fame. It was also the year that I had my first taste of what it was like to travel abroad with one of the most famous women in the world.

In August of that year I was assigned to accompany the Princess on the annual family holiday to Palma, Mallorca, with the Prince of Wales and their two young sons, William and Harry, at the invitation of King Juan Carlos of Spain. It was a trip that proved a defining moment in my relationship with Diana. Given that Prince Charles and his family were staying in the King's summer home, the Marivent Palace, complete with all his security already in place, it transpired that there was not enough room (and really no need) for me to stay in the Palace too. Instead I was billeted at the Nixe Palace, a five-star beachfront hotel close to the heart of Mallorca's primary city, Palma, and a short walk from the King's Palace. Directly opposite the hotel was a rundown English pub, which couldn't be a starker contrast to the opulent royal surroundings. Every night my sleep was broken by the shouts of rowdy, drunken British holidaymakers, who, it seemed, were hell-bent on making as much noise and trouble as possible. Sleep proved tricky.

I would make daily visits to the Royal Palace near Cala Major but Charles's personal protection officer, Superintendent Colin Trimming, was there so he took charge. The Royals were on holiday and unless the schedule changed, they were safe behind the high walls of the beautiful palace.

Truly a magnificent setting, it was originally known as Saridakis Palace after the Greek-Egyptian landscape painter John Saridakis. A friend and compatriot of Aristotle Onassis, Saridakis was a wealthy art collector too and had it built when he moved to the island in 1923. It was a stunning residence, with traditional Mallorcan and Italian influences, and contained hundreds of art antiques and a wonderful library of more than 2,000 books. After Saridakis's death in 1963 the Palace and its contents were gifted to the Spanish government to be used as a museum but when the Spanish dictator General Francisco Franco died in 1975, it was arranged that the newly installed Spanish Royal Family could use it as their holiday home. (The Saridakis family legally contested the arrangement in

1978 and insisted on the contents being returned. A ten-year court battle ensued before a settlement was finally reached.)

The weather that August was sensational. Every morning I was greeted by beautiful blue skies and it was not long before I was bathed in 29°C (85°F) temperatures. As I sat outside, looking out over the Balearic Islands archipelago of Spain in the western Mediterranean Sea, sipping my fresh orange juice over breakfast, I couldn't help but think how lucky I was. My career, I thought, had taken a definite turn for the better.

Most mornings, the Prince of Wales and King Juan Carlos would be up early to head off on the King's luxury bulletproof 136-foot yacht, *Fortuna* (he sold it for £6.6 million in 2014), leaving Diana to her own devices during the day. (On this particular day the boys accompanied their father on the King's yacht.) On one of her free days the Princess telephoned me personally and asked me to come and meet her at the Marivent Palace as she wanted to talk to me. I arrived at the gates, not quite sure if I had done something wrong or not. A Spanish sentry on guard who must have been told to expect me gestured for me to proceed into the complex. A second or two later, an immaculately attired Spanish royal official, clad in a dark uniform of heavy cloth clearly unsuited to the warm climate, arrived and then escorted me to the pool area, where the Princess of Wales was waiting alone. She got up from the sunbed where she had been relaxing to greet me. It was quiet, no one else was present and I really didn't know what to expect. She gestured for me to sit down on the chair next to her by the pool.

'It is so good of you to come,' she said, adding, 'I am so sorry I dragged you away.'

I took a second to take in the breathtaking views from the Palace's privileged position on the headland next to Cala Major. Then, the pleasantries over, out of the blue, Diana opened up about the terrible state of her marriage to the Prince of Wales. It was a total sham, she said, and she thought it important that I knew.

'I do feel extremely isolated, more than ever now. I am continuously misunderstood by those around me, and that upsets me,' she told me. It was a theme she would return to time and again during the years we worked together.

The Princess then went on to share secrets about her private life. She even explained that she enjoyed a 'close friendship' with a Life Guards officer, James Hewitt. I listened, just listened – it wasn't for me to sit in judgement. This was perhaps the most crucial moment in my burgeoning relationship with her. It was the moment she showed that she was placing her trust in me.

Of course the Royal Court is full of gossip and intrigue and like everyone working in that environment, I had heard the whispers about Charles and Diana's broken marriage. This was different, however, as it was coming straight from the horse's mouth. After about twenty minutes I tried to lighten the mood, but she would continue, determined to offload. Again, occasionally I would pitch in with another joke and the discussion would then be broken by the sound of her laughter. Within seconds, however, she would turn serious again.

'After Harry was born, our marriage just died. It was over before then, if I'm honest,' she went on. There was genuine sadness in her brilliant blue eyes, but although my heart went out to her, I completely understood how she felt, and despite my genuine concerns, there was little I could do but listen, if the opportunity arose, and reassure her. For now, I simply nodded and said nothing.

'What could I do?' she continued. 'I tried, I honestly tried, but he just did not want me. He just wanted her, always her. Do you know, I don't think I ever stood a chance.'

It did not take a policeman to understand that the 'he' referred to the Prince of Wales and the 'her' to his mistress, Camilla Parker Bowles.

Now and again Diana, wearing a bright orange bikini, would

lean back on her sunbed and run her fingers through her blonde hair as she soaked up the sun. Still learning the ropes of the job, I was surprised at her frankness and her informality. As our working relationship evolved over the coming years such intimacy would become commonplace but this poolside conversation was very early on in my time with her. Its importance lay in the fact that this was the first time that the Princess had confided in me, revealing the dark clouds looming in her life. At the time I felt a little uncomfortable as she spoke of her troubles, I must admit. Such familiarity between us, though, was soon to become the norm.

Diana's sad description of her failed marriage was in complete contrast to the one that the Palace officials were presenting to the press. Buckingham Palace was in fact part of a widespread conspiracy to deceive the press and the people. It was only a matter of time, I thought, before this precariously balanced stack of cards came crashing down.

Just days earlier, at the start of the holiday on 13 August, Diana, wearing a smart white blouse and orange skirt, had emerged from the Palace holding her sons' hands for a posed 'happy family' photocall with her husband and their host, the King of Spain, and his family. It had all been a 'sham', she insisted. Our conversation suddenly switched. It was just as awkward for me as she turned her attention again to her personal unhappiness. She explained that she had only agreed to accompany her husband to Mallorca in an attempt to put on a 'good show' in public. Above all, she said, she wanted happiness and security for her sons, and she knew that to achieve this the boys needed a stable life that included both their parents. After all, she was from a broken home herself, she reminded me. She was being completely open with me.

'You know, I don't go out of my way to be awkward but my husband just makes things impossible, totally impossible. I used to blame myself, even to hate myself. I used to think it was my fault, that

I was not good enough. Nobody ever praised me, can you believe it? After all I've done. I am an outsider and always will be,' she said.

As she spoke, Diana began to paint a picture of demoralising isolation and marital rejection. As previously mentioned I had had some idea that the Royal marriage was not in a good place – no one in her ambit, or the Prince's, could fail to know from the whispers at court – but I found it disturbing that she was prepared to talk so openly about it with me. I was not even employed by her, or the Royal Family, but by Scotland Yard. Either she was desperately short of sympathetic listeners, or she felt that she simply had to confide in someone she trusted, however new to her circle. In the same quiet, almost emotionless voice, she went on to explain that the gulf between her and Prince Charles was now so wide that nothing could bridge it. Her marriage was effectively over.

Loving a man who did not love her in return – and worse still, loved somebody else who predated the marriage – was tearing her apart. Of course I felt sorry for her, but who was I to advise or guide her? Was she expecting me to counsel her? This was dangerous territory. Instinct told me that all she really wanted was someone to listen to her, not at this moment to advise. As she recounted her fears for the future – her own and that of her two sons – the feeling of worthlessness that Prince Charles's overt and unrepentant infidelity with Camilla Parker Bowles engendered in her, and her overwhelming sense of marital claustrophobia, I could sense the weight lifting from her. Just by me listening to her wretched confession, she was somehow finding a moment of peace.

Then, for the first time in my hearing, she spoke what I would come to think of as one of her trademark expressions. 'Nobody understands me,' she said, although I felt I was beginning to do so. And, however self-pitying the remark, I was beginning to think she was right. It is important to view our conversation in perspective. It preceded the publication of Andrew Morton's book, *Diana: Her*

True Story, by four years, and although even then, in 1988, the national press was beginning to question the state of the Prince and Princess's marriage, no one had come close to exposing the reality. But Diana hadn't finished with me yet.

'We have not slept in the same bed for years,' she admitted, not without a touch of embarrassment, for me and for her. As she said this, I could not escape the feeling that, deep down, she believed the estrangement was her fault. Then, long before the rest of the world was to learn how depression had driven her to try to commit suicide (no matter how half-heartedly), she listed the occasions when she had tried to take her own life, and the reasons why: 'It was a cry for help but nobody ever wanted to listen,' she whispered.

As she talked, I had become increasingly aware of the depth of her unhappiness. Yet I remained unsure as to her reasons for confiding in me. Was it a test, a way to see if she could trust me? Was it simply, as I had at first thought, that she needed to tell somebody or else go mad under the emotional and psychological strain? Or did she so desperately need an ally as she faced an indifferent husband, an inimical Palace hierarchy, and the hostile coterie that made up Charles's 'Highgrove set'?

We sat and talked, she repeatedly returning to the core problem – her husband's relationship with Camilla Parker Bowles. She believed that his flagrant, even brutal, disregard for her feelings was a betrayal, the greatest of her young life, and, I have come to believe, that it was one from which she never recovered. She was unable to contain her tears as she recounted her story. There was no vindictiveness in what she said, just a pervading sense of misery.

Despite her palpable beauty, position and wealth it was clear that life had dealt her a cruel hand. I knew, of course, that there are always at least two sides to every story, but even so my heart went out to her and, perhaps against my better judgement, I told her so. I also gently reminded her that she had much to be thankful for,

15

not least two sons of whom she could be immensely proud. At the very mention of their names her sadness seemed to lift and the smile returned, lighting up her face.

'You are so right. I am so lucky – William and Harry, my boys, are so precious, so very precious,' she told me.

Diana's problems and her personal sadness were subjects the two of us would return to repeatedly over the next few years. There would be moments of great happiness, too, for she was not given to self-pity, or at least not for long. On that afternoon in Mallorca I had answered her cry for help (the fact that I had little choice in the matter would not have occurred to her). From then on, she felt she could trust me; in time I hoped she would respect my advice.

Our working relationship, as well as the friendship that developed subsequently, was rooted in the sense of mutual trust that brought us together in the Marivent Palace and I knew that, as a result, I would have a better chance of effectively protecting her from danger, and perhaps even from herself. For if the Princess knew that she could confide in me, no matter how great or how sensitive the secret, then there was no reason for her not to tell me exactly what she was doing or planned to do at all times.

After around an hour Queen Sofía of Spain entered the pool area with her sister-in-law, Queen Anne-Marie, wife of her brother, King Constantine II, the deposed monarch of Greece. I must admit I felt slightly relieved. At this point I tried to excuse myself, but the Queen insisted that I should stay. In an instant Diana's mood switched. Her despondency vanished (or at least, being the consummate actress she was, she was able to mask her personal problems) and she began making polite conversation as if she had no cares of her own.

Moments later, without giving me any warning, she repaid me for my attempts to switch our earlier conversation away from her troubles to my passion for music. Before I knew what was happening, she suggested that I give an impromptu singing performance for the two Queens. I'm sure none of the Royals present really wanted to hear what was to follow. I was flabbergasted when Diana leapt to her feet and announced, 'Ken has a wonderful singing voice. He wants to sing us a song.' Then to me, 'Go on, it would be wonderful if you'd sing for us.'

There was nothing I could do except take a deep breath and sing one of my personal favourites ('Myself When Young' from *The Rubáiyát of Omar Khayyam,* arranged by Lisa Lehmann). Scarlet from the heat, the exertion and the embarrassment, I earned polite applause from my audience, followed by an equally polite call for an encore that I tactfully declined. I said my goodbyes after a little bow. As I walked away, however, I caught Diana's eye, at which she mouthed the words 'Thank you' to me, and smiled.

Making my way back to my hotel room to the sound of cicadas and the rustle of bougainvillea in the warm breeze, I could not help laughing about my mercurial principal. So this is what it is really like to be protection officer to one of the most famous women in the world, I thought.

If nothing else, my solo effort that afternoon brought a result that I could never normally have hoped for. The Princess seemed captivated by my interest in music. She told me that she was fascinated by opera, which she said stirred her emotionally, but admitted she did not fully understand it. Enthused, I spoke of my own passion for the art and that evening gave her a copy of *Understanding Opera*, which she devoured. Moreover, my performance had led her and Queen Sofia into discussing their mutual love of music, and their admiration for the great opera singers. As a result, the Queen invited us to go and see José Carreras perform on the following day, which was the first time the singer had appeared in public since his recovery from leukaemia. The Princess joked that, after listening to my efforts, it would be a real privilege to hear another great tenor. Horrified by this comparison, I pointed out somewhat woodenly that I was actually a bass/baritone.

17

The next day, Saturday, 13 August, the Princess and I, together with Queen Sofia, her sister-in-law, Queen Anne-Marie of Greece, and the Queen's most senior aide Major Requena, flew in the King's private jet to Barcelona, once again leaving Prince Charles behind with William and Harry and the travelling Royal nanny. After landing, our car formed part of a huge convoy, mainly consisting of police, on a manic journey from the airport to a tiny village on the outskirts of Barcelona along an unmade dusty road. Unfortunately the lead car didn't seem to know the way and led the entire convoy to a dead end. We then experienced a reversing nightmare of scores of Mercedes limousines.

Eventually we arrived in the Spanish village. We were escorted to a small terraced house, the home of a friend of the Queen, overlooking a square. In the middle of the square was a grand piano on a raised rostrum. A small invited group of people was seated close to and around it. We stood on the private balcony and were introduced to the wonderful Spanish soprano Montserrat Caballé, a warm and vibrant woman full of charisma and charm. After enjoying a glass of champagne with us, the opera singer took up her position on the rostrum. On that makeshift stage, once the niceties were over, Ms Caballé, whose work became more widely known to the general public after her brilliant rendition of 'Barcelona' with the late Freddie Mercury, lead singer of Queen, performed a series of Puccini arias for around forty minutes. It was exquisite. Diana obviously loved the singing and was entranced by the spontaneity of the moment, alive with anticipation. At the end of the performance the diva joined us at a reception, during which she and the Princess chatted away in English like old friends.

This, as it turned out, was only the beginning. We returned to the cars and the Royal convoy then headed for the magnificent Peralada Castle at Girona, where Diana attended another reception (with me, as usual, never more than a pace or two away). It was here that she first met the England international footballer and now BBC presenter Gary Lineker. At the time he was the top striker for Barcelona, although he was by no means a typical soccer star. He had (and has) considerable natural charm, and the Princess seemed to enjoy flirting with him. Once the reception was over, we walked with Lineker to our seats in the auditorium within the castle precincts, where José Carreras was about to start the recital.

I have never seen a performance so faultless, nor so professional. If the great tenor had any nerves then he did not show them – and this, remember, was his first appearance in public after a long lay-off resulting from his gallant struggle with leukaemia. His performance was truly astounding and the finale left the audience in a frenzy of appreciation. Eventually, he encored 'Granada' five times, the ecstatic crowd showering him with flowers, so that by the end he was knee-deep in rose petals.

After the performance we were escorted to yet another reception, this one held in honour of Carreras. Even without her trademark high heels, Diana towered over him, as she did many of the famous people she met in the course of her royal duties, but his sheer presence commanded the entire room. He exuded a charisma to which she seemed drawn like iron to a magnet. The Princess had obviously studied the book I had given her the night before, determined not to appear ignorant in front of the great man. She asked him several very astute questions about opera and the art of singing it, and told him that she had been thrilled by his performance of 'Granada'.

On the return flight to Palma Diana was elated, bubbling over with enthusiasm for the day's excitements. The gloom of the previous day had dissolved, so that she seemed a completely different person. For someone whose private world was in turmoil and whose life was full of confusion, she was, for a few brief hours, wholly inspired. We got back late and she wanted to take a walk outside the secure confines of the Marivent Palace to see where I was staying. With a

Spanish security detail close by, we walked down to where my hotel was, and viewed with amazement drunken British holidaymakers outside the pub, who were oblivious to who was watching them. We strolled down to the beach before returning to the Palace.

The next day the Spanish security team, who had all to a man fallen in love with the Princess, extended a special invitation to Diana to a police paella party. She gladly accepted and at lunchtime a huge paella – some five feet in diameter – was served up. This was an invitation that Diana should have perhaps refused, but one I knew she would not; her style and her desire to be one of the party made it, for her, too great an opportunity to miss. For the young Princess, the chance to escape the small talk inside the Palace came as a huge relief. Inside the walls of the Palace and now surrounded by the entire protection team, she could not have been safer. I left her to talk and enjoy the moment. William and Harry meanwhile played games with a queue of police/security entertainers.

Immediately Diana was given a large ladle and attacked the sizzling cauldron of Mediterranean cuisine, serving those present. She was in her element, laughing and confident, even practising her limited Spanish – with no shortage of tutors! What her husband and the Spanish Royals were thinking is anyone's guess. One thing is for sure, this was fun outside of the Palace, and a moment she was never going to miss.

On the whole Charles and Diana were civil to each other in front of their sons, who were revelling in the sunshine, and to be fair, spending quality time with the father they adored but who was so often taken from them due to his busy schedule. On a few occasions Diana relented, after William and Harry begged her, agreeing to accompany Juan Carlos and Queen Sofia on the yacht *Fortuna* in search of private beaches on which to spend their afternoons.

I was attached to a clapped-out patrolling Spanish warship as part of the protection – a rusty hulk with a captain who, like his vessel, had seen better days. The vintage skipper had a penchant for vintage Rioja too, and it didn't seem to bother him whether he was at the wheel of the ship or not. His cabin was the only space where the air conditioning seemed to work. With temperatures in excess of 35°C (95°F), his company, or at least his cabin, was welcome. Our role in this circus was to shadow the *Fortuna*, and to keep the smaller press boats, packed with Fleet Street and paparazzi photographers and their long lenses, chugging along behind at bay. The only problem was that the smaller boats easily outpaced our warship, and more often than not we were last on the scene. So while the Royals enjoyed barbecues on idyllic uninhabited sandy coves and beaches and Fleet Street snapped away, getting their shots, I was left playing catch-up with a captain who reeked of booze on a warship unfit for purpose.

With the *Fortuna* anchored ahead we chugged to a discreet distance, and with engines idling, drifted in the Mediterranean. Small rubber dinghies crewed by Spanish security circled our warship. Through my binoculars I could see my team leader, Superintendent Colin Trimming, pretending to be invisible on a deserted beach. At this point, with most of the floating paparazzi in smaller craft easily capable of outmanoeuvring us, I questioned my presence on this ageing Spanish galleon. Signalling to a colleague, I abandoned my captain and went ashore in a rubber dinghy to where the Royal party was having lunch. Diana was quick to see me land, and walked briskly over to meet me, followed by William and Harry, who begged me to take them to 'The Battleship'. This conversation in the presence of my boss, Superintendent Trimming, led to my being ordered to return from whence I had come. I paddled slowly out in the azure water and deliberately fell into the dinghy, which brought laughter from the boys, and Diana too. Colin Trimming was not amused.

JANUARY 1989: NECKER ISLAND, BRITISH VIRGIN ISLANDS

My primary role as Diana's personal protection officer was to keep her safe. On my watch, she remained secure. Part of my role, however, was also to locate suitable holiday sanctuaries, where the Princess and her children could escape away from prying eyes. This was never easy, especially at a time when she was going through the worst personal crisis of her life and when she was hot 'property' to an insatiable media. But although this proved an almost impossible task, it was satisfying when my team of officers and I did achieve it on one or two occasions. We counted them as victories. At that time a set of photographs of a bikini-clad Diana on a beach was worth thousands of pounds to the almost ever-present paparazzi, and these shots were deemed essential to Fleet Street's picture editors and their money-making syndication departments, as well as to the foreign media. Finding and photographing the Princess in the 1980s and 1990s was big business, generating big returns.

Diana's favourite pastime, especially around December, was flicking through upmarket holiday brochures so she could escape the formality of a traditional royal Christmas as a guest of the Queen at Sandringham. She found the experience insufferable and in downtime imagined herself being whisked off to some barefoot luxury setting. She said she always felt suffocated and an outsider whenever she was there, even though it was a stone's throw from where she had been born and raised on the Queen's Norfolk estate at Park House, one of the houses Edward VII had built to accommodate his shooting-party guests. (It was later leased by his son George V to his friend, Lord Fermoy, Diana's grandfather, and the Princess's mother, Frances, was also born there.)

The Princess famously complained to her lover, James Gilbey, in the so-called 'Squidgygate' tapes of 1989, the telephone conversations intercepted and recorded around this time, that the Queen Mother used always to regard her 'with a strange look in her eyes', with a 'sort of interest and pity mixed in one'. But it wasn't her husband's family she really wanted to escape, but Prince Charles himself. At this point in the Royal marriage both had taken lovers – Diana was with Gilbey and Charles with Camilla – and often they were barely on speaking terms. The marriage was in fact by now a total sham, stage-managed for public consumption. Diana hated the charade and had she been anybody else she would have filed for divorce years earlier. It was around then that an exit strategy began to form in her mind: she knew she wanted out, the question was, how?

Previously I had experienced the frenzied chase for the Diana holiday picture when she and Prince Charles had stayed in Mallorca as guests of King Juan Carlos of Spain in the summer of 1988. On that holiday security was fairly straightforward as we had the advantage that the principals we guarded were staying at a royal residence with all the extra security and privacy that afforded them.

Going out on their own, staying in hotels or even privately rented villas, was always going to present a greater challenge for the police team, especially with the relentless royal press corps constantly on our scent.

Having spent another miserable Christmas at the Queen's Sandringham Estate, where, she complained, she had felt 'totally blanked' by the Royal Family, the Princess informed me that she had decided to take up business tycoon Sir Richard Branson's generous offer for her and her boys to see in the New Year of 1989 on his tiny private island. He had personally guaranteed her privacy. The invitation was not extended to the Prince of Wales, for the Princess had made it very clear he was not in her plans. He diplomatically told his sons that he had elected to stay at Sandringham while his wife was telling staff what to pack for their exclusive sunshine break – she could not wait to get away.

According to the sales blurb issued to those lucky enough to stay there, Necker Island isn't pretty, it's 'enchanting', and its millionaire – if not billionaire – guests don't come for a holiday, but to 'rejuvenate mind, body and spirit'. Branson visited the island in the late 1970s, and bought it for roughly £200,000 ($306,000) in the 1980s, at which time it was not much more than a mosquito-infested atoll. Many of the world's celebrities, including Barack Obama, Kate Winslet, Ronnie Wood, Kate Middleton in 2007 following a short break from her relationship with Prince William, and Prince Harry in 2012, have stayed on this tiny speck in the British Virgin Islands, which its owner proudly boasts is unlike any other holiday destination in the world (and at somewhere in the region of £34,300 [$42,000] for seven days in 1989, telephone calls not included, one would hope not!). Necker Island has, it seems, magical powers.

For this, the first of our two trips to Necker, the Princess brought her mother, Frances Shand Kydd, her sisters, Lady Sarah

McCorquodale and Lady Jane Fellowes, and their children, five in all, and her own two sons. She had provided herself with a perfect excuse for the trip by saying that she wanted to spend some time with her mother and sisters, but in reality she was desperate to escape the atmosphere at Sandringham. Indeed, as the boat bringing us from nearby Tortola approached Necker, and the island's beautiful white beaches came into view, the entire party seemed to breathe a simultaneous sigh of relief. The boys, alive with anticipation, could not wait to explore.

The unassuming billionaire was there to welcome the Princess and the rest of her party as we stepped on to the island. Back then, nearly thirty years ago (at the time of writing), it would normally have cost around £5,000 per day for the privilege of staying on the island, so Branson's gift of a holiday to Diana was an extremely generous one, even given the inevitable publicity that followed.

Necker was not quite what I had expected. The Great House, the main accommodation, struck me as being a cross between the lobby of a luxury hotel and a Surrey barn conversion. Inside, a snooker table had pride of place beneath a Balinese-style beamed ceiling. There were some stylish touches, like an outdoor claw-foot bathtub, giant beanbags and fridges stuffed with champagne specially produced for Necker Island. For guests for whom being on a private island just isn't private enough, there were separate cottages built in South-East Asian pagoda style, each one equipped with a meditation room, presumably to allow the hugely wealthy to play at being ascetic Buddhist monks. There was also a gym and a swimming pool, as well as four exclusive beaches, with a speedboat and several jet-skis at the guests' disposal.

Not only had Branson refused to accept payment for Diana's quite large party, but he had instructed his staff to spare nothing to make her stay perfect. As an example, a few weeks before we left, one of his assistants had telephoned me and asked what food I liked, my preferred 'colour, region and grape variety' of wine, and whether there were any books or records I particularly wanted. On the island itself, the staff were equally impressive, and obliging to a fault. I am sure that if the Princess had said she wanted freshly caught shark for supper, then one of the staff would have donned a wetsuit and set off to spear one single-handedly!

On the first evening our host held a magnificent lobster barbecue. As soft Caribbean music played and we watched the sun setting, Diana was in paradise. And so too, I have to say, was I.

While Diana and her family sunbathed on the beach and William, Harry and their five cousins romped about, I addressed my first official task, which was to liaise with officers from the local police force and senior officials from the British Virgin Islands. I told them that above all the Princess and her family wanted privacy, and they assured me that they would do their best to secure it, insisting no one would be allowed to sail within a mile of the island's shores. Even without the official back-up, however, Necker was a protection officer's dream. As the Princess and the Royal party wallowed under heavenly blue skies, the rest of the world was kept firmly away. There were no inhabitants on the island – other than the guests – and access was mainly by boat, from Virgin Gorda. Most of the staff came ashore every morning by boat and left each evening after dinner. If anything unexpected were to happen all I had to do was to summon a helicopter from Tortola and we could escape.

Graham Smith, Diana's former PPO, had accompanied her on the first trip, but by January 1990, when we made a second visit, he had been struck down with the throat cancer that eventually killed him, and although in remission, he was no longer fit for protection officer duties. Diana was desperately worried; she had somehow convinced herself that the stress of guarding her had led to Graham's illness. She hoped the holiday would at least help to revive his spirits, and insisted that he came as her guest. Even so

27

Graham was of immense help, and was able to relax and enjoy the comforts that Necker provided. On the first trip to Necker, both Graham and I had jointly headed up security. Although we had been able to keep the flight details secret – for the press couldn't follow if they didn't know where Diana was – I felt certain that the Princess would leak details of our destination. True, she insisted that 'All I want is peace and quiet and to be with my boys,' but I knew that she felt that this was just too good a PR opportunity to overlook.

Sure enough, it was not long before our peace was broken. Scores of press photographers arrived at the airport on Tortola, hungry for pictures of Diana in a bikini. Round one went to the local police, who promptly confiscated a number of cameras as soon as the pressmen arrived. But snatching a few cameras from the least experienced photographers at the airport, and other measures like banning flights over Necker and barring boats within a seven-mile radius of the island, were never going to deter the paparazzi and the elite of Fleet Street's royal correspondents. Within days Diana's haven was besieged by little boats bobbing around on the sea, filled with photographers desperate for pictures. Although some long-lens shots were taken and sent around the world, the effectiveness of the security measures limited the intrusion to grateful sighs from the Royal party and protection officers alike. The following year, 1990, they were back with a vengeance; better equipped and more determined than ever, and with the benefit of what they had learned from the Princess's first trip.

In the years since her death, it seems that Diana has increasingly been written out of history, so it is easy to forget that at the beginning of 1990 hers was the only story that mattered in Fleet Street. Editors, apparently, wanted nothing other than to fill their pages with the latest news of her. Pictures and stories about Diana sold millions of newspapers; circulations soared and that kept journalists and photographers in jobs, which is all that most of them really cared about. The royal reporting teams of the British tabloid press – nicknamed the 'Royal Rat Pack' – were tough and talented journalists. In particular, James Whitaker (who died in 2012) and Kent Gavin of the *Daily Mirror*, and Arthur Edwards and Harry Arnold (died 2014) of *The Sun*, who lived and breathed their work. Yet they were reasonable men, and despite the very different nature of our respective jobs, we tended to get along, and even to enjoy a measure of mutual respect.

MARCH 1989:
UNITED ARAB EMIRATES
AND KUWAIT

When in 1988 Viking Penguin published Salman Rushdie's controversial novel *The Satanic Verses* – portraying Islam as a deceitful, ignorant, and sexually deviant religion – all hell broke loose across the Muslim world. It set off a chain of events that included bookstore bombings, book bans and burnings, as well as accusations of blasphemy. The real low point in what came to be known as 'the Rushdie Affair' was when, in 1989, the Iranian Shiite Muslim religious leader Ayatollah Khomeini issued a fatwa (a ruling on a point of Islamic law) ordering Rushdie's death, forcing the writer into hiding.

It was amid this grave atmosphere and a spate of killings, attempted killings, and bombings arising from Muslim fury over the novel that the same year, in March 1989, the Prince and Princess of Wales were invited to visit the predominantly Muslim Arab states of the Persian Gulf. This promised to be a security challenge. The Prince of Wales's PPO, Superintendent Colin Trimming, took the lead on the Scotland Yard security recce and it was our hosts who 'guaranteed' Charles and Diana's safety, with hundreds of armed police and soldiers drafted in for the visit. Despite the Ayatollah's calls for mass demonstrations the Kuwaitis said they would remove anyone bent on causing trouble from circulation long before the Royals arrival. We received the same assurances from the leaders of the other Gulf States.

The visit itself was pretty standard – meeting ex-pats and joining members of the Royal Families in state dinners and desert picnics. The tour began in Kuwaiti and Charles and Diana stayed in the magnificent As-Salam Palace at Shuwaikh Port as guests of the Kuwaiti government. They enjoyed an audience with the Emir of Kuwait and also had an audience with the Crown Prince and Prime Minister of Kuwait, who hosted a lavish dinner in their honour. The Princess also visited the Kuwait Society for the Handicapped.

Throughout the visit the Prince and Princess remained diplomatically silent about Salman Rushdie, while their hosts treated them to lighter moments such as banquets in the desert and camel racing. It seemed everywhere we went, we were treated to old customs, drums, singing, dancing and having confetti thrown at us continuously. On a personal level Diana and Charles may have been at loggerheads, but on this tour both, when they had a mind to, were consummate actors when it came to royal duty. At one point the Princess even appeared to be flirting with the Prince when she didn't know how to dispose of a date stone until he showed her.

The couple had apparently agreed to put on a public display of togetherness when representing Queen and country on official overseas visits. Diana did her best, wearing bold colours and designs, to get the press writing about her glamorous outfits rather than speculating on the state of her marriage. In Kuwait she revelled in her love of attention and finery, smiling broadly as she posed in a stunningly ornate rich burgundy jalabiya, heavily embroidered with gold sequins, and impressing her hosts as she carried off the look.

From Kuwait the Royal party headed to Abu Dhabi in the United Arab Emirates, rich with its oil revenue, to be greeted by an immaculate royal guard and a double strip of red carpet. In just a few days Diana's fashion sense and warm smile won many hearts. Her favourite designer, Catherine Walker, had been busy ahead of the tour. The Princess wore a hot-pink and red dress for her arrival in Abu Dhabi, its clashing colours and large gold buttons very much style signposts of the 1980s. A peach suit with a flowing calf-length skirt and huge shoulder pads, paired with a single string of pearls and matching pearl earrings, was the outfit of choice for a trip to Emirates University, flanked by Sheikh Nahyan bin Mubarak and Sheikh Tahnoun bin Mohammed. The suit might seem outdated now, but it is worth remembering that this was the eighties, when the emphasis was on power-dressing, boxy suits and shoulder pads inspired by the TV soaps *Dallas* and *Dynasty*; Madonna was topping the charts, capitalism had yet to become a dirty word, and Margaret Thatcher, then Prime Minister and queen of the power-suit-and-pearls look, was running Britain.

Diana gave the so-called power suit a softer touch. At the camel races near Al Ain, she topped her peach suit with a pair of huge white-framed sunglasses and seemed to have relished the spectacle, giggling like a schoolgirl and chatting animatedly with the sheikhs, while her husband adopted the air of an awkward Brit abroad, sunglasses perched precariously on his nose as he grew increasingly hot and bothered in a suit. As the trip progressed, Diana's garb became more lavish: a navy-blue and white silk striped dress for an event at the British Embassy in Abu Dhabi, a light blue chiffon Zandra Rhodes floor-length gown for a reception at the British Consulate in Dubai, the plunging neckline thoughtfully covered with a cream pashmina for her meeting with Sheikh Mohammed, the Crown Prince of Abu Dhabi.

The two seemed completely at ease with one another, laughing as they chatted. One of the most charming pictures shows the welcome Diana received in UAE President Sheikh Zayed's private *majlis* (literally, 'place of sitting') in Al Ain. Sitting cross-legged on low cushions with their distinctive blue and white embroidery, wearing a floral shalwar kameez, her hair slightly tousled, Diana appears completely relaxed. Most endearing was the expression on her face: even the smiling public persona she normally had to adopt for the cameras gave way as she gazed in awe at the astonishing spread laid before her, complete with mounds of rice, an entire sheep and platters of fruit. Charles, sitting awkwardly, joked, 'It is much easier for women as they are double-jointed.' When their host asked why the UK photographers took so many photos, the Prince responded, somewhat disparagingly: 'So at least they can get one good one.'

A smiling Sheikh Zayed greeted the Princess – who suddenly looked a little unsure – with a warm grasp of the hand. They exchanged pleasantries with the help of a translator: Prince Charles joked about the weather in Britain and Sheikh Zayed asked after the health of his mother, Queen Elizabeth. Then the late President turned to the Princess to tell her of his plans to develop an island – Sir Bani Yas – with many gazelles. Sadly, neither Sheikh Zayed nor the Princess lived to see his dream finally come to fruition. Sheikh Zayed died in 2004 aged eighty-six, and one of the richest rulers in the world. By contrast, on a visit to the engineering faculty at Emirates University, hosted by Sheikh Nahyan bin Mubarak, Diana lingered behind her husband, arms crossed defensively, head bowed and a doleful air about her.

In Dubai, Diana was once again on top form. As the doors to the plane flew open, she emerged from the shadowy interior sheathed in a high-waisted, electric-blue skirt and a cropped white jacket with blue lapels. The ensemble was topped by a matching blue disc of a hat, surrounded by a broad white brim pulled so low as she concentrated on each careful step that the face beneath it was hidden from view. Her jaunty-angled brim tipped up to reveal a stylish blue turban beneath it. It was a moment that she knew would get tongues wagging as newspaper editors rushed to put her on the front page – once again showing her innate ability as a fashion trendsetter.

A quick change of clothing and then came a journey into the unknown desert for a special lunch arranged by their hosts. A convoy of 4 x 4s set off. After a bumpy, sandy drive across the undulating landscape we arrived at a small oasis literally in the middle of nowhere. A huge tent covered a stunning array of stacked oriental carpets and brightly coloured cushions. On a low table fruit and flowers edged an extraordinary display of food. Diana's attention was suddenly drawn to two men in Arabic dress digging a hole nearby. With a smile on her face she murmured to one of the hosts, 'Surely not the best place for gardening?' 'No – come quickly,' he replied. 'See, this is the best underground cooker you will ever see.' This diversion was certainly not part of the scripted tour, but nevertheless fascinating in the extreme.

Suddenly from the hole two well-cooked lambs appeared! Diana's laughter turned to shock as she was told of the ancient custom of cooking lambs on a bed of cinders, then burying them until they were ready to eat. Once the lambs were released of their charred coats, the meat was placed on a large wooden platter and carried ceremoniously to the tent. Not a meal for a vegetarian, but the flavour was truly exquisite. Cross-legged on the raised carpets, Diana impressed her hosts with her voracious appetite for the tender meat, while giving a wide berth to the sheeps' eyes that stared at her from a close distance. The Prince of Wales, however, with a love of lamb, sat crossed-legged enjoying this desert feast.

There was no outward sign of Iran's call for demonstrations against the Royal visit despite the large numbers of Iranians living in Dubai at that time. Indeed, there seemed no appetite for demonstrations at all, but our hosts were taking no chances. The white Mercedes we used, loaned by a local chef, was armoured against bombs and bullets. Diana had been well-briefed on respect for cultural sensibilities by her private secretary, Patrick Jephson, and she knew that with the Philip Somerville turban hat that subtly covered her hair and a demure Catherine Walker suit, she did it in the most stylish way possible, mesmerising her hosts, male and female alike.

It was while on an official visit to an all-female event in Dubai that, during an arranged lunch, Diana would meet informally with local women to discuss personal and local issues. My presence was deemed inappropriate, and although I could have insisted that I stayed, I decided that the correct protocol was to allow the Princess the privacy to get on with the job. The organisers, while grateful to me, now seemed more concerned with finding me a place to eat alone. Within minutes I was escorted to a large outside area with lush manicured lawns and plants. While sitting at a single round table and one chair with a parasol I was served a midday banquet by a brigade of waiters. Wading through this Middle Eastern feast, I was aware of laughter, one particular screech immediately identifiable, that of Diana, now waving from a rooftop overlooking my 'table for one' with all her assembled female guests. So the personal protection may have been temporarily suspended, but my one-man show alone in Dubai did bring laughter and a moment of happiness.

This is where Charles and Diana, no matter what the state of their marriage in private, were a brilliant double act, super envoys for Britain. Both had been well tutored on the growing importance of Kuwait, Abu Dhabi and Dubai in global trade and this visit was arranged as a whistle-stop charm offensive. Diana was uniquely adroit at fusing with any environment, instantly putting anyone she met at ease. She looked so calm, so in control, I thought, even though her own life was in turmoil, embroiled in adultery and betrayal. What her Muslim hosts would have made of that behaviour had they been aware of it, who knows?

Whenever there was a photo opportunity, Diana's hosts from the United Arab Emirates wanted to sit next to her and be photographed with her. They were completely absorbed by her and she was absolutely charming to them in return. The Princess, who was making her first and only visit to these states, appeared astounded by everything she saw unfolding around her. In contrast her husband was well respected in the Arab world and had always shown a profound interest and admiration for Islamic culture, art and customs.

Now and again, however, Diana let slip her personal frailties. At odd moments I could see her distress starting to show. To me it was really obvious, but not, perhaps, to the wider world. It must have been so disconcerting for her to have to maintain an effervescent façade, but she was after all by now a consummate performer, seemingly able to cloak her private anguish with the humane public face.

On the last leg of this Gulf tour, in Dubai at a dinner hosted by the Emir, Rashid bin Saeed Al Maktoum, who had reigned for thirty-eight years from 1958 until his death the following year, 1990, Diana was in conversation with the Emir's son, the Crown Prince Maktoum bin Rashid Maktoum. She was talking about her return to the UK that evening. The Prince then asked her what aircraft she owned. Diana, despite being very tired, both physically and emotionally, was able to laugh and say that she did not know what type of aircraft British Airways was laying on, all she knew was that it was coming via Delhi and she had been told it had been delayed. The Prince was clearly baffled by Diana's story, not really believing that she was about to take a scheduled airline flight after being a guest of the Emir.

'A scheduled flight, seriously?' he said.

When Diana confirmed it was so, he was astonished. There then followed a little confusion as the Prince summoned and dismissed a series of genuflecting royal flunkeys, followed by some conspiratorial whispering. Satisfied by the outcome, he then turned to Diana, and said, 'Your Royal Highness, you cannot possibly do that. You must take our Royal plane.'

The Princess's tiredness drained away and there then followed an exchange with her husband, as she sought approval for the last-minute scheme. The Prince of Wales, who was not joining us on the return leg home as he was heading on to Saudi Arabia for some private time, looked a little mystified by this sudden change of plan, but nodded his approval and we left the Emirate in style.

The Royal aircraft, a Boeing 747 with a lavish interior refit, was apparently always on twenty-four-hour standby. Permission was granted for us to land at London Heathrow in the early hours of the morning. Ascending the steps to what would be the 'First Class' compartment at the front of the plane, we found a restaurant with five round tables, each one beautifully laid with fresh flowers, gold cutlery and a mandatory gold telephone. The 'Business Class' section was a luxury lounge with TV screens, with bedrooms behind. Our travelling party on board consisted of just five people including the Princess and was outnumbered by the crew by a ratio of four to one.

This era of pre-social media meant that advance warning of our sudden change of travel arrangements could be relayed via the gold telephone – a first for me in all of my travels with Diana to date. I recall speaking with her personal chauffeur, Simon Solari, at his home in London to update him on our arrival at LHR. The inevitable question of 'Where are you, Wharfie?' was posed, my answer abused in a friendly manner with a string of expletives when I told him.

Diana, having already eaten, turned down the chance to feast on fresh king prawns and caviar, only to remark to a fluent English-speaking crew: 'I don't suppose you have any baked jacket potatoes with beans?'

As we cruised at an altitude of 30,000 feet, the entire plane went into a sudden shake of enforced turbulence, albeit in the cabin, after Diana's teasing remark. A glass of champagne proved irresistible, with the Princess herself toasting the crew and us 'happy few' for the success of the tour. With that, she retired to the comfort of a luxury full king-sized bed for what she later described as the most comfortable night's sleep ever in the air.

We landed in the early hours at London's Heathrow, outside permitted hours, having been granted special permission. As always Diana's chauffeur, Simon Solari, had secured an airside pickup. It was the perfect end to an extraordinary day, and prelude to the reintroduction of reality inside Kensington Palace.

The trip to the Gulf had ended with much hilarity and high jinks on board the Emir's jumbo jet, but in reality those of us closest to the Princess knew that this was a defining moment in the already troubled Royal marriage. Prince Charles would later admit in an interview with the presenter Jonathan Dimbleby to mark his twenty-fifth anniversary as Prince of Wales that by this stage the relationship had 'irretrievably broken down'. In reality it had happened at least three years earlier, but I now sensed Diana was getting ready to break away. At this stage she had no idea how she was going to do it, though.

The cracks of marital disharmony were undeniably starting to show publicly, too. As I stepped off the Emir's plane I wondered how much longer the Royal couple could keep up the charade – or how.

SPRING 1989:
AIX-EN-PROVENCE,
FRANCE

I soon learned to my cost that when she put her mind to it Diana, Princess of Wales was a difficult woman to please. When she was on top form there was no one in the world better to work alongside, and when she was not, it was best to give her a wide berth – not that easy when you were her personal protection officer with a duty to keep her safe. Then you had two choices: confront the situation head-on, or simply tread on eggshells until in a flash her mood would change, which it invariably did.

'I want to go away on holiday but I don't want any special treatment, no fuss. I want to be just like everyone else. I want to be like normal people,' she insisted. It was a curveball that just came from nowhere and I knew this one was going to be particularly tricky to manage.

'Really? Are you sure, Ma'am?' I asked. 'It will present some... well, shall I say, logistical challenges. Of course I can make the arrangements as you wish, Ma'am, but to be frank... Well, you're not like everyone else.'

It was a response she didn't want to hear. She flushed a little and puffed out her cheeks, psyching herself up.

'Ken,' she breathed deeply, always a sign that I might have overstepped the invisible mark when she was in one of her moods, 'can you please just make the arrangements as I said? That is what I want.'

This wasn't a question, more a directive. Her heels were well and truly dug in. Not the time nor the place to spell out the pitfalls of her flawed plan, I thought. It was best to go along with her madcap idea – at least on the surface.

'Of course, Your Royal Highness, as you wish,' I said after a deliberate pregnant pause. 'I'll come back to you.'

I knew full well that this scheme would go one of two ways: either it would result in a total calamity, for which I would doubtless be blamed, or it would be scrapped altogether and normal service would be resumed. Time, when guarding Diana, was often a healer. While I hoped common sense would kick in, I also knew there was no guarantee; I had to prepare for all eventualities.

The truth was Diana was not like any other passenger. Yes, she did have a passport, but that was as close to normal as she got. Diana's number – 125580 – was the old dark blue British one with her title, Her Royal Highness The Princess of Wales, emblazoned across the front. Inside, where nationality was required, it simply read 'Princess of the Royal House', which always made her giggle. Where it asked for the name of the bearer, it read 'Her Royal Highness Diana Frances The Princess of Wales nee: Lady Diana Frances Spencer'. On page two she listed her place of birth as 'King's Lynn (Norfolk)' and her date of birth as '1 Jul 61' – and signed the document at the bottom in pen with the bold and distinctive one-word signature 'Diana' underlined. (Note: Her Majesty Queen Elizabeth II does not require a passport when travelling overseas – the documents are, after all, issued in her name as Sovereign. Other members of the Royal Family must carry one. However, the Queen is made to go through an identity check every time she flies in and out of Britain, giving her full name, age, address, nationality, gender and place of birth to immigration officials.)

Travelling can be dreary: standing in line at security, luggage allowances, plane delays, jet lag, and strange hotels. But it was not like that for the Princess of Wales. Commercial airlines were acceptable, but so too were private jets, royal helicopters and billionaire's yachts. The Royal Family, even Diana, are under economic restraints and must justify spending taxpayers' money on travel. (It was something the Princess enjoyed reminding me of when she had pangs of guilt over her extravagant and privileged lifestyle.) Today, the Royals' travel expenses are made public; back then they were not. Diana's son Prince William and his wife Kate have been known to skip chartered royal jets. They have flown commercial and William and his brother Harry have flown with budget airlines, too. As a general rule, just as in Diana's day, British Airways is still the go-to airline for the British Royals.

Back in those days we would never see a queue, let alone experience the drudgery of getting stuck in one. The Princess, with me at her side, would be driven straight to the plane by limousine, or we would be temporarily entertained in one of the VIP lounges, with a reciprocal arrangement at the other end. Her documents would be dealt with separately, her luggage handled by the airport Special Services if travelling privately, while on official overseas tours a specially appointed 'baggage master' would accompany the Royal party, whose job it was to ensure the baggage got to the right hotel or official or private residence. Packing for Diana, especially for a royal tour, was a grand affair. On official visits she would have her belongings neatly labelled with colour-coded tags. Diana's would often be pink, with a number and her name, The Princess of Wales, on them. Another tag, usually in yellow, would denote where the bag should be taken: 'residence', for example.

There would be carry-on bags of all shapes and sizes. On Diana's joint tour of the US with Prince Charles in 1985 the Royal couple had around 7,000 pounds of luggage that would cost a traveller around £6,000 in excess luggage fees today. Her luggage was emblazoned with the letter 'D' surmounted by a crown. She had more than twenty outfits during her trip to the US in 1990. Even on flights Diana travelled in style and arrived looking smart and polished. She was always a stickler for protecting her skin with products from her favourite beauty routine. Always swift, always easy, travelling was one perk of the job, I admit, that I miss to this day.

On our private overseas trips – holidays, usually – Diana would pack much more lightly for herself and her sons. The two of us used our fictitious names, Mr and Mrs Hargreaves, for the bookings. British Airways Special Services would be alerted and when we boarded the aircraft the cabin crew, of course, had not been remotely duped. It was just the pseudonym I adopted for security reasons and of course to try to throw the tabloids, paparazzi and any other undesirables off our scent. Wherever we went, Mrs Hargreaves – Diana – was big news. Photographs of her doing the most mundane things would fetch thousands. She could barely sneeze without it making front-page news. Part of my job was to keep her movements secret, by whatever means possible. Unfortunately for me, the Princess was so famous she was instantly recognisable wherever she went. Had she lived in the era of camera phones her life would have been made even more unbearable whenever she stepped out in public, something her son Harry has often complained about during interviews.

I had hoped Diana's hare-brained scheme to go on holiday with her friend Catherine Soames to Aix-en-Provence without special treatment would just be forgotten, but when we returned to the subject the Princess was adamant that she wanted to travel without the special facilities afforded to VIP royalty. I completely understood her there, and wished this were possible. Sadly, being a Royal means not being normal, and I was right to anticipate problems.

When the day came I arrived very early at Kensington Palace so that we could head off to catch the Gatwick Express train from Victoria.

'Why do we have to leave so early? The flight isn't until 3pm and I have a hair appointment at 11.30am,' Diana complained. She failed to see the irony of the situation. Her idea of normal was not that of the hundreds of holidaymakers setting off that day to catch their budget airline.

'Well, I cannot see how you can make that appointment, Ma'am, and queue for luggage, then go through security in time. We will miss the flight as we have to take public transport, too.'

She looked at me quizzically and said, 'Really, as long as that?'

At last, it was beginning to sink in. But she was not about to lose face. We compromised and I asked her chauffeur, Simon Solari, to take us to Gatwick Airport as soon as Diana's hair appointment was over. When we arrived at the terminal building, the queues were horrendous. We made our way to the check-in, trying to look as inconspicuous as possible. Diana was dressed down in jeans and a T-shirt covered by her favourite blue blazer – her standard uniform when travelling. Clearly the first time the Princess had stood in a queue since she was married, it had become alien to her. She tried her hardest not to be noticed, but a rowdy group of girls from Essex on their way to a hen-party weekend recognised her and couldn't believe they were ahead of her in the queue.

'It's bloody Diana! Look, it's the Princess!' observed one in what she thought was a whisper.

'Bloody hell, so it is!' said another.

'Shouldn't she be in First Class?' chipped in another, seemingly oblivious to the fact that there wasn't a First Class cabin on any of the short flights.

Within seconds we were surrounded and as a result other people at the check-in had begun to notice her too. It was, as I had warned, developing into a security situation where I would have to make a call.

'Can we have a photo together, your 'Ighness? It's her hen weekend,' another of the hen party said, pointing towards one of her friends.

By now we were ringed by around twenty people, all vying to get a better look at the Princess. None, I felt, presented a serious security threat so perhaps slightly mischievously, I allowed the situation to unfold for a little longer, just to prove my point. After a minute or two Diana gave me the look – without saying a word, her signal was clear: 'I am a Princess... Get me out of here!'

Fortunately, I had a Plan B. Without telling the Princess I had privately contacted Special Services at the airport the day before and explained the situation. They had, as always, promised to assist, should we need it. And so, in an instant, we were gone.

'Where are you going, Di? I wanted just one more photo!'

Within seconds normal service was resumed and we were whisked through security. The Princess was offered a glass of water in the sanctuary of the exclusive VIP area, which she accepted with a smile.

She didn't say a word, but she knew exactly what had happened. The security of the VIP lounge restored her calm, but the experience of being at the centre of overexcited hen-party revellers was one she would repeat many times with screeching laughter. She claimed in the retelling of this story to her friends that she would have been happy to join in the fun with the all-female party en route to Ibiza. I knew in reality that nothing could have been further from the truth.

Arriving in Marseille, we drove in a pre-arranged hire car to Aix, with no additional security, taking in the beauty of the countryside: endless undulating lines of grapevines interspersed with typical

Provençal architecture, painted in soft faded pastel blues or pinks contrasting with brightly coloured shutters, and scenes of rustic beauty resembling a Paul Cézanne masterpiece. The villages we passed through looked as though they had been around forever, with their steep winding paths, eye-catching towers and cosy squares with bistros and cafés. Diana was in her kind of heaven. With William and Harry back home with their father, Diana was for a few days at least freed of parental duties.

A sign by the roadside directed us to a honey farm along a narrow dusty orange track. I parked our rented Renault under a tree to shelter us from the hot sun. Chickens and geese wandered all around us. It was somewhat surreal and hard to imagine this could happen so soon after the 'hen party' explosion at Gatwick, and now we were alone in the middle of Provence, buying jars of honey from two unsuspecting French farmworkers, who had not the faintest idea that they were selling honey to HRH the Princess of Wales. Diana loved it – this was the 'normality' she craved.

With gifts for her guests secured, we continued our journey and arrived in a village just outside Aix an hour later. The villa was small, but set in isolation, with a wood extending for miles at the rear and the smell of dried Provençal herbs wafting from the woodland floor. Diana met with her friend Catherine Soames and immediately headed for the open swimming pool. An elderly woman served lunch: trays of fresh salad vegetables, so that peppers, onions, and tomatoes with fresh basil formed the centrepiece of our Provençal lunch, with of course the odd bottle of blush-pink rosé to wash it all down.

On this occasion, knowing that Diana wanted privacy for just three days, I insisted my French colleagues in the local police 'lay still' in Aix-en-Provence, visiting me only if I specifically requested assistance. I had informed them of our presence as a matter of courtesy and I'm sure they had a local team assigned to us, but they kept their distance. Diana assured me that she would not leave the villa without me in tow, so extra policing was not needed and I was happy with my arrangements. Her hosts were very accommodating and while invited to join them at mealtimes, I declined, to afford her as much privacy as possible. Three wonderful lazy days in glorious weather followed. The Princess simply relaxed, soaking up the tranquillity of the natural environment that embraced us.

The day before we left, Diana asked if we could go for a drive after lunch for an hour or so. Of course I agreed and was happy with map in hand to do so. Driving towards Aix-en-Provence, an avenue of plane trees gave shelter to a family group, all playing boules. Close by was a gurgling moss-covered fountain, producing the only sound apart from the dull thud of a metal ball landing on the open ground.

'What is that game?' the Princess wanted to know as we drove past.

I explained that it was a favourite game played in the South of France, a bit like bowls, but with metal balls, where the aim was to toss them as close as possible to the wooden ball (known as the 'piglet' or 'jack') while standing inside a circle with both feet on the ground.

'How do you know all this? Shall we have a game?' she said, laughing.

I told her that I would see if I could borrow a set so we could give it a try.

We turned around and patiently sat watching these local French folk play while enjoying the beauty of the countryside. There were a couple of other interested spectators, both sipping small cups of espresso, though heaven only knows where they had got it from. The players were totally oblivious as to the identity of the blonde woman watching them and Diana loved the anonymity.

I spotted a set of unused balls nearby and with my limited French language skills was able to secure our game. Never for one moment did I think I would ever play pétanque with the Princess of Wales in France without being spotted by the paparazzi. This visit, which had started out so badly, like so many others that followed, proved that anything is possible. It was the one we got away with, without the media knowing anything about it – an added bonus for the both of us.

AUGUST 1989:
SEIL, SCOTLAND

A great deal of nonsense has been written about the allegedly indifferent relationship between Diana and her mother, the late Frances Shand Kydd. What I witnessed in private was that whenever Diana was at her most troubled, and really needed the most private of counsel, it was always to her mother that she would turn.

Whenever we went to her home near Oban in the west of Scotland, William and Harry were ecstatic. They loved visiting 'Supergran' and the freedom it afforded them. Diana too would benefit from her mother's experience as Frances was an excellent listener and mediator. It was a welcome break for the Princess and her sons when they needed a healthy dose of normality. At the time Diana's mother lived in a whitewashed farmhouse on remote Seil, one of the Slate Islands, twelve miles south of Oban. Its main village, Ellenabeich, then comprised neat white terraces of workers' cottages crouching below black cliffs on the westernmost tip of the island. Frances had moved there in the early 1970s after she married Peter Shand

Kydd and they set up home in an eighteenth-century farmhouse at Ardencaple, overlooking Mull.

As with any proposed visit by the Princess, private or otherwise, I would be sent in advance to ensure the place was secure. Although such an investigation would be very discreet, it was essential to liaise with the local police at Oban, who enjoyed a good relationship with Frances, and to ensure there were enough rooms in the nearby Willowburn Hotel at Balricar for back-up protection officers. It is not too much to say that Seil was the setting for one of the best holidays Diana and her sons ever took together, far outshining the more glamorous and exotic foreign trips she made that the press highlighted. In August 1989 the three of them spent a week's holiday with Frances. It could not have come at a better time, for the Princess was close to breaking point from the continuing unhappiness of her marriage. Seil and the surrounding area had everything that two active and adventurous small boys could hope for. With the sea on its doorstep, open countryside, river inlets and rowing boats, it was better than any adventure playground.

Good forward planning meant that we arrived there undetected by the media. It delighted the Princess that here her boys were able to play as normal children away from snoopers, and away from the restraints of Royal life. Diana, too, had complete freedom – she was able to go off on long solitary walks without the back-up officers or me.

I knew that she was relatively safe on the island, but as a precaution I insisted that she always took with her a police radio tuned to my waveband in case she encountered difficulties. This, I think, was a measure of the level of trust that had developed between us since I had taken over as her senior personal protection officer in the summer of 1989. True, I was not acting by the book, and doubtless my superiors would have been horrified, but it worked. The Princess appreciated our working relationship and the freedom it brought her, and for weeks afterwards her feelings of being trapped would seem to evaporate.

One of Diana's many qualities was that she really was, at heart, a natural girl who liked taking care of others. She took no domestic staff with her when she went to visit her mother. It meant she could really be herself. Perhaps curiously for a woman of immense privilege, she relished the domestic chores that the absence of her sometimes over-attentive staff allowed her. She delighted in doing the dishes after dinner and in washing everybody's clothes; she even offered to iron my shirts, though I initially declined. Eventually, however, I relented and handed one of them over, joking with her that I could not imagine the Queen ironing one of my colleague's shirts. The image of Her Majesty standing at an ironing board with one of her shirtless bodyguards before her sent the Princess into fits of giggles. As she stood in the kitchen with just a towel wrapped around her, ironing my shirt, William joined us. He had developed the idea that his mother had a crush on me and put this to her. The Princess told him not to be so silly, at which he suddenly tugged at her towel so that it dropped to the floor, leaving the wife of the heir to the throne naked before me. Diana slowly picked up the towel, covered herself again, and promptly burst out laughing.

There was a relaxed family atmosphere to those holidays on Seil that was especially welcome because it was so rare in a life filled with official functions and all the other trappings of royalty. I helped prepare the meals that the family and I would enjoy at Frances's old table. We would sit there eating, drinking and regaling each other with stories far into the night. Such times were truly golden, and I'm glad to have been able to share them. Much of this was owed to Frances, a decent, down-to-earth woman, humorous, intelligent and kind, who has been, and sometimes still is, much maligned. During the days, as I kept the two Princes occupied, the Princess was able to discuss with her mother the full implications of her increasingly desperate situation. Frances was the perfect sounding board. Not only was she a sympathetic ear, but she also had a wealth of experience in marital disharmony, having been through one of the most celebrated divorces of the sixties with her then husband Viscount Althorp (later Earl Spencer)..

Frances knew of the private relationships of both her daughter and her son-in-law, but gently urged Diana to fight to save her marriage, knowing that she still loved Charles, if only for the sake of her sons. She, more than most people, knew the agony of being separated from her children.

Just over a year later, Frances came to stay at Highgrove for the weekend at the invitation of the Prince who, curiously, for he liked her, timed it so that he was away and Diana had the run of the house. It was wonderful for the Princes to have Granny Frances around, and they could barely contain their excitement when she arrived. As always, Frances revived her daughter's flagging spirits. It was one of those beautiful September weekends when the summer seems to have forgotten that autumn is already here. The weather was perfect for lounging beside the pool, and there the two women, so similar in character and looks, sat and talked for hours. It was not difficult to guess what they were discussing. Both were genuinely sad to be parting when Monday morning came. They promised not to leave it so long before they met again, then Diana embraced her mother on the steps before waving her off.

I had a great deal of time for Frances. A pragmatic personality, she was sharp-witted and thoroughly decent, seemingly wholly content in her Scottish fastness. She appreciated the more relaxed attitude to class in Scotland, and often lent a hand in a shop that she owned fourteen miles away in Oban. While perfectly friendly to everyone she met, she never encouraged intimacy. I, however, got on extremely well with her. In my view she did everything she could to support her daughter, but also to save Diana's marriage, if only for the sake of William and Harry. Her wisdom, her experience, her kindness, were always at Diana's disposal, and the Princess knew it, and was glad of it. Sadly, however, by the autumn of 1990 matters had reached a point beyond any person's repair.

Having witnessed their closeness, the claims of a rift between Diana and her mother particularly rankled with me. I felt it was important that I should speak out in defence of Frances and so I decided to release a number of private letters giving a vivid picture of a strong and loving relationship between the two women to the respected *London Evening Standard* newspaper.

These hitherto secret letters written to me showed that the Princess thought of Frances as her 'best chum'. And the revelations, showing a warm and loving relationship based on trust, which I had offered to the inquest hearing in 2008 roundly contradicted claims by Diana's former butler, Paul Burrell, that the Princess had fallen out with her mother. I had become a friend and confidant to both women during my time as Diana's PPO. In a series of letters to me, Frances – who sadly died in 2004 from brain cancer, aged sixty-eight – shared family secrets and discussed Diana's agonies during the break-up of her marriage to Prince Charles. I was furious at the evidence given by Burrell at the inquest and felt it would be wrong for this to go unchallenged just because Frances was no longer there to defend herself. It damaged her memory and I, for one, knew how close she and the Princess had been. Like any mother and daughter they would have the occasional spat – that's family – but whenever Diana needed real help, her mother was the one she turned to.

One of Frances's letters to me, written from Ardencaple late in 1991, at the height of Diana's distress over her marriage, begins: 'Dear Ken, I can't let another day go by without writing to record a huge thank you to you for your great help viz Angela [the code name we used for Diana]. She sees life colourfully and believes me to be her best chum – a compliment and a responsibility. I do seem able to get her to throttle back a bit on her real fears, whether they are imagined or not, so I couldn't be more grateful for your help. I'm humble enough to say I don't know the cure for her deep anxiety; I do think she was intimidated.' The letter goes on to say that 'Angela' was 'truly grateful' for the support I and other members of the Royal Protection team were giving her. She signed herself 'Supergran', her nickname from happy times with Diana and the Princes William and Harry.

That letter refers to a particular incident in which Diana was labelled a 'trollop' – but by her maternal grandmother, Ruth, Lady Fermoy, not by Mrs Shand Kydd. Diana told her mother that Lady Fermoy – the late Queen Mother's lady-in-waiting and closest friend – had called her a trollop after she wore close-fitting leather trousers at Kensington Palace in around 1990. But far from agreeing with Lady Fermoy and the Queen Mother – who apparently had also criticised Diana – Frances confided, 'My mother is a jealous, interfering old faggot, and I'd better not say what I think of the other one.'

By then barely on speaking terms with Charles, the Princess believed the entire Royal Family was hostile towards her and turned to her mother for moral support. When, in 1993, I moved from the role of protecting the Princess to take up other duties, Frances wrote to me. It was a kind and warm letter: 'I do want to say my biggest thank you to you for your truly magnificent caring of her – you probably know her better than me!' I had acted 'in good and bad times as a wise adviser and robust cherisher' to the Princess, she wrote. Her words meant an awful lot to me, for Frances was right: I had cherished Diana, and done my best by her.

MARCH 1990:
NIGERIA

There were very few joint engagements with the Prince and Princess of Wales scheduled for the visit to Nigeria. Officially, the reason given was that they could achieve more and would be able to interact with more local people on their travels. On one of the rare occasions when they were slotted together, however – to visit Yerwa-Maiduguri in Borno State, in the northeastern region of the country on 17 March 1990 – Diana relished making her husband decidedly uncomfortable. It gave us all a compelling indication of what was to come in her story.

The visit started well enough when the couple met the Shehu of Borno, Mustafa Ibn Umar El-Kanemi, in the Emirate in northeast Nigeria. Charles, who had been in a foul mood earlier, seemed buoyed by a splendid Durbar. In turn, Diana played her role immaculately, allowing her husband to take the lead. But when the couple visited a leprosy hospital at a village just outside the city, it was she who took charge. Charles followed along behind her and was far less at ease, and noticeably reluctant to go round embracing lepers. His grimacing smile said it all, and Diana instantly knew that her personal genuine contact annoyed him greatly.

She, in contrast, clearly savoured the visit, making a point of shaking hands with the lepers, seeking out physical contact to demonstrate that leprosy is not contagious, that lepers should and must not be shunned – just as she was later to do with HIV/AIDS victims. She wore no gloves, defying the taboo, trying to show in a single act, touching the sufferers with her bare, 'healing' hands, her own special brand of magic.

'When I see suffering like this,' she whispered as she walked to the next room, 'this is where I should and must be. Shining a light on these poor, poor people.

'I just want to show that in a simple action – touching – they are not reviled and nor are we repulsed,' she added.

It was to become her mantra.

Prince Charles, following along behind, was far less comfortable. It just wasn't his style, or perhaps he interpreted Diana's actions as an attempt to embarrass him. The Prince in these circumstances was beyond embarrassment; in public he was the consummate professional, but nevertheless angry and at worst annoyed that he could not bring himself to applaud his wife for an act of genuine sincerity.

The Royal couple had arrived by plane and were met at the Murtala Muhammed Airport by the Chief of General Staff, Admiral Augustus Aikhomu, and Mrs Rebecca Aikhomu. From there they were taken to State House Marina, where President Ibrahim Babangida was waiting to receive them with a beaming smile. That banquet seemed to last an eternity and the Royal couple were somewhat fractious by the time we made it back to Lagos marina and the Royal Yacht *Britannia*, our floating palace. Diana reviewed the 'beating the retreat' played by the band of the Royal Marines (also aboard *Britannia* for the tour) on the quayside alongside the

Prince of Wales (who was in an exceptionally bad mood). On board his demeanour soon worsened as conditions were far from ideal here either – the air-conditioning failed and temperatures were well over 32°C (90°F). Desperate to keep up appearances, Diana was continually being battered with asides from Charles, which irritated her immensely.

Commenting on the conditions, the Prince remarked, 'What the hell am I bloody doing here?'

'Shut up, Charles! For Christ's sake, it's your duty,' Diana hit back.

When His Royal Highness reached his serene quarters in the magnificent State Apartments to the stern of the Royal Yacht, he was infuriated by the stifling heat and sent a message to the commanding officer, Rear Admiral Sir John Garnier, asking why this was. God alone knows what it was like for the crew in the cramped conditions forward of the ship's funnel, where it was like entering a different world. It was later discovered that the cause of the problem had been a floating corpse bobbing in the water alongside the yacht. (Apparently, it was not uncommon for local people to dispose of their dead in this way.)

Earlier that morning I had carried out a recce with local police, who were aggressive. A car containing a family of seven had broken down on the Royal route. Police lashed out across the bonnet with a metal chain without any words being exchanged – the family abandoned their car and escaped down the embankment while the police made arrangements for the car to be removed. When I attempted to explain that this procedure in dealing with members of the public, albeit a potential security threat, was not how we handled such incidents in the UK, I was abruptly informed that this was not the UK – and that was how they dealt with such incidents in Nigeria.

This early morning recce ahead of the Royal visit by Diana underlined the extreme poverty in Lagos. Later, the Princess and the

President's wife, Mrs Maryam Babangida, inspected products made by women as part of the Better Life For Rural Dwellers programme, a pet programme of Mrs Babangida. Diana and Mrs Babangida hit it off immediately. There was an unusual chemistry, and Diana was forever praising her for her multi-coloured choice of national dress and splendid headdress. Diana's designer mint-green dress was lost against the vibrancy of colours worn by the ladies at the exhibition held at the Tafawa Balewa Square, the commercial heart of the capital named after Nigeria's first Prime Minister, in the shadow of the twenty-six-storey Independence House.

'How long are you staying in my country?' asked Mrs Babangida as farewells were being planned, 'Why?' asked Diana. 'Well, I could send some dresses to your boat for you to take back to England.' Diana laughed and gently embraced the President's wife, saying, 'That's so lovely of you, but my husband would probably suggest I stay in Nigeria.' With her classic high-pitched giggle and arching of her back, Diana waved goodbye. It was a happy day.

As the press struggled and sweated and argued with the ever-present oppressive Nigerian security, Diana remained cool in her rather 1930s dress. The reporters and photographers looked like they were about to boil over at any moment, spilling off their media buses, the snappers clutching aluminum stepladders as if they weren't taking photos but at a decorators' convention.

This West African tour was officially meant to be for Prince Charles, as a potential future head of the Commonwealth, to familiarise himself with the volatile but important region. In reality, for Diana at least, it was very much more about getting the right kind of coverage in the British press.

It was, however, a low point in the Royal couple's popularity; for the first time the novelty of the pair was wearing thin. The 'stuff of fairytales' notion that the late Archbishop of Canterbury, Robert Runcie, had used to describe their romance and marriage had long left the public imagination. And although the world didn't know the real extent of the sham marriage they knew enough. The problems – the affairs and the arguments – had not yet made the newspapers and somewhat naively, the Palace Press Office was keen to revive flagging public interest in the future 'King and Queen'.

The Palace and the Foreign Office chosen solution was a punishing round of activities that took the pair to every corner of Nigeria and Cameroon – Charles opened a British Council Library, walked in the rainforest, and greeted war veterans in a tropical botanic garden, while Diana visited children's hospitals, traditional handloom weavers and women's development projects. And wherever the Princess went, the Royal press pack followed. None of the press seemed to be in the slightest bit interested in Charles. Diana was determined not to let the side down – she looked like she had just stepped out of a movie. In a blue print day dress, presenting an incubator to a newborn babies unit; Diana in pink and white lawn, amid the brown dust of an African village; Diana laughing as the youngest and smallest member of an Ibo dance troop took a running leap into her lap; Diana in a safari suit, greeting patients and children with a warm, beaming smile.

I went ahead from Lagos to Maiduguri, travelling on a scheduled flight with the press, and arrived at a government hospitality barracks with travelling chef Mervyn Wycherley and baggage master, the late Ron Lewis. Our accommodation was truly shocking – barrack-style, with beds that had been made up months before. When I removed the blankets, my bed was alive with insects. The three of us decided not to sleep in the barracks.

That night Ron Lewis, always most dutiful with supplies of gin and tonic, and I sat in chairs under a tree, and with the medicinal drinks to hand fought off the mosquito attacks, assisted by our wall of smouldering protective candles. Those who chose to use the beds later in the morning complained of being bitten alive and feeling unwell. The chef joined us early after midnight, following the collapse of his sink and bath and part-collapse of a wall – this could hardly have been described as a fine-dining experience!

Once again I was to advance the next leg of the tour to neighbouring Cameroon. I left with the travelling press officers, Dickie Arbiter and Kiloran McGrigor. Arriving at a hotel in the capital of Yaounda with a day to spare prior to the arrival of the Prince and Princess, it was time to wind down. I challenged Dickie and Kiloran to a round of golf. It was a surreal settling; the sprawling city set over seven hills was our backdrop. Unfortunately we had to make a madcap exit at pace when we were forced off the first hole by an aggressive venomous black mamba, one of the speediest snakes on the planet. We decided to vacate the course as quickly as possible and golf has never appealed since that moment. That evening I mischievously persuaded Dickie to let me buy him supper, knowing that it would be far cheaper for me to settle the bill for food rather than wine.

'Only if you buy the wine, Dickie,' I said to double-check he had bought into my ploy, knowing I was on to a winner.

That evening a meal of local delight costing only a few dollars was in complete contrast to the hefty three-figure sum for two bottles of French Sauvignon.

Back at the hotel, the general manager was informing all male guests that it was 'ladies night'. Since I was alone, although with Kiloran close by, it passed me by. However, at 7.30pm, two luxury coaches arrived at the hotel entrance and some thirty to forty 'ladies of the night' arrived and began their solicitous moves within the hotel. The following day, Kiloran let Diana know that I had been under female attack from what the Princess dubbed the 'Night Fighters'. That evening she wanted to know the full story – slightly edited, of course, but laughingly added, 'Was my husband there anywhere?' 'I didn't see him, Ma'am,' I joked.

The Royal couple were received by President Paul Biya of Cameroon shortly after their arrival in that country, where they discussed Cameroon's application to join the Commonwealth as well as British aid to the country. And so the gruelling schedule went on. The Princess visited the Yaounde Deaf and Dumb School and other charitable causes. It was relentless and towards the end you could see that Diana's caring campaign was beginning to take its toll.

The official banquets were tedious and at the final one the Princess practically ignored her host, the President. I watched as her eyes kept drifting sideways to where the Royal press corps was sitting, giving them conspiratorial looks and flirting as only she could with their cameras.

Back in the State Rooms aboard the Royal Yacht *Britanniu*, Diana invited me in for a chat. She looked shattered but there was self-satisfied glow about her.

'I am spent, Ken,' she told me. 'I need a break.' Sadly the journey was not yet over, but I could see just how tired she was, both emotionally and physically. Being the consummate professional, her duty was always to HM The Queen. We laughed, with her saying 'What the hell are we doing in Lagos?'

APRIL 1990:
NECKER ISLAND,
BRITISH VIRGIN
ISLANDS

Exhausted, Diana had arranged it so that she had no more engagements until the end of April 1990. She had also arranged another trip to Necker, once again through the generosity of Richard Branson. For her it was the perfect escape and she was buoyant with excitement at the thought of spending time with her sons away from the Prince. What she had not foreseen, however, was that her decision to take a pre-Easter break on the island, once again without her husband, would send Fleet Street into frenzy. It became headline news.

Charles was blamed, even though it was Diana who had arranged the solo holiday. He chose instead to spend the time in the Scottish Highlands, thereby accidentally emphasising the gulf between the couple. The tabloids unfairly lambasted him as a bad father. One headline screamed: 'This Is Your Father – He's Hardly Seen the Boys Since Xmas', while a second read: 'Another Holiday Apart! They'll Be Forgetting What Dad Looks Like'. The accompanying articles labelled the Prince an absent father and reported that he had seen his sons for only two days in the previous two months. (In fact, it was three days.)

For this visit to Necker, Diana had decided to play Cupid to her brother, then still Viscount Althorp, and his wife of a few months, Victoria, inviting them both along for a surprise second honeymoon. Once again, William and Harry, her mother, Frances Shand Kydd, and sisters, Lady Sarah McCorquodale and Jane Fellowes, with their children, also joined her at the hideaway. I headed up the security team alone, for although Graham Smith was in the seventeen-strong party, he was there this time as the Princess's guest. She knew that he was seriously ill, and hoped that the sun and relaxation might help his recovery. It was good for me to have Graham around, too, because I knew that this year the paparazzi were determined to win their prized pictures. With so much speculation in the British press about the holiday before we left, there was not the remotest chance of keeping this trip a secret.

Within hours of our arrival the press and paparazzi were back. A small armada appeared on the horizon, with more than sixty journalists and photographers packed into chartered boats of all shapes and sizes, cameras primed and at the ready. Diana was almost incandescent with rage. 'How did they know we were here?' she demanded, before adding bitterly, 'Someone must have told them.' When I suggested that it would not have taken much to work out as the Princess was known to have a penchant for exotic islands in the Caribbean (especially if her holidays there were gratis), she flashed me one of her stony stares – she was not in any mood to see the funny side.

The presence of the journalists and paparazzi, albeit offshore, irritated her and the rest of the party enormously. No matter how much I urged them to try to put it out of their minds, assuring them that I would make sure that it would not affect their security, the Princess became obsessed with the problem. She kept saying, not very helpfully, that I should 'do something' about it. She also insisted that the media were frightening her sons. I was not at all surprised for she had filled the young Princes' heads with a great deal of nonsense about the press, telling them that they were all 'bad, bad men', with the result that the boys' reaction to journalists and photographers was all too predictable. (Diana was not altogether straight in this. She would later maintain a friendship with the *Daily Mail* journalist Richard Kay, and it was she herself who secretly selected Andrew Morton, once a royal correspondent on the *Daily Star*, to write the book that would, in the end, help her to escape from her marriage.)

I weighed up the odds. There were three other protection officers and myself against the crack troops of the world's press. Even Custer had better odds than this, I thought. There was also Graham Smith – and although he was a sick man and was not there officially, I took the lead from him. He and I agreed that we had to be proactive. The media knew exactly where we were, and since they weren't going to go away until they got what they wanted, we had to try and strike a deal, or pack up and abandon the holiday altogether.

Once again, Diana had not brought any staff with her and so without the luxury of a private secretary or a press secretary, it was left for me to deal with the problem. Until then, no one had really ever had to face such a situation before. In the past, Royal holidays had either been taken within the almost fortress-like Royal estates, like Sandringham or Balmoral, or as the guests of foreign royalty, as when the Prince and Princess had stayed in Mallorca. A combination of the large numbers of encroaching journalists and photographers, the absence of any effective means of deterring them, the Princess's ill-humour about the whole business, and my own desire not to see the holiday cut short, meant that I was going to have to act as some sort of press liaison officer.

I could have told the Princess that this was really not my problem. She had decided to come to this island for a holiday; she knew perfectly well that she was always going to be open to press intrusion wherever she went and whatever she did. I might have added that my job was simply to ensure her safety, and that although the presence of the media was an irritation, it did not present a major breach of security but I did not. After talking over the situation with Graham Smith, I decided to arrange to meet some of the senior Fleet Street journalists to see if, between us, we could broker a deal in a bid not only to restrain the more intrusive hacks, but to clip the wings of the rogue elements among the foreign paparazzi, who tended to be a law unto themselves.

There is a piece of received wisdom in my line of work that, in effect, states that to ensure effective protection, information is essential. If I was to find out what the paparazzi were doing, I needed to secure allies from Fleet Street. The professionals tended to be more reasonable because, unlike the freelance photographers, their pay cheques were assured whether they got the pictures of Diana or not (unless they were fired for failing, of course). They wanted the scoop for reasons of professional pride as much as from a desire to beat the competition; in other words, they were not motivated by money alone.

With this in mind I climbed into a small boat with Dave Sharp and sailed out to where most of the press boats were. I spotted James Whitaker's rotund frame and pulled up alongside. As I looked out at the gathered photographers and reporters, many with sun-reddened faces and ample bellies, binoculars slung around their necks, I couldn't help smiling. They reminded me of *Sun* reporter Harry Arnold's apt description of the Royal Rat Pack when he wryly told Prince Charles, 'We may be scum, sir, but we are *la crème de la* scum.'

We sailed in among them, and by a mixture of yells and gestures

APRIL 1990: NECKER ISLAND, BRITISH VIRGIN ISLANDS

I signalled that I wanted them to meet me at Biras Creek on Virgin Gorda, about fifteen minutes away by motor boat. Sensing a deal, Whitaker, who always tended to assume the mantle of commander-in-chief of the Rat Pack, gave the order for the rest to follow. Settled in a calypso bar, cocktails or beers distributed to everyone, we talked over and around the situation. I knew that I was in dangerous territory here. Technically, dealing with the press was well beyond my remit, and doing so could cause problems for me with my superior officers back at Scotland Yard. Yet in the end I felt I had no choice. I made it clear to the gaggle of hacks and photographers that the Princess was there on a private holiday and was under no obligation to give a photo opportunity just because the media happened to be intruding on her privacy. To sweeten the pill, I told them a few minor details about the holiday, without giving too much away. The senior journalists there – Whitaker, Kent Gavin and Arthur Edwards – sat quietly surrounded by the rest, listening to what I had to say. There was a moment's silence after I delivered my 'leave-us-alone' speech before James Whitaker gave his response.

James's bark was worse than his bite. The 'Red Tomato', as the Princess had dubbed him after seeing him packed tightly into a red ski-suit as he tried to give chase on a Royal holiday in the Alps, adopted the mantle of spokesman-in-chief. With a manner somewhere between that of a retired colonel from the heyday of the British Raj and a female pantomime character played by a man in drag, he put the case for the indefensible. Mercifully, he spared me any 'freedom-of-the-press-and-public-interest' cant, adopting instead a more realistic approach.

'Ken,' he rasped portentously, 'we have a bloody job to do, and if we work together we can make everybody's job, including yours, a damned sight easier!' I knew he had a point, although I kept quiet. 'If you could just persuade the Princess to go along with the idea of a photocall, she would get a peaceful holiday, you would not have to worry about security and we would have the editors off our backs, get the snaps and go fishing.' Everyone, including Dave Sharp and I, burst out laughing but James silenced us all with a glare.

He went on to point out that the genuine newspaper journalists and photographers were the least of my problems, as the real concern was the foreign paparazzi. I knew that it was true.

Daily Mirror photographer Kent Gavin, or 'Idle Jack' as he was known, 'Widow Twankey' Whitaker's pantomime partner-in-crime, was the quiet one of the team. Unlike James, however, whose loud protestations usually went over people's heads, when Gavin spoke he commanded respect from his peers. The Princess knew and liked him; indeed, he had even been invited to photograph Prince William's christening in 1982 (and in 1996, the year before the Princess was killed, he was voted Royal Photographer of the Decade). He loved the good life and covering Royal holidays, as well as official events, was an important part of his professional jet-set life. For once, Gavin backed Whitaker, pressing home the point that the Fleet Street journalists were not really the problem. 'Tell the Princess she looks a million dollars, and I'll make sure the pictures of her in the *Daily Mirror* do her justice. She'll knock 'em dead back home.' Kent Gavin understood that the real impact of the Princess upon the public was in pictures of her. He also knew that she was vain, and that the idea of appearing on the front pages, showing off her beautiful and bronzed body, would secretly appeal to her.

For my part, I realised that the key to any deal depended on the Fleet Street journalists' ability to deliver full co-operation from the paparazzi, the men who, in the slipperiness stakes, make the most active eel look positively inert. Nevertheless, the Fleet Street teams did wield significant power over the paparazzi back then, since it was their editors who would pay the big cash for any pictures the freelancers got if they ignored a deal and struck out on their own.

Additionally, the paparazzi were not stupid, and knew that it was better to secure a deal that got them some pictures than risk getting absolutely nothing at all.

With some satisfaction, I noted that as Dave Sharp and I left the bar the Royal Rat Pack were locked in discussion with their French, Italian and German rivals. It puts the UN into perspective, I thought, as I glimpsed a red-faced Whitaker berating some unfortunate French photographer who had dared to challenge his authority.

On the journey back to Necker I mentally weighed up how I was going to win Diana's support for a deal with the media. I knew I would need allies, notably Diana's brother, Charles Spencer, and Graham Smith, if I were to persuade her to co-operate. We might have found paradise, but I was well aware that if I failed to win over the Princess, then as far as she was concerned, mine would be a paradise lost. Graham supported me, as I had known he would; so too did Charles. He told the Princess that in his expert opinion we had no choice; we either negotiated a truce or it would be all-out war, and the local police simply did not have the resources to drive off fifty or sixty determined pressmen. Even with help from the guests, I and the two other protection officers would never be able to prevent some of our unwanted visitors from landing on the island and trying to get pictures of Diana and her sons; meanwhile, others out in the boats would come as far as they could inshore and snap her whenever she appeared. That was not intrusion, but full-scale invasion. As a clincher, Graham added his belief that if Diana did not agree, then we might have to decamp and either look for another holiday destination at very short notice and with no guarantee that the media would not find us again within a day or so, or return to Britain.

While the Princess was considering this, I explained that if we arranged one photocall there was a good chance that once they had got the pictures they had come for, the press would leave her and her family alone for the rest of the holiday.

'But can you guarantee it, Ken?' she wanted to know. This, of course, was the question I least wanted to have to answer, and the crux of the whole problem. I had to admit that I could not, but that there was very little alternative. Unlike in the previous year, the local police could not provide the additional cover we needed to cope with the numbers of journalists and photographers homing in on the island. They were busy chasing drug dealers, and had already withdrawn the night boat patrol they had originally offered. This, coupled with the fact the year before I had dispensed with the services of the local night-time beach patrol after I had found the police team asleep over their rifles, meant that my security team was stretched well beyond its capabilities. There was nothing we could do to stop the press invading Necker at any moment, day or night. True, their mission was to take photographs, and they were therefore not life-threatening, but it would still have been hugely embarrassing if any of them had made it up to the house. It would also have driven the Princess, and probably some of her guests, into a paroxysm of fury, with who knew what consequences. The last thing we wanted was a PR disaster brought on by complaints from aggrieved journalists or photographers. As it was, the Princes William and Harry were already muttering darkly about exacting revenge on the intruders.

I explained to Diana that while I appreciated that she was on a private holiday and that she was entirely justified in complaining that her privacy was being shamefully invaded, we had to agree to the picture deal. I assured her that I would not allow any of the press to set foot on the island, and that she would not have to pose for the cameras in any way. I suggested that she should just go about her normal business on the beach with the two boys, and I would do my best to oversee the operation from a boat alongside the press boats offshore. Once again she immediately grasped our main problem.

'But can they be trusted?'

Of course, I had no way of knowing, but I tried to reassure her by saying that I felt the press could be relied on to deliver their side of the bargain, since it was in the interest of all parties for the deal to hold up. After a few minutes, and with a little gentle persuasion from her brother, Charles, for which I was extremely grateful, she agreed. I was almost certain that Kent Gavin was right, and that, deep down, she was quite looking forward to having pictures of herself, looking sensational in a swimsuit, splashed across the front pages of the world's press, but of course she was not going to let me know that.

I called Kent at once and told him the deal was on, adding, as ominously as I could, that if he or his colleagues broke it then I would never trust him or Fleet Street again. The laid-back photographer said that he would do his very best to deliver what he had promised and so at eleven the next morning I boarded a small boat and sailed out to the press launches moored offshore. On arrival the hacks and photographers were in fine form, jostling for the best position and joking with each other. They were obviously relieved that their expensive journey had not been wasted, and that their editors – and ultimately the public – were going to get the pictures and stories they wanted.

The paparazzi were grouped together on a smaller boat moored a few yards away. They were deathly quiet, acknowledging my arrival with a nod almost in unison. Unlike the Fleet Street crew they were not interested in glory or lavish picture by-lines on the front pages, they were in it just for the money. I repeated the rules of engagement and briefed them all about what was going to happen. I then bluntly refreshed their memories about the deal we had struck, pressing the point that after this photocall they would leave the Princess alone. Again there were a few nods, this time of agreement, but I knew that in trusting them, I was going out on a limb.

Within a few minutes the Princess and her family appeared on the beach. She looked sensational, and played her role to perfection. I had suggested that she should play with her sons on the beach, within sight of the cameras, but what followed surprised even me. Surrounded by her sons and their five cousins, she proceeded to let them bury her in the sand, laughing all the while. Then, having extricated herself, she threw off her sundress, revealing her bikini underneath, and raced William and Harry, then aged eight and five, down to the sea to rinse off the sand. Her body gleamed with water in the hot sun, and the camera shutters clicked in frenzy. It was, as ever, a masterly display by the consummate public-relations professional.

After about twenty minutes I called a halt to the photo shoot – if they hadn't got enough pictures by now, then they shouldn't be in the job. To a man, paparazzi included, they all stopped immediately, clearly elated at the photographs they had got. We fired up the boats' engines and headed for Biras Creek, where I told them in no uncertain terms that this was the end and that, no matter how much I normally loved seeing their smiling faces, I did not want to see any of them again on this trip.

All of them agreed that it had been a fantastic photocall, one of the best they had ever had. They gave me credit for it, but it was the Princess who had made it work. Once again I asked them to leave us alone. I was convinced that some would stick around, but most of them, mainly the British freelancers, would leave. But somehow I knew that the French, who never took no for an answer, would be back for more. James Whitaker left me decidedly sceptical as he led Fleet Street's chorus of approval.

'Never mind all that, James – just deliver your side of the deal,' I told him as I left.

Back home in Britain, the newspaper editors were delighted. Diana, looking absolutely wonderful, was splashed across the front pages of most newspapers, especially the tabloids. Under banner headlines, she sent her message back to her errant husband, who she suspected would have been enjoying secret trysts with his married lover, Camilla

Parker Bowles, while she was far away on Necker. 'I'm here without you, and I'm having a wonderful time,' it might have read.

The photo shoot out of the way, Diana and her family could relax and enjoy themselves. The press did manage to miss one scoop, though. I remember a dramatic moment when Diana saved her mother's life during her first holiday on Necker Island in 1989. The banana boat they were all riding through the waves veered suddenly, throwing them all into the water. Everyone swam back to the vessel except Frances Shand Kydd, who we feared might be in difficulty. Diana and I spotted her simultaneously and the Princess dived in and pulled her to the surface. As I pushed her onto the vessel from the rear, Frances in typically Frances manner joked, 'Ken, will you please get your hand out of my c***!'

However happy the press and the Princess might have been, my superiors at Scotland Yard were furious. When I contacted Head Office by telephone, I was told that the photocall had caused quite a stir back in London, and that senior officers were not happy about my involvement, which had been reported in the press.

Senior management of the Metropolitan formally reminded me that my role was not that of a press officer, but a protection officer. This time it was my turn to be incensed. I told them in no uncertain terms that I would be sending them a full report of what had happened on Necker, in which I would explain exactly why I had acted as I had done (with, I might add, Graham Smith's full support). Warming to my theme, I added that I was looking forward to hearing exactly how the geniuses who sat behind their desks in Scotland Yard would have handled the situation, a situation for which there had not, until then, been any precedent. Finally, I reminded them that I had a difficult job to do there, and that I was getting zero assistance or guidance from London, either from Scotland Yard or Buckingham Palace. I then stormed off in indignation to have a cocktail – virgin, of course, since I was on duty – to calm myself down. It worked. As I watched a spectacular orange sunset sink below the horizon I could not help laughing out loud at the way the whole business had turned out.

To my astonishment, and to their credit, the deal with the press held up for the next three days. I think the Princess was surprised, too, because she changed her swimsuit every day, just in case she should be photographed again – she was never one knowingly to disappoint her public. She and her party suffered no press intrusion whatsoever, and I basked in the glory of having brought about this almost unthinkable state of affairs. Diana and her family were able to walk on the beach, swim and snorkel without a press boat in sight. At last she was able to unwind.

There was no daily plan of activities, but William and Harry looked to the men in the party to organise their day so while the Princess and the rest of the women lounged around the pool, watched over by Dave Sharp, I was tasked with keeping her two extremely active sons occupied. It was not an onerous task, not least because Richard Branson's island had everything in place to make this, for boys, the adventure holiday of a lifetime.

One of William's favourite games involved the children unleashing billiard balls across the snooker table at high speed in a bid to smash their opponents' fingers, almost the only rule being that the contestants had to leave their hands resting on the table's cushions until the ball was unleashed. I had to put a stop to this, as gently as I could. As a diversion, I took them snorkelling with their Uncle Charles, but this was not enough to beguile the inquisitive Prince William; he wanted to explore. So he and I hatched a plan to recce the island, and one morning set off together armed with knives, and with only bottled water, fruit and some sandwiches to sustain us. William could not contain his excitement as we ventured deep into the island's interior.

For the next three hours the boy destined to be King and I hacked our way through the undergrowth, climbed rocks and forded streams, re-enacting our own version of *Robinson Crusoe*. William loved every minute of it. At one point I began to worry as the midday sun beat down on us and I realised that I had lost my bearings. I kept this to myself, however, and eventually, albeit two hours later than I had anticipated, we made it back to the main house. William raced in, desperate to tell his mother every detail of his great adventure. Harry, too young to journey off into the island's jungle, had spent the time playing in the pool with his cousins.

Throughout the three-day truce I kept in daily touch with Kent Gavin by telephone. This was a way of briefing reporters, who had asked that I should let them know if anything untoward had happened to the Princess or any of her party that might constitute a legitimate story. I thought the tale of how the heir apparent had gone missing while exploring with his mother's police protection officer might make a good story, but for obvious reasons I said nothing.

I honoured my side of the bargain, though, allowing the journalists harmless snippets about what the Princess and her party had been doing, and repeated that I expected the media to keep theirs. On the third day after the photocall, however, Gavin warned me that something was afoot. He told me that Fleet Street could no longer be held responsible for the French paparazzi that he feared would soon be out in force again. At this my heart sank – I knew that the Princess would be furious if their peace was to be broken by the media once again. Gavin suggested that I should persuade her to do another photocall, which, he thought, would probably placate the ever-hungry paparazzi, but when I put the proposal of a second photocall to Diana she was predictably reluctant.

'You said that if I did the first one they would leave us alone, so why have I got to do another one?' she complained.

She had a point, but I reminded her that at least the deal I had struck had kept the press away for the last three days. I continued by saying that although many of the photographers had left the area, my information was that there were a few hardcore paparazzi preparing to invade her privacy once again. I then suggested that the best solution, however annoying, was for her to do a short, ten-minute photocall, at which point the deal would be reinstated – with any luck until the end of the holiday. After a few minutes' consideration she saw the logic of this and agreed, and the shoot went ahead the following day. She did not like being forced into a corner, but relaxed and beautifully tanned, she saw the advantages to both sides.

Yet even after this a few paparazzi determined to try to get something different. The rest of the press honoured the agreement and left the immediate area, but a handful of freelance photographers remained. They were, from a security viewpoint, considerably easier to handle than the original fifty or sixty, and I felt my decision to negotiate had been fully justified. But the young Princes in particular still wanted their revenge on the ''tographers', as seven-year-old William called them. It was not long before they got their wish.

Richard Branson's manager on the island, Dan Reid, had returned from one of his business and supply trips to Tortola armed with three giant handheld catapults and hundreds of balloons, which he gave to the children. I have no idea where he found them, but they proved a big hit with the Princes and their cousins. The catapults were huge. To fire the balloons, which for maximum effect would be filled with water to the size of cricket balls, the catapults had to be tied to posts or held by two people while a third loaded, aimed and fired the missile. Initially, they caused much hilarity as the children and the protection officers fought pitched mini-battles against each other. There was, however, one moment of slight anxiety when young Fellowes – son of Lady Jane and her husband, the Queen's private secretary, Sir Robert (now Lord) Fellowes – known as 'Beatle', received a direct hit in the chest when William launched an attack on him from the helicopter pad. Poor Beatle went down severely winded and was left with a huge bruise on his chest for the rest of the holiday. But after a brief cooling-off period, during which the Princess considered a complete ban on our war games, the balloon battles were allowed to continue. As the children perfected their warlike activities, William had a brainwave that he felt sure would get his mother's backing.

'Ken,' he said, his eyes lighting up with excitement, 'when the photographers come back in their boats, why don't we catapult them from the house?' There was a perfect vantage point; set upon rocks about eighty feet above the shoreline. William – whose ancestors had led troops into battle – was ready to get his revenge on the snoopers who had upset his beloved mother. Without me knowing he rallied his troops – Harry and their cousins – and they set about constructing two sites in readiness for the return of the press boats.

It didn't take me long to find out what they were up to. When I told the Princess what her sons were planning for the media she thought it was hilarious and approved it immediately. I was dispatched to supervise the battle plans, feeling rather like Captain Mainwaring from the British comedy *Dad's Army*, in charge of a unit of the Home Guard. I even adopted his catchphrases – 'Now gather round, everybody' and 'There's a war on, you know' when addressing my troops. Within hours, true to form, the press boats appeared on the horizon, which sent the children into a frenzy. 'Steady, lads,' I said, 'don't fire until you see the whites of their eyes.' It was not quite Britain in 1940, but to the two Princes it was just as vital to defend their post from invaders.

As boats carrying the hardcore paparazzi approached, I gave the children the order to unleash their stack of coloured water bombs. The unfortunate photographers did not know what had hit them, and after twenty minutes and several direct hits they retired hurt and did not return. To be fair, they had the good grace to see the funny side. For William, protecting his mother was a matter of personal pride, and he rushed back to tell her of his victory, very much a hero in her eyes.

Everyone was in high spirits. The Princess, revitalised by her holiday, wanted to bid farewell to Necker in style, and to that end arranged a lavish beach party. That night, clad in a diaphanous blue silk dress, she was in real party mood. As the reggae band, the Bitter End Steel Orchestra, played, she grabbed me, looked me straight in the eyes and ordered, 'Let's tango!'

As we swept away to the music of the steel band the rest of the party joined in. Diana's brother, Charles Spencer, had no choice but to follow our lead, being hauled onto the dance floor by his mother, Frances. Then, one after the other, Diana's sisters teamed up with the other detectives. Just to infuriate my Scotland Yard superiors even further, one of the band members sold the story of our last-night party to the *News of the World*. An article about our merrymaking appeared the following day, under the banner headline 'Di Tangos With Cop On Necker Island', and the accompanying text described me as a 'smoothie' who 'sees more of her than Charles'. For once, Diana joked when she saw the article from the now-defunct Sunday tabloid.

Above: The Princess of Wales with her police protection officer, Inspector Ken Wharfe; royal correspondent James Whitaker can be seen between them in the background. The Princess was visiting flood victims in Carmarthen, South Wales with Prince Charles in 1987.

Below: Prince Charles, Diana and Princes William and Harry with members of the Spanish Royal Family at the Marivent Palace in Mallorca, 13 August 1988.

Diana in Mallorca as a guest of the King of Spain. It was during her holiday there in August 1988 that she confided in the author about the state of her marriage to Prince Charles.

Top: Diana, Princess of Wales, with Prince Harry, aged four, during her private family holiday on Necker Island, 9 January 1989.

© Getty Images

Centre right: A view of Necker Island in the British Virgin Islands. The island is entirely owned by Sir Richard Branson, Chairman of the Virgin Group.

© Getty Images

Left: Unwinding on Necker. An excellent swimmer, the Princess was always the first in the water.

© Getty Images

Above left: Sitting cross-legged on the raised carpets and wearing a relaxed outfit by Catherine Walker, Diana is about to enjoy a special lamb feast in the inland oasis city of Al Ain, United Arab Emirates, 15 March 1989.

Above right: Earlier on the same day, in Dubai, emerging from the aircraft in a show-stopping ensemble. Always careful of others' sensitivities, she is wearing a tactful Philip Somerville turban hat.

Below: Abu Dhabi, United Arab Emirates, 14 March 1989: the Prince and Princess of Wales during their Gulf Tour. Ken Wharfe is standing to the left of the Princess, and just visible at far right is the Prince's own PPO, Superintendent Colin Trimming.

Above: Diana, Princess of Wales, and Maryam Babangida (left), the wife of the Nigerian President General Ibrahim Badamasi Babangida, attend the Rural Women's Fair in Tafawa Balewa Square, Lagos, during her and Prince Charles's official visit to Nigeria, 16 March 1989.

© *Getty Images*

Below left: Diana and Mrs Babangida shared an unusual chemistry. Wearing a discreet mint outfit by Alistair Blair, the Princess kept praising Mrs Babangida's colourful choice of dress.

© *Getty Images*

Below right: Back on holiday on Necker Island, with Prince William playing by her side, 11 April 1990.

© *Getty Images*

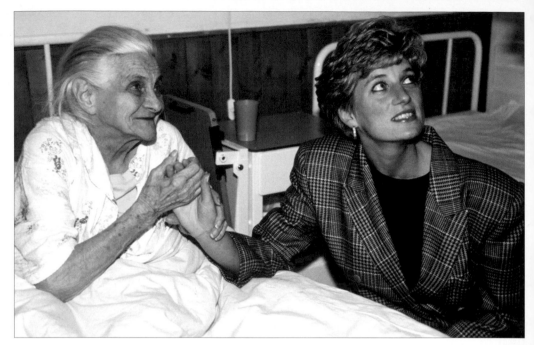

Top: Visiting the Nagyatad refugee camp during an official tour of Hungary in 1992.
The camp housed refugees from the dissolution wars in the former Yugoslavia.

Below left: Diana wearing a white strapless dress, embroidered with pearls, designed by
Catherine Walker, for a banquet during her official visit to Hungary, 7 May 1992.
A pearl and sapphire choker completes the look.

Below right: wearing a Moschino outfit at Victoria station, London, for the arrival of the
Italian President on a state visit, October 1990.

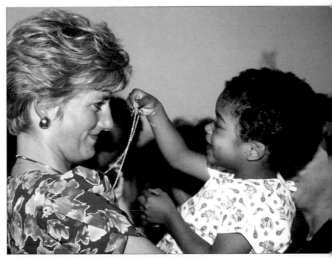

Top left: Brazil, 23 April 1991: Diana walks hand in hand with two pupils from the elementary school in Carajás she is visiting. The Princess is accompanied by her police protection office, Ken Wharfe, and, to his left, by her friend Lucia Flecha de Lima.

Top right: Holding a baby at a hostel for abandoned children in São Paolo, Brazil, 24 April 1991. The hostel cares for HIV-positive children.

Below: Visiting patients suffering from AIDS at the Hospital Universidade in Rio de Janeiro, Brazil, 25 April 1991. Few people worked so hard or did as much to remove the stigma attached to AIDS as the Princess.

Top: The famously poignant image of the Princess, trapped in an unhappy marriage, in front of one of the world's most celebrated monuments to love, the Taj Mahal in Agra, India, 11 February 1992.

© Getty Images

Centre left: Walking with bare feet and with her head covered with a headscarf during a visit to the Badshahi Mosque in Lahore, Pakistan, 25 September 1991.
© Getty Images

Centre right: Another informal photograph of the Princess in India, engaged, as always, with those to whom she is speaking.
© Rob Jobson

Left: Speaking to the nuns at Mother Teresa's Hospice in Calcutta during the Prince and Princess's visit to India, February 1992.
© Rob Jobson

MAY 1990: HUNGARY

I t wasn't the most auspicious of starts to the historic four-day official visit to Hungary, the first by members of the British Royal Family to a former Warsaw Pact country. The Queen's Flight BAe146, taking the Princess of Wales to Budapest on 7 May 1990, diverted to Gatwick Airport shortly after take-off from Heathrow because of an electrical fault. The four-engined jet spent an hour and twenty minutes on the ground at Gatwick while the fault was repaired. The aircraft then left for Italy, where Prince Charles was picked up, before travelling on to Hungary's capital city.

The tension between Charles and Diana was high when they set off for Budapest on the official visit. By now this was not a royal team, but rather two royal star performers determined to steal the limelight from each other. Of course this meant that the army of staff there to attend to 'The Boss' and 'The Boss Lady' – including private secretaries, equerries, press officers, personal assistants, a hairdresser and a valet – were treading on eggshells. It was never as bad for the security team as we were not technically on the Royal payroll.

On walkabouts in Hungary they did their own thing, as if not even aware of the other's presence. The Princess was in mischievous mood from the moment she set foot in Budapest. The Royal couple were met at the airport by their host, newly elected interim President Arpad Goncz, a liberal writer jailed for six years after the 1956 anti-Stalinist uprising. Diana seemed determined to steal the headlines away from her husband. For some inexplicable reason she held the hand of the President's wife, Zsuzsanna Göntér, and the cameras focused on that. It was seen as a moment of solidarity of unity.

Upon arrival, their first stop in the first city of Hungary was Heroes' Square, with its iconic statue complex featuring the Seven Chieftains of the Magyars, where the Royal couple placed a wreath at the Tomb of the Unknown Solider. About two thousand people gathered at the square and many applauded as Charles and Diana emerged from their car. Around a hundred members of the British ex-pat community in Budapest had turned out to see them.

President Arpad Goncz presided over a gala dinner held for the Royal duo on the Monday night. Charles hailed Hungary's role in 'changing the face of Europe' with its early moves towards political reforms and drew applause when he said his great-great-great grandmother, Countess Claudine Rhedey, was Hungarian.

'This evening I am especially proud of the Hungarian blood in my veins,' he declared, before adding, 'Making democracy work is never easy, but the effort is well worth the bother.'

In return, President Arpad Goncz said that Hungary now had a 'unique opportunity to irreversibly return to developed Europe'.

Diana seemed nonplussed when her husband gushed about Kenneth Branagh and Emma Thompson bringing *King Lear* to Budapest. She was not on top form but worse still she was in an obstructive mood, which again signalled that she was ready to do her own thing. The only moment of light relief came at the Ambassador's residence breakfast. The Ambassador, Sir John Birch, was not the usual smooth diplomat and host. He insisted there be no talking at the table because it was 'customary and essential' that the World Service be listened to by all. Not surprising thereafter that Diana ate in her room, as did the rest of the Royal party. The Ambassador's chauffeur, however, was a little more accommodating and asked Diana if she was 'into caviar'.

'Oh, that's the black bead stuff, isn't it?' she replied.

'There is a good black market here in Buda for caviar, I could get some for you,' he offered conspiratorially.

'Don't worry, I'll stick with my baked jacket potato,' Diana told him with a deadpan face.

Although privately the Prince and Princess remained at loggerheads, publicly the outward show of togetherness continued. Nonetheless, the situation within their marriage had gone from bad to worse by the time the couple set out on the official tour of Hungary. As it would turn out, Hungary was to be one of their last great acts of togetherness. Amazingly, the press swallowed the Palace spin and focused on how well Charles and Diana appeared to be getting on.

But that was in public and behind closed doors nothing could have been further from the truth. Perhaps Fleet Street's finest cynics had for once been overcome by the history and romance of the setting, and by the tour's timing. After all, the communist system was collapsing in Russia and all over Eastern Europe, and the beautiful city of Budapest and its people were once again free from authoritarianism. It is even possible that the wonderful romance of the place and the moment had an impact on the Prince and Princess, although I doubt it.

Diana would return again in March 1992 for a whistle-stop visit, where she attended an evening at the State Opera House for the performance of the English National Ballet, but this time alone.

AUGUST 1990: VENICE AND VERONA, ITALY

We slipped into the famed open-air Roman Arena di Verona undetected and settled into our front row seats of the ancient theatre just minutes before the performance started. Diana, her mother, Frances Shand Kydd, our host, the Contessa Maria Cristina Loredan Guerrieri-Rizzardi (a longtime friend of Diana's mother, Frances), and myself were tense with excitement as we awaited the arrival on stage of the great maestro Luciano Pavarotti for his performance of Verdi's *Requiem*. What followed was simply magnificent as the finest of operatic tenors held his audience spellbound. Diana was in awe of the genius before her – we all were.

Then suddenly, sadly, about halfway through the *Requiem*, the heavens opened, and even our umbrellas could not stop the torrential rain from soaking us to the skin. Nothing, however, could dampen Diana's spirits that night. She was elated, by the music, the atmosphere, and the dramatic setting, and wanted the evening to go on forever. Sadly, however, the downpour meant that for the first time in the city's recent history, the concert had to be cancelled.

Pavarotti had spotted the Princess during the performance, and as he left the rain-drenched arena, he invited our entire party back to his dressing room. There, in his broken English, the great tenor wooed the already smitten Diana.

'You were absolutely marvellous,' she told him. 'It was truly unforgettable. I was so profoundly moved.'

The great man returned the compliment and flirted with her outrageously. Then, even though her green flowered dress and matching hat were dripping wet, she spoke to the director and asked for the leaders of the chorus and the orchestra to be presented to her.

After chatting with them for ten minutes, she turned to leave the arena. Instead of the quiet exit she had imagined, however, Diana found her route lined by around one hundred and fifty members of the cast, who applauded her and sang 'Auld Lang Syne'. By now she was on fire. In contrast to her mood, the rain was still falling so heavily that the emergency services had been called out to deal with serious flooding in the area. But nothing could deter the Princess. As we stood beneath a tarpaulin, sheltering from the rain, waiting for the cars, she suddenly declared that she wanted to go to Venice. Diana always craved privacy so on the occasions when we did 'get away with one', as she put it, it made the moment even sweeter.

'Ken, we've got away with it. Nobody knows we're here, not even the local press. Let's live a little,' she beamed.

It was close to ten o'clock, but I knew from her expression and her manner that nothing was going to stop her seeing Venice, the City of Love, that night, even if she had to walk there. Much to the consternation of the local police assigned to us for the evening (I had contacted the Carabinieri on our arrival), I sanctioned it. The Italian officers said the rain made driving conditions dangerous and it would take at least two and a half hours to get there, although the distance was about seventy miles. They might just as well have saved their breath, for nothing was going to stop the Princess.

Within minutes, Diana, her mother, the Contessa's chauffeur, Tony Pezzo, who was related to the Rizzardi family, were heading for Venice, along with Sergeant Dave Sharp and myself. The flabbergasted British Consul, Martin Rickerd, also joined the party, somewhat bemused by our lapse into what appeared to be insanity.

The Carabinieri provided an escort in a Saab, and I did my best to keep up with them all in a Fiat Punto, aquaplaning most of the way. After one of the most treacherous drives of my life we arrived at the police headquarters of Venice just after midnight. The entire place was flooded in about a foot of water, and as the escorting police car turned the corner on the approach to the building the driver lost control and crashed into a brick wall. The Princess burst out laughing, which did not amuse the police officers that had gathered to greet her. Thankfully no one was hurt, just the pride of the driver who had driven so brilliantly in appalling conditions from Verona

At that precise moment it stopped raining and the clouds obligingly parted to let the moon through. Diana jumped out of the Contessa's car and starting kicking the puddles, as if she were Gene Kelly in *Singin' in the Rain*. The Venice police then arranged for two motorboats to take us off to enjoy the astonishing beauty of the city by moonlight. As we sped off along the canal, the driver of the crashed police car at last broke into a smile.

'I thought it was only we Italians who are crazy,' he said, his ill humour evaporating in the wake of the Princess's mood.

There was no one else around. For the next hour we saw Venice as few have ever been privileged to do. We sailed along the Grand Canal, with the ancient city silhouetted against a stormy sky pierced by a full moon. Armed with a flask of coffee and a bottle of chilled Pinot Grigio, from which Diana would take the occasional swig, as we had no glasses, we were midnight tourists in an empty city. She then announced that she wanted to walk through Saint Mark's Square. The Italian police, who by now had embraced the mood, agreed. We docked our launches at the Hotel Danieli and, still with the tarpaulin over our sodden heads since it had started to rain again, walked towards Saint Mark's Cathedral at the end of the square.

It was a surreal experience. With the exception of a couple of vagrants dossed down above the water level near the famous landmark, we were the only people there. Then, from nowhere, Dave Sharp appeared with a tray of hot croissants and small loaves of freshly cooked bread, which earned him a round of applause from the by now ecstatic Princess.

As she took another swig from the bottle of white wine, Diana, her eyes alight with pleasure, turned to me and said, 'If only I could have this freedom once a month, it would make the job worth it all the more.'

Sadly we had to depart. The Princess took graceful leave of the Venetian police officers, who were equally charming in return. We returned to Lake Garda just in time for breakfast, snatched two hours' sleep, and then set off for Milan's Linate Airport for the flight home. It was there that the press finally caught up with us.

One paparazzo snatched shots of the Princess, still animated after her three-day holiday, kissing the Contessa's chauffeur, Tony Pezzo, on the cheek as she made her goodbyes, while *The Sun* had printed pictures of Italy in an attempt to flush out a source to support their story of Diana's visit, but had failed to do so. By this time, however, Diana was back at Kensington Palace, her private memories locked safely away.

* * *

That blessed weekend at the Villa Rizzardi, near Negrar, a few miles from the ancient city of Verona, lived long in my memory.

Diana was so happy. At last she could be a private person, able to wander around the shores of Lake Garda almost unnoticed. It was a wonderful weekend. After lunch on the day of our arrival Contessa Rizzardi accompanied us to an area of the vineyard where staff were cleaning in preparation for the next harvest. Huge shiny vats were being meticulously scrubbed.

The Contessa summoned her manager and two bottles of wine – one red, one white – were produced with glasses, very much to the excitement of Diana's mother, Frances, who did enjoy her wine, and openly encouraged by Roger Bramble, her long-time friend. Bramble was excellent company, an intellectual jester. As the wine was quaffed rapidly, further bottles followed. Then suddenly the sound of live guitar music echoed through our cavernous space.

An elderly man with a Spanish guitar appeared from a nearby cellar and climbed into a small hole at the base of one of the recently cleaned wine vats – with guitar. This prompted much laughter – even more so when the elderly Italian began to sing favourite arias from within. The acoustics were superb. Diana and her mother, now with the support of Bramble, almost forcibly pushed me towards the vat with the Italian, equally encouraged by the Contessa. I relented and climbed inside. With little or no communication, the vineyard employee and I, with guitar, mumbled our way through a selection of Italian arias, 'Take Me Back To Sorrento', with 'O Sole Mio' getting an encore from the audience out of sight. I emerged from the vat, only to find Diana and Frances creased up with laughter at this bizarre performance. Bramble stepped forward with the Contessa, and with outstretched hands to us both said, 'Bravo, yum yum blessings!' Breaking a golden rule of protection, a glass of the Rizzardi white was necessary and then we all returned to the house.

Later, Diana and I took the speedboat on Lake Garda, as our host's wine estate was on its edge, and raced over the glass-like waters. For the Princess the Villa Rizzardi had proved the ultimate sanctuary, a place where she could abandon her innermost fears and just be herself – even if it was for only three days.

APRIL 1991:
BRAZIL

Prince Harry was close to tears on hearing the story of forty-one-year-old Cristina da Cruz Nascimento. It was June 2014 in São Paulo. Just over twenty-three years earlier, his late mother had visited Brazil on an official visit with his father in one of his parents' last joint Royal tours together. He heard how Nascimento had raised her two granddaughters, Karina, eight, and Carolina, nine, because their mother was murdered at just twenty-four years old and their father was in jail. Cristina's account led Harry to share the painful story of losing his own mother in a car crash in 1997.

'I was completely overwhelmed and shocked,' he said of the time, when he was just twelve years old. 'There are two little girls – I'm quite emotional – just looking at them. I wanted to talk about my own experiences, but there is no point because it is just so far removed. The bravery of them looking at me, smiling at me... I wanted to use my own experiences in a very small way, to try to give them a bit of understanding about the fact [that I understood what they] are going through,' he said. 'I've never blubbedin public as far as I can remember, but I was pretty damn close. It was amazing to hear those stories,' he added.

It was one of the first times the Prince had opened up about the profound impact of the loss of his mother. Over the next few years he and his brother, William, for so long silent about her death, began to talk about it.

When I heard him talking about his mother in this way, I couldn't help but think how proud she would have been of her sons, particularly Prince Harry, who like Diana wears his heart upon his sleeve. Like the Princess, Harry is prepared to take risks, to *do* rather than just *say*. His comments took me back to Diana's official visit to Brazil, where for the first time she truly showed the confidence to do what she wanted to do and not just follow a path scripted for her by royal aides and government. In so doing she broke the Royal mould and in an instant launched herself as the 'Queen of People's Hearts', shaking up the poised royal brand forever.

In April 1991 the Prince and Princess of Wales flew to Brazil for a five-day trip aimed at boosting environmental issues and trade relations between the two nations. The highlight was supposed to be a day-long seminar on environmental conservation aboard the Royal Yacht *Britannia*, near the northern city of Belem, at the mouth of the Amazon River. Among those scheduled to attend were the Brazilian President Fernando Collor de Mello, William Reilly, director of the U.S. Environmental Protection Agency, British Environment Minister David Trippier and his Brazilian counterpart, José Lutzenberger, along with several top US, European and Brazilian bankers, businessmen and environmentalists.

The trip was billed as a mission of environmental co-operation between Brazil and Britain, which had been intensified since they signed an agreement in 1989 to work closely on environmental issues. While in Brazil, Charles was to visit two successful conservation projects: an iron mine in Carajás, in the state of Para, and a reforestation project in Espirito Santo, sponsored by a British-Brazilian paper company, Aracruz. The Royal couple's first stop was Brasilia, where they were to meet with the President, and then it was on to São Paulo, Brazil's financial capital, where the Prince met with local industry leaders. For Charles, who saw himself as a champion of the environment even then, it didn't get more important. But Diana had another agenda — her own. And it was soon apparent, much to Charles's chagrin, that the British press were only interested in what his wife was up to.

Images of Diana holding hands with a child during a visit to a school in Carajás or posing alone in front of the Christ the Redeemer statue in Rio de Janeiro were all Fleet Street editors focused on. And when the Princess, in a bright floral dress, visited a hostel for abandoned children in São Paulo, where many of the street kids were HIV-positive, the press went into overdrive. She was photographed holding the small children in her arms, in an instant spreading her message of love and dispelling the stigma of those suffering with HIV/AIDS. Diana was doing exactly what she wanted to do — breaking down barriers in a way only she could.

'They just want a hug,' she whispered to me. 'Heaven knows, they need it, don't you think?'

This was Diana at her best – raw, real and true to herself. It was inspiring to witness. There was nothing calculating about the Princess and her work with children and AIDS, it came from the heart. When she scooped the children up into her arms it was a perfectly natural act of love. For the first time I saw Diana blossoming into the public figure she wanted to be. She had the courage of her own convictions and was now, at last, prepared to tear up the old rule book and replace it with her own.

We flew around Brazil in two British Aerospace 146 jets, which England exports to Brazil, and on the streets of Rio de Janeiro and Brasilia, the Prince and Princess were promoting the best of British by riding in a Rolls-Royce Silver Spirit II automobile. Under President Fernando Collor de Mello's economic plan, Britain would export the cars at the beginning of the following month at a retail cost in Brazil of about $350,000 (£260.000). These luxurious vehicles nearly led to me becoming embroiled in our own controversy. We were staying at the Copacabana Beach Hotel. Unusually, so too were the Princess's chauffeur, Simon Solari, and her chef, Mervyn Wycherley. Upon arrival in Rio, I accompanied Simon to a private building just outside Rio to take possession of a Rolls-Royce saloon that had been donated privately for the Royals' use while they were there. Security was of paramount importance – vehicles of this description were rarely seen in Brazil – and with an exceptionally high crime rate, the security of this vehicle, given its intended use, was crucial.

Driving back to the hotel, the vehicle drew large crowds. Short of fuel, we pulled in to a petrol station. I fuelled the car while Simon paid. The vehicle was attracting large crowds, and I sensed a potential problem – and summoned Simon to 'hurry up'. Suddenly, three women, scantily dressed, rushed to the car, opened the rear door opposite me, and clambered in. These women were in fact three transsexual men. The incident now had the real potential for very negative media and of course the risk of serious criminal damage. Using the best of my interpersonal skills and offering a small amount of cash, I was lucky with hindsight that they agreed to vacate the Royal Rolls without any negative media coverage. Simon and I left the garage laughing.

Back at the hotel we told Diana, who as expected found the whole story hilarious, leaving the Prince of Wales somewhat baffled. The Princess couldn't wait to tell him the story herself.

'Ken and Simon have just given some transsexuals a lift in your car, Charles.'

The Prince looked even more confused, before replying, 'Oh *really* – are they to be part of the Brazilian security team, Ken?'

Diana's hairdresser, the irrepressible Sam McKnight, was also travelling with the entourage. Sam, who would later be described as one of the most important image makers of the late twentieth and early twenty-first centuries by the *New York Times* no less, was still a rookie on Royal tour at this stage. I had previously made a point of personally advising all the travelling staff to be very careful when venturing outside the hotel. Crime was rife, slick teams of pickpockets operated in the tourist areas and I had warned them all not to leave any belongings on the beach outside. Sam went for a stretch of sunbathing across the road from the hotel. Some time later, a hotel porter/doorman approached me in the foyer to say that he thought that a member of our party was in difficulty on the beach. Fearing perhaps a swimming accident, the late Ron Lewis, who was the travelling Yeoman (baggage), and I ran to the beach. Lying on his back was Sam, surrounded by a circle of bikini-clad trannies throwing peanuts at his torso. I sensed he was frozen in confusion as to what to do next. Although it was an incident not likely to have been life threatening, two transsexual incidents in two days for members of the Royal party was enough. Rumours travel fast on tour, and the renaming of staff was quick to follow – the hairdresser now with the nom de plume of 'Peanut'.

Diana then left Rio for São Paulo as part of the Brazilian visit. Travelling in an aircraft of the Queen's Flight, a Boeing 146 piloted by Squadron Leader Graham Laurie, we encountered a severe storm en route. We were all belted in our seats and the plane was being severely buffeted, with the wings flexing; Diana and the entire crew and passengers were nervous. We could see through to the cockpit. Hail pellets the size of golf balls were pounding the aircraft – it was like being in a corrugated tin hut being hit by machine-gun fire. The cockpit window was completely covered in thick ice. After a demonstration of complete pilot brilliance – Squadron Leader Laurie landed the plane at São Paulo to rounds of applause from the few of us inside – Diana rushed forward to the cockpit and embraced him.

Fearful of damage to the aircraft, Squadron Leader Laurie left the plane first to inspect the nose. He then summoned us all before we left for our next engagement and showed us the nose of the aircraft that was now bereft of paint. The hail had been so powerful that during the storm it had pummelled the paintwork and taken it back to the bare metal.

Diana and her team returned from Brazil to London on a chartered British Airways Boeing 747 from Belem in 1991 as the Prince of Wales set off for the Amazon rainforest. It was my birthday and Diana had informed the crew. With many of the economy or as the Princess would say 'goat-class seats' removed, the aircraft was certainly in a party configuration. Covered tables carried a selection of fine wines from the business-class cellars. Once airborne, a call to order was made, and a BA stewardess carried in a large cake in the shape of a Gordon's gin bottle complete with lighted candles to a chorus of 'Happy Birthday'. How lucky was I. As for the cake, now that was *The Great Belem Bake Off*. Mervyn Wycherley, with his customary, 'I know nothing about it', later confessed to raiding the kitchens of the Copacabana Hotel in search of appropriate ingredients.

'Why the Gordon's gin bottle, Mervyn?' I asked.

'It's English, Wharfie, and the Princess's idea, not mine,' he told me.

With doors set safely to manual, this was a long-haul flight that would be remembered by all those lucky enough to be present.

SEPTEMBER 1991: PAKISTAN

'I don't think my husband has ever had the occasion to use one, *seriously*,' Diana blurted out somewhat indiscreetly as somehow the conversation between the Royal staff and the Princess on board the Queen's Flight BAe146 had turned to the subject of condoms.

We were flying high above the snow-capped Himalayas to Chitral, a former princely state, in the shadow of Tirich Mir, the highest peak of the Hindu Kush range. Diana had become locked in discussion about the subject of contraception and condoms, perhaps because one of the visits on her official tour of Pakistan had been to a family planning centre in a village outside Islamabad.

Then came one of the most bizarre occurrences I'm sure has ever taken place on a Royal flight. It was supposed to be the exotic end of our visit that got frankly a little too exotic. We were all a little demob happy, when the staff member decided to reveal that he had a party trick where he could blow up the condom and put it on his head, fully inflated.

'Really? Go on then, show me,' Diana said, intrigued, and laying down the bizarre challenge excitedly. Within seconds everyone was falling about the place in fits of giggles as the staff member accomplished this extraordinary feat in a matter of seconds. Squadron Leader Laurie of the Queen's Flight must have wondered what on earth was going on as he prepared to make one of the trickiest landings in Chitral with just 5,741 feet of runway. He was surely mystified by the laughter coming through the fuselage from the Royal Cabin – he might have expected applause at the very least. It was just as well he didn't witness the performance going on inside.

As we stepped off the plane to be greeted on the tarmac by the Commissioner of Malakand Division and the Deputy Commissioner of Chitral, Diana was soon back to demure 'Princess mode'. She watched a local dance and was presented with a traditional Pakol, a woollen Chitrali cap with feathers indigenous to this region, and an embroidered coat. Members of the Chitral Scouts lined the route by car from the airport to visit the Aga Khan Rural Support programme projects established in Bilphok, a village where Diana visited a school constructed by the locals and briefly looked at an afforestation project. I had to laugh when the press was warned not to use the school roof, which looked a tempting vantage from which to take photos but was to be avoided as it was made of mud and would not support human weight! From there we pressed on to the Chitral Fort, the ancestral home of the former ruling family, the Mehtars of Chitral, where the Princess was met by the former Mehtar, Saif ul-Mulk, who escorted her through the grounds of the fort, which stands on the bank of the Kunar River, close to a large mosque. The former royal prince (for Chitral had ceased to be a princely state in 1969) then escorted Diana into the main dining hall, where she studied the collection of photographs before being taken on to the balcony for a view of the Tirich Mir peak.

As I stood next to her, admiring the astounding scenery, Diana poked me and whispered, 'I need another one of those caps, I can't take one back for William and not have one for Harry.' There was urgency in her voice – she knew there would be war in Kensington Palace if Harry didn't get one too.

'I will do my best,' I whispered back.

So, as the Chief Minister of the North West Frontier, Mir Afzal Khan, was hosting tea and local dancing for the Princess, with the help of an interpreter I headed back a short way to a market place, but to no avail. Finally, I persuaded another village elder to surrender his cap. For a time those two hats were the favoured nursery toys for Indian games by William and Harry, I recall.

It had been the then Prime Minister Benazir Bhutto on a visit to London who had invited the Prince and Princess of Wales to Pakistan but it was decided this would be a good opportunity for Diana to make her first solo visit of substance. It was seen as a test to see if she had what it takes to use her celebrity to promote British interests abroad. Sir Nicholas Barrington, the High Commissioner, had met with the Princess and mapped out the overview for the visit and what should be included in the programme. Benazir Bhutto's unexpected dismissal as Prime Minister meant the visit had to be cancelled until her replacement, Nawaz Sharif, had extended the invitation again – everyone wanted to meet the Princess.

It was decided that Diana would stay at the High Commissioner's official residence in Islamabad. With patrolling guards, it was safest and the swimming pool was well out of range of the photographers so she enjoyed a swim every morning. I knew exactly what type of schedule she wanted and it was one that went far beyond the issue of security.

'I am a humanitarian, Ken,' the Princess told me before I left. 'I want to touch the people and I want them to touch me.'

She was making it clear that she wanted to smash down old barriers and set a new and exciting agenda. It was her chance to establish the caring Diana brand. This wasn't a cynical move, however, it came from the heart.

Diana's decision to get up close and personal with people who had not been vetted during her first ever official solo visit to Pakistan was not a request, it was unequivocal. It may have been before 9/11 and also before the rise of the so-called Islamic State, which would not take place for many years, but visiting this predominantly Muslim country presented me with one of my toughest security challenges of my career to that point. Somehow I had to make sure that Diana was not put at risk while fulfilling her wishes.

The Princess saw her first official solo visit to Pakistan as a great opportunity and she was anxious not to fail. She felt the visit provided her with a chance to emerge from the shadow of her husband and be seen not only as a worthwhile member of the Royal Family but as a person in her own right. The Prince of Wales, meanwhile, was undertaking a separate visit to Nepal, and it was arranged that he would collect the Princess in Pakistan for the flight home. However, the media spotlight was on her, not him.

At the end of August 1991, before I set off for the reconnaissance, during which I hoped to pave the way for a safe and media-friendly tour, Diana requested a private meeting. She urged me to ensure that her character was reflected in the working visit and it would not be Foreign Office led. She wanted, she said, to show the world what the Princess of Wales was all about. Her private secretary, my good friend Commander Patrick Jephson, took directives from the Foreign Office and the High Commissioner's locally based team about what they wanted to achieve from the Princess's visit, as well as seemingly endless instructions and advice from the Palace. With his considerable diplomatic skills he had to chart a course that accommodated them and his boss, Diana. Formal directives were all very well, we both knew this was a visit on which the Princess would take the lead, with or without our help.

The Pakistani government and people could not have been more helpful or hospitable, and were clearly delighted – 'honoured' was the word they used – to be hosting such a high-profile tour. I quickly found that nothing was too much trouble for them. I was put up in the old Government House in Lahore, a fantastic building dating from the days of the British Raj, and immensely comfortable, and was assured that nothing was too difficult. At one point I asked if they could arrange a back-up car for security use, and emphasised that it had to be reliable. At this, the eyes of one of the local organisers lit up with excitement.

'Don't you worry, Inspector, don't you worry. I have something very, very, very special for you.'

Three 'verys', I thought, God help me! A few hours later, I was taken to see it, and could barely contain my laughter as I was proudly shown an old but classic pink Lincoln convertible.

On my return I gave the Princess a detailed briefing. She had received a formal outline of the visit from Patrick Jephson and the High Commissioner, but she wanted me to reassure her not just that all the proper security measures were in place, but that the trip was going to be a huge success and would showcase what she was all about. I did my best to set her mind at rest on both points. She was going to get her way – she would be seen as the caring Princess of the People, not a ribbon cutter. I could tell Diana was nervous before we left for the visit; she was on edge, snapping at her domestic staff. She even experimented with a Bach flower remedy to soothe her nerves before the visit. I told her not to bother, reassuring her that she was strong. But Diana never wanted to let anyone down, she was determined to use her fame to help make the world a better place. It was to prove a visit that would have a profound impact on her and her future role.

Diana flew out to Oman, Muscat, on a scheduled British Airways plane. From there, we joined a BAe 146 of the RAF's Queen's Flight, waiting to take her on the last leg to Islamabad. Wearing a stunning, flowing three-quarter-length pale green dress, she was greeted at the foot of the aircraft steps by British High Commissioner Sir Nicholas Barrington. On landing, she went straight to her first engagement, giving the world and her detractors back at Buckingham Palace a clear message that she meant business.

Her first stop was at a ceremony at the Commonwealth War cemetery in Rawalpindi. There, after a prayer by the Reverend Graham Burton, the Princess chatted to Pakistan's Victoria Cross recipient, Jamadar Ali Haider. She then went on to visit Sir Syed Academy For Hearing Impaired Children, where she demonstrated her skills in sign language. Then, in a move that particularly pleased the Princess, she was invited to call on Pakistan's Prime Minister, Nawaz Sharif. He greeted her and then escorted her to the main drawing room for a 'call'.

This, Diana wanted to stress, was official business, sanctioned by and undertaken on behalf of HM The Queen and the Foreign and Commonwealth Office. She ended this exhausting first day by flying the flag for Britain, and delivering a scripted speech, in which she spoke of the close economic ties and friendship between the two countries at an official dinner hosted by Mr Sharif.

The Princess, in a long black jacket over white Shalwar trousers, was clearly nervous about delivering her speech but handled the situation with aplomb. She certainly did not let anyone down, although there were many lurking in the corridors at the Palace who would have loved for her to fall flat on her face, as she was well aware. Diana was not a timid girl, however, but a determined woman. She may not have had much in the way of formal education, but she was extremely canny and had a highly developed instinct for other people and their expectations. Before she retired after that first testing day, both elated and exhausted, she again sought reassurance from me.

'How did I do?' she asked me, a little apprehensively.

Sometimes I felt like a trusted uncle reassuring his precocious but nervous little niece.

'You were bloody marvellous,' I said, 'Bloody marvellous!'

At this she smiled, said goodnight and headed off to bed.

The Princess was now on a roll. She performed brilliantly the next day too, carrying out her duties with energy and enthusiasm, visiting commercial operations where British firms were working with locals; she met students back from the UK at a lunch in the Margalla Hills overlooking the city, always, as was her trademark, squatting down beside the smaller children to talk to them on their level. Then there was a call on the President, Ghulam Ishaq Khan – an independent – at his newly constructed residence in Islamabad, Aiwan-e-Sadr, before he escorted Diana to a dinner on the seventh floor.

Unfortunately, by the third day Diana's sullen demeanour had returned and she didn't say a word to me on board the Queen's Flight to Lahore Airport. The Governor of the Punjab, Mohammad Azhar, as well as smiling local schoolchildren there to present flowers, met her on the tarmac. My new best friend, the local Chief of Police, was as good as his word and there waiting to collect us in Lahore was our very own open-top 'special and reliable' pink limousine. Diana could barely contain her giggles as she climbed inside the classic old vehicle, looking every inch Lady Penelope Creighton-Ward from the popular children's TV show, *Thunderbirds*.

'Can we now call you Lady Penelope, m'lady?' I asked.

'As I long as I can call you Parker,' she joked.

Thanks heaven her mood was lifting, I thought. For the rest of the day I referred to her as 'Penny', which got her giggling every time. As previously mentioned, Diana was an inveterate giggler – the slightest thing could set her off.

Lahore was a cauldron. The crowds were huge, six or seven

persons deep on both sides of the road. Our motorcycle escorts were somewhat nervous drivers astride barely combusting aged BSA 125cc Bantams – the archetypal 'truly British' lightweight motorcycle produced in Birmingham after the war. Two of them crashed and went careering off the road in front of us, but luckily no one was seriously hurt. Diana was concerned too about the static uniformed police hitting the ankles of onlookers, although they seemed to accept this ritual police punishment.

'Do they really have to do that? It looks really over the top,' she said.

My colleague, Sergeant Dave Sharp, tried in vain to reverse their aggressive tactics by speaking to the local police chief, but he was having none of it. An effective way of preventing enthusiastic crowds from getting too close to the car, it had worked for years and he saw no reason to change it now. The ankle striking continued; if anything, they seemed to step up the ritual as though the police chief was telling us to butt out.

Diana visited the Christian Kinnaird Girls College, founded in 1913, where she was greeted by the gushing principal, Dr Mira Phailbus, with a colourful song and dance routine tracing the evolution of Pakistani women, while covering the Royal party with rose petals. The schedule and the heat were stifling. From there she went on to the King Edward Medical College, where, in the detoxification rooms, she would sit on the beds of patients and chat freely with them about their problems. I could tell, however, that the heat and dust were getting to her – she was flagging. By the time we reached the great courtyard in the old walled city, the main monumental centre of Lahore, the Princess was exhausted. Diana laid a wreath at the red sandstone tomb of the celebrated poet-philosopher Allama Iqbal before entering the Badshahi Mosque, one of the world's finest Islamic monuments, built by Emperor Aurangzeb in 1674, with a courtyard that can hold 100,000 people for open-air prayers. She left her shoes at the entrance and was greeted by the Imam, Maulana Azad, who escorted her around the prayer chamber and cloisters.

The Princess wore green and wrapped a flowing dupatta around her head. But the High Commissioner, Sir Nicholas Barrington, was flapping about her dress not being long enough – I thought he was about to explode in the heat. Diana had been given the advice but chose to wear a skirt that only reached her knees. She was conscious of what was expected, but went ahead with what she was wearing anyway. By the time we reached the final part of the Lahore visit, she kept looking at me with weary eyes. I encouraged her to keep going, but when we got to the Shish Mahal, the place of mirrors, her patience snapped.

'I want this to finish now,' she whispered to me. 'I want no more delays. Make it happen.'

There was a huge surge of people wanting to get close to Diana that spoilt the atmosphere. She did not want to attend some of the events planned for her, and was beginning to make things difficult for those around her, especially Patrick Jephson and her press secretary, Dickie Arbiter. Things came to a head as we sat in the aircraft at Lahore Airport, waiting to return to Islamabad for a dinner she was due to host at the High Commission.

I tried, as diplomatically as I could, to snap her out of her petulant mood, but it was to no avail – by now everyone, in her view, was out of step with Diana, it seemed. Then news reached us that a violent thunderstorm had hit Islamabad, which meant that we would have to stay on the ground for perhaps as long as another hour. Diana spoke to the High Commissioner who was accompanying her, and learned that the dinner had had to be cancelled, which seemed to brighten her mood visibly.

'Oh dear, Sir Nicholas,' she said, 'what a terrible shame,' just about concealing her inner delight. He tried to suggest that if the

Princess made an appearance there, however brief, it would create much goodwill.

After we had finally reached Islamabad (at a time that would have made the dinner still possible) and as Sir Nicholas moped over the empty tables and his chance to show off the best of British for the banquet that never was, I realised that with no formal engagements, we now had the evening to ourselves since my back-up protection officer was looking after the Princess. When Diana retired with a snack, I therefore suggested a 'boys' night out' – after all, why waste the opportunity? Patrick Jephson agreed and so, with Dickie Arbiter in tow, the three of us embarked on what proved to be a riotous evening. Next morning, a much brighter Diana could not wait to hear about our night on the tiles.

'How's your head? Did you boys get up to no good last night?' she asked.

Naturally, I adopted a choirboy expression and admitted nothing.

The next day, we headed to the Khyber Pass, first flying in the Queen's Flight to Peshawar, the capital of the Pakistani province of Khyber Pakhtunkhwa. It evokes images of romance, chicanery and real danger – the paradigm dusty frontier town. Set at the foot of the Khyber Pass, for centuries it has been an important trading town and staging post for invasions, its fortunes often more closely linked to affairs in Kabul. As we drove with Retired Brigadier Amir Gulistan Janjua, the Governor of the North West Frontier Province, I watched out of the window as groups of men, tall Pashtuns, huddled together conspiratorially, many of them armed. It left me a little uneasy.

En route to the Khyber Pass we stopped to visit a prosthetic centre outside of Peshawar, established by the former television foreign correspondent (and later ITN newsreader) Sandy Gall. The plight of the children in the conflict-ravaged area had a profound impact on the Princess. It was here that she first became aware of the terrible scourge of landmines that was to occupy so much of her time towards the end of her life. Little children had been left maimed for doing nothing more than going out to play. A visit to a war-torn area like this would today be totally off-limits to a member of our Royal Family, as it would be deemed too dangerous.

The main road running westwards from Peshawar curves for around thirty-five miles towards the Afghan border at Torkham. During this course it runs through the historic Khyber Pass, cutting through the Hindu Kush, dotted with carved and painted insignia of the various British regiments that served there. As we headed there, accompanied by members of the paramilitary Khyber Rifles Regiment raised from local tribes as extra protection, we passed a number of forts spaced along the road, among them Shagai Fort, a seemingly impregnable red building built by the British military in the 1920s, and Ali Masjid Fort, high above the pass.

We drove through the Khyber Pass and walked to the briefing platform at Minchi Point, which looks across the Afghan border.

On our arrival one of the Palace press officers, Kiloran McGrigor, was at the centre of a narrowly avoided diplomatic incident. As we approached, accompanied by the Commandant of the Khyber Rifles, Lieutenant-Colonel Khizar Hayat, and other senior officers, she had insisted that the photographers were roped in, despite there being acres of space for them to operate in, much to their displeasure. Some senior officers in their splendid uniforms surged forward to greet Diana – one of those wonderfully unscripted moments that happens on Royal tours. Kiloran in her role as press officer quickly responded and tried to restore order. Regretfully – being a woman – she made the mistake of pulling on the arms of the army officers and trying to re-position them. Those touched by her were furious.

'No woman *ever* touches me without my permission,' roared one fierce-looking officer.

I could see the situation getting out of hand but decided not to intervene and to stick with the Princess. Poor Kiloran looked acutely embarrassed and moved away slowly while order was restored with a few quiet diplomatic words from the British High Commissioner. Diana, who was on fine form after a rest, smoothed everything over. She looked amazing in a scarlet blouse and floral skirt and was able to charm all the local men with a smile. Every single one of them – some in military uniform, others in white traditional clothing – wanted to be in the photos and she was happy to oblige. They posed with her as she signed a book placed on a desk to mark her visit. She then posed looking through military binoculars for the view across the border into Afghanistan, where there was still fighting around Jalalabad. It was an unbelievable backdrop of arid, broken hills of shale and limestone.

We finally made it back to the colonial residence of the Governor in Peshawar for lunch in the drawing room. Afterwards Diana viewed the gemstone collection and was presented with a large ruby by the Chief Minister, Mir Afzal Khan. Then, as the media filed their dispatched reports and photos before returning to Islamabad, the Royal party with one photographer, Martin Keene from the Press Association, boarded the Queen's Flight for our last hurrah in Chitral.

Back in the UK the newspapers lapped up every minute of Diana's solo adventure – the tabloid editors couldn't get enough of it. Headlines screamed that she had taken Pakistan by storm and that her visit had been a resounding success. The tabloids somewhat predictably hailed her vociferously as the jewel in the Royal Family's crown, one of them claiming, employing a typically lame pun, that she was 'ALL THE RAJ'.

The Princess could barely contain her elation. As far as she was concerned, she had arrived as a public figure on the world stage. From then on until the end of the visit, she performed her duties with good humour and considerable élan, and people flocked to see her. Above all, her natural sympathy shone through on even the most formal of occasions, making her countless new admirers.

Diana may have been buoyed by her solo success, but the triumph of her visit to Pakistan was almost inevitably regarded in a different light by traditionalists at the Palace, as well as those in Prince Charles's camp. She undoubtedly had the private backing of the Queen, who had sanctioned the visit, as had the Foreign and Commonwealth Office, but there were many in senior positions within the Palace who felt that it had been not only unwise, but also foolhardy.

The Old Guard feared that once Diana's free spirit escaped the confines of the Palace there would be no stopping her, much less controlling her, as they once had. In this they were absolutely right: Diana had no intention of looking fearfully over her shoulder ever again. Convinced her errant husband would never love her, she was determined to chart her own course in life. As usual, however (as was perhaps my policeman's lot), I urged caution, *extreme* caution. As I knew only too well, the Princess was prone to over-excitability, but on this issue there was no point in warning her to hold back. Her mind was made up, and I knew from the way she was speaking that her life was never going to be the same from this moment on.

At one stage during the tour the Queen's Flight BAe 146 arrived at Lahore to collect us, bringing Prince Charles with it. As we prepared to leave for Islamabad aboard the aircraft, a curious incident happened that left the Royal party vastly amused at my expense. The RAF group captain commanding the flight was ready for take-off and was going through his final checks when we heard a loud banging at the back of the jet. The noise was so alarming that the pilot aborted the take-off, but the banging on the fuselage continued.

With the engines shut down, the steps were lowered so that the crew could investigate further. Suddenly the local chief of police, a large and imposing man with a huge handlebar moustache, appeared at the door, clutching a furled umbrella, with which he had obviously been knocking on the aircraft's metal skin. He was badly out of breath and seemed quite alarmed. Had he, just before we had taken off, uncovered some sinister plot to blow up the flight? No. Apparently oblivious to the fact that he had halted the Royal flight, he began to explain, panting deeply.

'I had to stop you,' he gasped, with all of us hanging on his every word. 'You see, I forgot to let my wife say goodbye to Inspector Wharfe and she made me promise that I would do it.'
We all burst out laughing.

The Prince of Wales, who was sitting in the Royal apartment at the rear of the aircraft, turned to me and asked, deadpan: 'Have you known her long?'

I thanked our visitor with as straight a face as I could manage, and he departed, his marital duty done, while the flight crew readied the aircraft for take-off once more. As we lifted off, Diana turned and nudged me and whispered mischievously, 'You obviously made an impression with the Chief of Police's wife.'

Her success in Pakistan crystallised the Princess's determination to 'go solo', a phrase she loved to use. No one, and especially not her husband, was going to stop her now. As she repeatedly told me, she was still in love with Charles, but she was not going to let him get the better of her. Her optimism was one of the most attractive features of her character and when she was in one of those moods she was a pure joy to be with.

**

Benazir Bhutto's government was dismissed from office on 7 August 1990, the year that Diana's visit to Pakistan was first scheduled. Following a recce that year, it was decided that because of the political unrest following the dismissal of Bhutto, a high-profile visit by the Princess would, for security reasons, be unwise and the visit was therefore postponed. It was after Diana's successful solo tour of Pakistan a year later that privately in London she met with Benazir Bhutto. The Princess often talked of the admiration she had for Bhutto for her career had been celebrated as a triumph for women in the Muslim world and for the global fight against Islamic extremism. Alas, Mrs Bhutto was assassinated in 2007 while leaving a campaign event in Rawalpindi.

Following Pakistan, however, Diana realised that she had more cards to play. After all, she had wooed and won the media. Cynics had written her off as nothing more than an upper-class girl who had left school with no qualifications, a pretty accessory for the Prince of Wales and a useful mother to his heirs, but they had missed the point: she had become adept not only in the art of survival but also flourishing in the world in which she found herself. She knew who to flatter and how, even if it was sometimes to deceive. Above all, she knew how to get what she wanted. After the struggles and disputes of the previous months, she was primed and ready for the fight to come, in which she would take on not just her husband and his supporters and cronies, but the Palace as well.

* * *

The Queen was suffering from a bad cold, and her voice, weary and hoarse, summed up the worst year in recent Royal history when, in a speech she made at the Guildhall on 24 November 1992, she described that year as her '*annus horribilis*'. The Latin expression was her first public admission of failure, an acknowledgement that the state of affairs within the Royal Family was in many ways dire, and she knew it, although it was also a reference to the disastrous fire at Windsor Castle on 20 November.

At the beginning of the year, however, many in the Queen's inner circle believed that the Prince of Wales's marriage could be saved. There was a feeling that a working arrangement could be put in place that would suit both Charles and Diana. Yet those in Diana's camp knew that nothing could have been further from the truth.

By early 1992 the couple were effectively separated in everything but name. Charles was living his preferred life as a bachelor. He rarely saw his sons or wife, and threw himself into his work. Camilla Parker Bowles, of course, was the soulmate who consoled him, and appeared to attend to his every need. Effectively, he had made it clear to Diana that although she was his wife, the mother of his two sons, and Her Royal Highness The Princess of Wales, she had no place in his heart, now or in the future. Diana, although resigned to this way of life, had long since decided that she was not prepared to abide by the rules her husband had laid down. True, she had engaged in extramarital affairs, as he had done, but she was not willing to make life easy for him. I felt that she was, in some ways, still in love with the idea of being in love with him, and when we were alone together she would often ask me what she should do.

I continually urged her to try and win Charles back, or at least for the sake of the sons they both loved to come to some kind of amicable arrangement that would keep the marriage intact, but in my heart I knew that this was never going to happen. I believe that if the Prince had offered her even the smallest morsel of love then she would have clung to it, and tried to rescue their dysfunctional marriage; but he did not. To this day, I remain convinced that Diana never wanted to divorce him. In a fit of pique she would fly off the handle and say that divorce was her only way out, but she knew from her own experience as a child, when her parents had divorced so publicly and bitterly, as well as from her work with the relationship-counselling charity Relate, that to end the marriage might have a catastrophic impact on their two sons.

There was also another factor, namely that the actress in her, bolstered by occasional descents into self-pity, also found the chance to play the wronged wife too compelling to miss. As I have said, it never seemed to occur to her that she was just as guilty as the Prince, that her own adultery was equally relevant to the breakdown of their marriage. We would talk for hours about that breakdown and the conversation always came back to the same question: should she stay, or go? My answer was invariably that she should stay and fight from within because it would be terribly cold on the outside. I knew, however, that the time would come when there would be no other option. More importantly, so did the Princess. To the outside world, the charade went on. Although their joint public appearances were rare, people essentially mistrusted what they read in the newspapers about the rifts in the Royal marriage.

Even if I had not worked directly for the Princess, the lighter moments of the job would have made being a protection officer worthwhile. One memorable occasion made a particular impression, not least because I found it funny, but also because it summed up the distance between the couple, as well as Diana's absolute lack of appreciation of her husband and his sense of humour. It was the evening of the state banquet held for the King of Norway in London. The Prince's policeman, Colin Trimming, had the night off, and I had said that I could handle security for both our principals.

That night, Diana was in a particularly impatient mood. She was not above tapping her feet to express her frustrations, in this case at having to attend this most formal of functions, at her husband, at having to dress to the nines, at delays and any other irritations that came to mind. In complete contrast, the Prince was extremely relaxed. He knew the form on state occasions like this, when all senior, and many of the so-called 'minor' members of the Royal Family, were on parade. Everything had to be done in almost military fashion. Royalty would arrive according to ascending order of rank, with the most senior, the Queen herself, arriving last at exactly the time listed in the programme. It might sound a little absurd, but this is how the business of monarchy works (and has done for a very long time), and state banquets, when the principals turn out in all their finery, tiaras, dress uniforms, evening dress, decorations and all, is when the business of royalty becomes very serious indeed. But Diana did not quite see it like that. As far as she was concerned, a state banquet was just an irritation, something to go to, to be seen at, and then get home from as early and unscathed as possible. In the mood she was in tonight, this was doubly, or even trebly, the case.

The Princess and I, in full evening dress, were in the hall of the apartments at Kensington Palace, waiting for the moment when we would set off in the limousine according to the prescribed order of precedence. She sighed and turned to me. 'Can we go early? I don't want to hang around here any more,' she said. There was a faintly childish whine in her voice.

'Ma'am, it's really not as simple as that, there is an order...' I started to tell her, but before I could finish she snapped back, 'I know all about their bloody orders, I know all about them! I want to go now. Simon [her chauffeur] is ready, and I want to go now.'

Fortunately, Charles, also in evening dress, appeared in the hall right on cue, tugging on his cuffs in his slightly nervous manner, like an actor in a West End comedy. He clearly sensed an impending tantrum from his volatile wife.

'Are we ready to go?' he asked me.

There was a stony silence from both of them as I pointed out that it was not our slot yet.

'Have I got time for another Martini then?' he asked politely.

I don't know why, but I couldn't help smiling broadly. It struck me as vaguely absurd that the future King was asking me if he had time for another drink, even if the question was rhetorical. I told him that he probably did have time. The frost emanating from his wife became icier.

'Is anything the matter?' he asked, not directing his question to anyone in particular.

I decided to say nothing, aware that the impending storm was about to break. Diana was ready for a fight, if not spoiling for one.

'Well, Charles, there is, actually. I want to go now, I don't want to hang around here. Why can't we go now?' There was a dangerous edge to her voice.

'Diana,' he replied reasonably, 'you know the system. We have to go at the set time, so that we arrive just before Her Majesty.'

He took a step back as though preparing himself for an onslaught and he was right to do so. Diana, drawing herself up in her high heels (or 'tart's trotters' as she called them), turned on him.

'But Charles, why can't you go on your own? I can get there earlier, nobody will worry about me,' she said.

Of course she knew that if she turned up without her husband the waiting media would plaster it all over the front pages, speculating, quite rightly, that the Prince and Princess had had yet another row. When Charles pointed this out to her, however, she became even more frustrated, repeating angrily that she wanted to go now, and that he could follow her when he wished.

The Prince, who clearly did not want a fight, retreated, asking the butler, Harold Brown, for a Martini, his favourite tipple, en route to his study. As soon as he left, I told the Princess that I thought the whole row was silly. It was not what she wanted to hear, and she sounded off again. I was actually trying hard not to laugh, partly at the ridiculousness of the situation, and partly at her husband's antics. A few minutes later, Charles emerged into the hall again, as his wife paced up and down like a caged animal.

'Charles, I have really had enough of this. I'm off,' she fumed.

'No, Diana, we really have to wait,' he rightly insisted.

Charles then ordered another Martini from Harold and departed again and at this point I let out a little chortle.

'What is the reason for the delay?' the Prince asked, reappearing.

'Actually, Sir, the Princess Royal is stuck in traffic at Hammersmith,' I told him, to which he replied with a wry smile, 'Oh, not again!' He then carried on with his drink.

'Do you find my husband funny?' Diana snapped, by now extremely irritated with me, as well as everything else. 'Well, *do* you?'

I paused for a second, and then said, 'Well, actually, I do, Ma'am. I think he has a great sense of humour.' Foolishly, I then added, 'It's not too far removed from my own.'

From her expression, Diana was clearly exasperated. At that moment she and I were simply not on the same comic wavelength.

'So, what kind of humour is that?' she retorted curtly.

Too late I realised that I had said the wrong thing. The Princess did not find her husband funny, nor should her protection officer. For the rest of that night she said not one word to me, other than a few perfunctory answers to my necessary questions. It was an amusing incident – to me, at least – but also a sad one. It demonstrated the extent to which the relationship between Charles and Diana had deteriorated, and how difficult that could be for members of their household, for by this stage, early 1992, Diana had to be handled very carefully. Not surprisingly, she had become increasingly unstable emotionally and felt betrayed if a member of her inner circle demonstrated any empathy with the Prince or his team of advisers.

The formal separation of the Duke and Duchess of York, announced on 18 March 1992, had a huge impact on everyone in the Waleses' household. We all knew that if the Yorks' marriage was over – something the Queen must have sanctioned – then it could only be a matter of time before the inevitable happened, and the Prince and Princess of Wales followed suit. Whatever her emotional state, however, Diana kept a very cool head. As the Yorks' separation played out in public, she scanned the newspapers to learn how it was affecting her own popularity. Of course this was cynical, but in the prevailing climate it was wholly understandable.

FEBRUARY 1992:
INDIA

E ven before we set off for the official visit to India in February
1992, it was obvious all was not well within the Royal
marriage. They were practically living separate lives, Diana at
Kensington Palace and Charles at his beloved Highgrove Estate in
Gloucestershire, around one hundred miles apart. For me it made
life considerably easier as the distance between them helped calm the
Princess's moods, but when the diplomatic mission forced them to
spend time together and put on a show, it ratcheted up the tension
for all those around them considerably. Their diplomatic mission
was pretty clear: their visit to India was a symbol of the long-standing
ties of common interest and affection between the two countries. It
was about the liberalisation and development of India, about the
environment and architecture, and of course, where Diana came in,
the underprivileged. That's as may be, I thought. My job was to keep
her safe and to try to get to the end of the visit without the Princess
exploding with rage at her estranged husband.

Even before we had touched down at Palam Air Force Station, Delhi, the press fired the first salvo when *The Sun* published an exclusive front-page article revealing that Diana would be visiting the Taj Mahal, the immense white marble mausoleum, near Agra, built in the seventeenth century by Shah Jahan in memory of his favourite wife, and perhaps the world's greatest monument to love, alone. 'DI TO VISIT TAJ MAHAL ON HER OWN,' the tabloid trumpeted triumphantly, once again delighting in exposing the growing void between the Prince and Princess of Wales. Gleefully, the accompanying report quoted Prince Charles, who had visited India as a single man, aged thirty-two, in 1980. Sitting on a stone bench in front of this great jewel of Muslim art, he had vowed to return one day with the woman he loved. 'One day I would like to bring my bride here,' he had declared. Yet, when the opportunity availed itself, when he was back in the country some twelve years later with his wife, he chose not to. His message could not have been clearer.

Diana knew that they would come under the microscope during the visit, but I truly believe she no longer cared very much who knew – press or public – the depths to which her marriage had sunk. Their first official engagement in India was the ceremonial welcome at Rashtrapati Bhavan, the remarkable marble and pink sandstone former Viceroy residence designed by the architect of New Delhi, Sir Edwin Lutyens, and completed in 1929 at an astronomical cost of £1,253,000. The Cambridge University-educated Vice President, Dr Shankar Dayal Sharma, and his wife, Mrs Vimla Sharma, greeted the Royal couple. Diana, with me close by, was escorted to an enclosure, while the Prince walked to the dais to inspect the Guard of Honour. As they presented arms, the national anthems were played – the Indian military in their splendid, immaculate uniforms were quite a sight.

One of my abiding memories, however, was of Diana resplendent in a white and turquoise outfit with wide-brimmed hat later on, looking as if she had stepped out of a moment in time from the British Raj. She looked every inch the princess as she posed for photographs in the breathtaking formal gardens known as the Mughal Gardens, a stunning array of fountains and pools, extensive flowerbeds in full bloom and shaded walks. It is a moment in time that will live with me forever.

Then Charles and Diana, with an essential police escort to get through the New Delhi traffic, headed to Raj Ghat, the memorial dedicated to Mahatma Gandhi. A simple square platform of black marble marked the spot where the great man of peace was cremated, following his assassination in 1948. The peaceful memorial was surrounded by a beautiful park with labelled trees planted by such notables as HM The Queen, US President Eisenhower and the Vietnamese Communist revolutionary leader Ho Chi Minh, to name but a few. Two museums dedicated to Gandhi are nearby. The Prince and Princess took off their shoes and put on special footwear before walking slowly towards the memorial. Both bowed their heads in tribute before Charles laid a wreath. Before they left in the convoy they were presented with a packet of books about the great man. They then returned to Rashtrapati Bhavan at the north court to be greeted by a member of the India Presidential staff. He led the Royal couple to the first meeting with the softly spoken President Ramaswamy Venkataraman and his wife Janaki. That night, despite clearly flaking a little, Charles and Diana threw themselves into their packed schedule and the couple were the guests of honour at a banquet given by Vice President Sharma at the Lutyens-designed Hyderabad House, once a residence for Osman Ali Khan, the last Nizam of Hyderabad.

The first day was over and it had been an undoubted success but even at this moment Charles insisted that he would not change his schedule and said he would still attend a business function in

Bangalore on the day when Diana visited the Taj Mahal. Everyone in the Royal Household could see the symbolism of this decision but the sycophants surrounding the Prince were simply not prepared to tell him how shortsighted he was being and that for the good of the visit he must change his plans. The reality, however, was far more complicated. After they both visited Mrs Sonia Gandhi, the Italian-born widow of assassinated Prime Minister Rajiv Gandhi, at her residence, 10 Janpath, New Delhi, the Royal couple went their separate ways to complete busy schedules. Diana and I went straight to Palam Air Force Station to fly down to Agra, while the Prince carried out a number of engagements, including a stag lunch at the residence with the President in New Delhi.

Royal Tour programmes can be complicated to plan and in often fast-paced humid conditions like India even more difficult to execute for all concerned, the principals, the Royal Household and the press. Tempers can fray very quickly and it is essential that the security team remain calm (and well hydrated) at all times. In the case of Charles and Diana, the biggest media stars at that time, the only way to achieve all that was required diplomatically was having separate itineraries. It also suited the state of their relationship and gave the press officers a legitimate excuse to hide behind when questioned about the couple's personal life.

The accompanying press team, led by Dickie Arbiter, was in an invidious position. Dickie was on a hiding to nothing over the Taj Mahal visit. The idea of the Prince and Princess going there together had been discussed at length during the recce and a joint visit would have given the world's media the money shot. But at the time Diana was scheduled to be in Agra, Charles was committed to a number of engagements in New Delhi, including delivering his major speech of the tour. It would, in his view, be too complicated to change things at the last minute and would let too many people down. So, as Diana and I and a small team were in the air en route to the Taj Mahal (along with pretty much the entire press corps travelling with the party), the Prince was at a School of Planning and Architecture in New Delhi with zero press coverage. Rightly or wrongly, no one was interested in his programme that day, only Diana's.

As the Prince was giving the 'major speech of the tour' at the Indo-British Industrialists Forum, accompanied by Dickie Arbiter, a garlanded Diana was already at the Parivar Seva Sanstha (Family Help Institute), a family planning organisation, where she was told how the project was promoting the use of 'non-clinical methods of family planning and the prevention of AIDS'.

'You mean condoms,' the Princess interjected with a smile.

Afterwards came a tour of the red sandstone sixteenth-century Agra Fort with its exquisite grape garden, known as the Anguri Bagh, a formal garden with a marble tank in the centre. Diana welcomed it, as there were plenty of places to find shade out of the searing sun. From there we headed for the money shot: the Princess in front of the Taj Mahal. She was not supposed to say a word at her photo opportunity. Even if Charles had seen the error of his ways, however, and wanted to join his wife after all it was far too late. The reality was he never had any interest in changing the arrangements. Perhaps the real reason he chose to stay away was that he knew his marriage was doomed and since both of them had been involved in adulterous relationships, he perhaps felt it too hypocritical to go along with the media sham.

The Princess, who told me she was genuinely upset by her husband's refusal to join her at the Taj Mahal, had privately decided to drive home the point. Diana's guide, M.M. Rawat, a lecturer at Agra University and Uttar Pradesh's retired director of tourism, greeted her. I could sense Diana was cooking up trouble although she played her role to perfection – I could see it in her eyes. It was 1.20pm and the heat was insufferable, especially in a jacket and tie.

The Taj Mahal, the tomb of Mumtaz Mahal, the favourite wife of Mughal Emperor Shah Jahan, who died in 1631, is a truly spectacular sight. A complex of buildings, the tomb itself stands on a square podium with minarets at each corner. It is an awesome structure. The triple-domed mosque to the east is an identical building – the mosque's *jawab* (echo), which cannot be used for worship, it was simply built for symmetry. In front of the terrace is a large garden with a marble pool at its centre. A high wall, punctuated by pavilions and turrets and on the southern side by a stately entrance gate, borders the terrace and garden. When you first see it, it truly takes your breath away, undoubtedly a wonder of the world. (In fact, in 2007, the Taj Mahal was declared winner of the New Seven Wonders of the World.)

For Diana the visit to the world's greatest monument to love had even more significance to her personal story. With a few carefully chosen words, it would be the place where she would effectively declare to the world that her marriage was over. When the then Sky TV News reporter Simon McCoy shouted out to the Princess, asking her what she thought of the magnificent tomb, she paused for a few seconds before delivering her devastating rapier thrust.

'What do I say, Ken?' she whispered out of the corner of her mouth.

Completely unprepared, and with no script to work on, I whispered back, 'Just say it is a healing experience.'

'It was a fascinating experience – very healing.'

Pressed to say exactly what she meant by that, the Princess paused again. 'Work it out for yourself,' she added with a glint in her eye. And so the press pack had their story, as well as their picture to go with it, and Diana had effectively given them carte blanche to write what they liked about the state of the Royal marriage.

As soon as she had uttered those words I visualised the headlines that would follow yet I could not help but sympathise with her. The Prince might very easily have made the visit to the Taj Mahal a positive statement about his marriage, and impressed his wife in the process. Instead, his refusal to accompany her made it clear that he did not care about her, and that he did not care what people thought about his marriage either.

I believe the Prince of Wales never intended going along with what was in fact a complete charade, no matter what anybody did to try and make him see the wisdom of doing so. To do so would have made him a total hypocrite. Of course he had loved his wife, but by now that love had fizzled away. He therefore drew the line.

The inevitable negative headlines followed. The *Daily Express* criticised Charles for his PR blunder, publishing a huge photograph of a demure princess sitting alone in front of the Taj Mahal under the banner headline: 'Temple of Loneliness'. For her part, Diana had done her best to ensure that she got her message across, although it should be noted that it was not she who had arranged that sad solo picture, but the press. On arrival at the Taj Mahal photographers bellowed at me to keep her entourage and the accompanying dignitaries back. I duly obliged, and they got the picture they wanted, out of which they made such capital. Diana did not mind – as I have said, she was past caring – but it is wrong to describe the setting-up of the photograph as one of her guerrilla raids in the PR war against her husband. Had he wanted to, Prince Charles could have turned the whole thing on its head, simply by agreeing to go with her to the Taj Mahal. Instead, he chose to let matters run their natural course and so the die was cast.

In all honesty who could blame the press? This was a self-inflicted wound. Prince Charles's unyielding decision not to accompany Diana to the Taj Mahal made it clear to his wife that he was no longer concerned about what she or the public at large thought. Later, Charles publicly admitted that he had got it wrong, claiming 'some people' might have thought him a fool for not joining her. 'A wiser man,' he reflected, 'probably would have done so.' That's as may be, but he didn't, and it was a conscious decision.

If that scoop wasn't big enough for the travelling media, the Royal couple were about to hand them another on the eve of Valentine's Day. Charles and Diana had been reunited on the tour in the ancient city of Jaipur, the capital of the north Indian state of Rajasthan, where the Prince had been asked to play in an exhibition polo match. He was thrilled at the chance but the same couldn't be said of his wife, who was determined to get him back for his snubbing her at the Taj Mahal. And she did so with another devasting blow.

The situation reached a head on Valentine's Day. It was a stunning backdrop. The city is circled by hills dotted with forts and the old city, also known as the Pink City. At the same time a public relations exercise was organised. After the match, the Princess was to present the cup to her husband with a kiss. Diana, however, was in no mood to be used, something that Charles's aides should have foreseen – they had, after all, had enough warning. On the day of the match thousands of local people ringed the polo field in the heat and dust, making it, in security terms, almost impossible to police. As far as any protection officer might have been concerned, a thousand assassins could have been lost in the crowd, and we would not have known until it was too late. I looked on anxiously, but everything went off safely. Diana, however, had a public slight up her sleeve. Any exhibition match requires an official prize giving at its conclusion and it was understood that she would hand out the prizes, and it was also assumed that, win or lose, she would plant a kiss on her husband. I could tell she was in no mood to play the doting wife, however.

During a break for lunch, we were told Diana had changed her mind and would not be attending the polo. Alarm spread. The tour's private secretary, Peter Westmacott, who later became British Ambassador to the US, had to conjure up all his diplomatic skills to persuade her otherwise. Peter, Dickie Arbiter and I went to see her in an attempt to urge her to turn out.

'No, I don't want to go,' Diana insisted. 'I have no intention of doing so, none whatsoever.'

The two courtiers were crestfallen but they kept on trying.

'Do you honestly think I even care? You really think I even care any more? Because I don't,' Diana raged. 'I'm at the point where I don't care what they think, much less what they write in the papers. I'm not going to present the prizes and that's that!'

Eventually she relented. Tens of thousands of spectators were pouring into the grounds to watch the match. They were there, Peter and Dickie said, to see her. The last thing Diana wanted was to upset her hosts, who had been so generous and kind. One couldn't help but feel sorry for her. But she still had one last card to play.

The actual polo match was a success. The Royal couple, accompanied by the former Maharaja of Jaipur, arrived to cheers before the ball was thrown in at 4pm to start the match. After four seven-minute chukkas Prince Charles was on a high. He even managed to score three of his winning team's four goals and was flush with the glow of victory. By contrast, the Princess had a face like thunder. When her husband, now wearing a smart jacket over his polo shirt, walked up to the rostrum in his sweaty polo outfit to collect his prize and kiss his wife on the lips, she turned her head to the side, forcing him to air kiss, and worse still, humiliating him in front of the world's press. He was furious. Diana, in a cool lemon outfit, had made him look a fool, and he was not about to forgive her for that. Later, when I asked why she had behaved as she did, she replied: 'Ken, I am not about to pander to him. Why the bloody hell should I? If he wants to make a fool out of me with that woman, he deserves it. But I am not about to make a fool of myself so all his friends can laugh at me.'

Diana had clearly intentionally humiliated the Prince and he was furious. 'She is nothing but a spoilt schoolgirl,' one of Charles's household told me. There was no advantage in defending her

125

position: she had made her point. I could see her reasoning, and even sympathised with it, but that was not how the Prince and his staff saw it. They accused Diana of petulance. 'Surely she could put on a show just once?' one of his senior aides said bitterly. Actually, I thought, she has been doing just that for almost all her adult life. Surely she is allowed some time off for good behaviour?

The following day *The Sun* published a front-page photograph by Arthur Edwards under the banner headline: 'THE KISS THAT MISSED!' Charles was pictured grimacing as the Princess bluntly rejected his kiss. Inside the newspaper cruelly published a guide for the Prince, showing him how to kiss a woman properly. Diana had shown her husband up as unfeeling by the Taj Mahal stunt – now she had made him look a fool. After that there was no going back. We travelled on to Hyderabad and they carried out a joint visit to Nalu village, where they visited a carpenter's shop, looked at a pottery and the village hand pump, but for the Royal party accompanying them the entire experience was excruciating. As far as Charles was concerned Diana had publicly humiliated him and he was in no mood to forgive and forget. The battle lines had been drawn up and the Prince and Princess hardly spoke to each other during the rest of the tour.

The Royal couple went their separate ways, both literally and metaphorically, soon afterwards – the Prince headed to the mountainous Kingdom of Nepal in the foothills of the Himalayas while Diana made for Calcutta.

By now these joint tours were anything but displays of togetherness. The Prince and Princess effectively ran their own shows, Diana acting as chief executive and publicity director of her own roadshow: her own 'tour within a tour'. There were so many standout moments – all great photo opportunities that ensured she was front-page news. I remember at the Mianpur Old Age Welfare Centre in Hyderabad an elderly woman reached out to touch Diana's feet as a sign of respect during her visit. The Princess then shook hands with members of India's lowest caste, known as 'the Untouchables', during her visit there. It was perhaps not a 'Taj Mahal' moment but for me it resonated what Diana was all about. The 'Untouchables' historically ostracised from Indian society were untouchable no more.

As fate would have it, however, Mother Teresa was not in Calcutta. She was reported to be seriously ill and had been taken for treatment to a hospital in Rome. Thus, to Diana, the perfect photo opportunity featuring the inspirational Albanian nun and the 'Princess of Hearts' could not happen after all. Sometimes it's easy to become immune to poverty. Working alongside Diana in the late 1980s and early 1990s, I saw a lot of it firsthand. Calcutta was an exception to that rule. I was not feeling on top form there – I had a bad fever, having been struck down by a dose of malaria after a security review at the most appalling place I have ever visited in all my life, the mortuary attached to the hospice run by Mother Teresa's Missionaries of Charity. Indeed, the hospice itself was effectively a mortuary. The wretched souls in there barely had a living cell in their emaciated bodies, while some of the assistants, many of whom had travelled from the West, were themselves infected with AIDS. Outside on the streets, others, near death, were wrapped in sheets.

It might seem strange, then, to say that the actual Royal visit to the hospice was a success, but it was. One desperately sick man, who doctors said had just hours to live, had amazed everyone by staying alive for twenty-four hours after he was told that the Princess was coming. In her spotless pink dress, surrounded by the grime, dust and despair, she crouched beside the dying man and clasped his hand in an almost biblical scene. The hordes of pressmen were quick to snap pictures when she knelt and prayed for him. The blackboard above the door that led to the mortuary read that fifteen of the hospice's patients had passed away that day.

Within half an hour of her departure, that figure had risen to sixteen as the poor man's wasted body was carried in to join the rest. The sisters had asked me earlier, as they showed me into the mortuary, if the Princess would want to see it too. It was a depressing place, sad beyond words and with an atmosphere that seeped into every pore of one's body. I declined – even Diana, I thought, would not want to go this far.

The tour of India plumbed new depths of despair for the Princess. For her there would be no turning back and a formal separation was now inevitable. The strain of hiding the real story – the truth behind the relationship between the Prince and Princess of Wales – was taking its toll, not only on the principal players but also on the staff of both households. After India, I vowed to try and sidestep these joint ventures. Frankly, the tension these trips caused was too much for anyone to cope with. It stressed Diana to such an extent that she became hell-bent on destroying everything to do with the tour that had been so carefully worked out and organised by advisers after months of planning. Like the little girl in the Longfellow poem, 'When she was good, she was very, very good. But when she was bad she was horrid.'

On her own Diana was a different person, and her solo events were essentially pleasurable experiences. I was left to organise her holidays with her sons. They were great fun, not least because they were often set in idyllic locations. With the Prince off the scene, Diana and her team of trusted members of her inner circle could relax. Since her death, and even before it, a lot of nonsense has been written about her mood swings. True, she could be petulant and, at the very least, changeable, but she could be damn good fun too, and had the graceful gift of knowing how to make people feel very special.

As we returned from the Indian sub-continent, Diana had only one thing on her mind – escape. Before that process could be put in hand, however, relations with her husband were to deteriorate further. Accepting the inevitable, Prince Charles began to take the first steps in preparation for a legal separation. Lord Goodman, the leading lawyer and government adviser, had been suggested to the Princess as a man who could be trusted and she took soundings too. The so-called 'War of the Waleses' was about to go public.

MARCH 1992:
LECH, AUSTRIA

T he Princes William and Harry had been plaguing their parents to take them skiing. Harry in particular was desperate to learn and his father had promised to arrange it. To his frustration nothing ever materialised. It did not, however, stop the Prince from making his annual pilgrimage to the Swiss Alps and his favourite resort, Klosters. Charles, being a creature of habit, made it clear that he would do exactly what he wanted, and that if Diana did not care to join him then that was her prerogative. The Princess, however, had made it clear to her husband after the avalanche in Klosters that claimed the life of their friend and equerry, Major Hugh Lindsay, in 1988 that she would never return there.

Privately, Diana had determined that she would answer their sons' wish. Her good friend Catherine Soames, the former wife of Charles's long-time friend and Tory minister (and grandson of Sir Winston Churchill), Nicholas 'Bunter' Soames, suggested that the exclusive resort of Lech would be the perfect place for William and

Harry to learn to ski and it would be a fun holiday for the Princess too. Thrilled, Diana asked Catherine to book it for her, oblivious to (or at least choosing to ignore) the security implications involved.

A few days later she broached the subject with me, knowing that security would be a potential nightmare, given the inevitable press attention her holiday would attract. I told her that I would have to check the resort out as such a visit could have serious security implications. Armed with little information apart from the name of the resort and the hotel she had picked, I made arrangements to travel to Austria.

I immediately made contact with the Chief of Police (protection) in Bludenz, Austria, and a pre-holiday recce was arranged. I then telephoned the Arlberg Hotel and spoke with the manager, Mr Hannes Schneider, but at this stage made no reference to Diana. After booking my flight, I headed for the Austrian mountains. Upon arrival by hire car from Zurich it was soon obvious to me that the location was perfect. The wooden chalets, the mountains dusted with snow and peppered with trees, and the people – protective, discreet and professional – made the ski resort of Lech an ideal royal retreat. For many years it had been the haunt of European and Middle Eastern royal families, but now it was about to be exposed to the ultimate test – Diana, Princess of Wales, one of the most famous and sought-after women in the world. I knew it would not take long for the foreign paparazzi to find us.

I had arranged to meet the Austrian police representatives at the hotel the day after my arrival. Schneider was a most impressive man, as was his entire family. The five-star hotel situated in prime position in the village was a picture postcard example of the very best of absolute skiing luxury. Once we had established the purpose of my visit, we examined the initial booking via Catherine Soames, which showed a request for two separate adult rooms and rooms for four children. At this stage no request had been made for a nanny, three protection officers, two police skiers from London, a night duty protection officer, and two Austrian liaison police skiers. With a beaming smile on his face Hannes Schneider ripped up the initial reservation and told me, 'I think it is best to start again. It really is no problem.'

'Mr No Problem' soon became his catchphrase and was synonymous with all future royal visits to Lech with Diana. The hotel hosted many European dignitaries and Herr Hannes Schneider was the perfect 'mine host', freely doling out top advice and making recommendations. In my experience he never made one bad recommendation. A section of the hotel was placed at my disposal to accommodate the entire party that worked perfectly.

'What about the snow, Hannes, can you guarantee that?' I asked.

'Only God can to do that,' he observed. 'But the village is set at a modest altitude of 1,450 metres and each year we receive up to double the amount of snow of some of its French rivals.'

Hannes had an answer for everything, it seemed.

I then went to the local police station to inform the police of the dates for Diana's arrival. Before my departure I travelled to nearby Zurs as Lech shared its ski area with the smaller village. There I visited numerous restaurant chalets to take back as much information as possible for the Princess and her sons. Before leaving, I telephoned Diana and suggested we meet the following day to discuss the new arrangements.

Excited, she took a deep breath and sighed, then said, 'At last – I have done something for my boys on my own.'

I travelled back to London, really pleased with the arrangements and the prospect of discussing them with the Princess. I knew that this would be the skiing template for years to come, and so it proved to be. Back in London Diana invited me to her drawing room at Kensington Palace. We discussed the arrangements and were both excited at the plans made.

Weeks later, on leaving Kensington Palace we travelled by car to London Heathrow, where I boarded a British Airways plane bound for Zurich with my two colleagues appointed to protect William and Harry. Arrangements via the consular office in Zurich ensured that my request for a twelve-seater mini bus be in position airside to meet the aircraft. On this occasion a representative from this office travelled with us from Zurich. All passport formalities were cleared via the consulate, and we left the airport escorted by police until the motorway. After that we continued on the two-hour journey escorted only by my police colleagues travelling behind a vehicle carrying the luggage.

A beaming Schneider family in traditional Austrian dress was waiting to greet us on arrival, a Royal greeting for sure. I could see Diana was blissfully happy as her excited sons ran into the hotel. The plethora of stuffed animals on the floors and walls of the hotel immediately transfixed the boys – Herr Schneider senior was a big game hunter and his trophies adorned the hotel walls. Harry spotted immediately a huge black bear on the floor and attempted to climb inside, much to the embarrassment of his mother, but this delighted the Schneiders, who immediately transferred the beast to his room.

With an indoor swimming pool at their disposal, Diana and the boys were quick to change. Herr Schneider had also made arrangements with the local ski school, Stroltz, to visit the hotel and fit them all with boots. Ski instructors were introduced, one for the two boys and one for Diana. With little snow, and it being their first skiing experience, William and Harry had no time to waste and with help from their instructor made for the nursery slopes accompanied by their protection policeman, Sergeant Dave Sharp.

Diana, in a reflective mood, requested a walk to the shops. Meanwhile the nanny – the late Olga Powell – organised the luggage and the unpacking. The Princess was content and with no press or paparazzi at this stage, it was a poignant moment. After a brilliant supper at the hotel the Royal party turned in. I briefed the night duty corridor officer who had travelled out in advance; an experienced police officer and a crucial cog in the overall security plan.

After breakfast the next day William and Harry left the hotel with their ski instructor for the nursery slopes. With little snow, Harry was frustrated and chose not to listen to the instructor. Clearly having watched too much *Ski Sunday*, he placed both arms and skis tightly under his body and skied off at speed, only to end up on his backside in a chalet garden, wedged against a small pine tree, having run out of snow and ended up skiing on mud.

Diana and friends Catherine Soames and Katie Menzies, with the instructor and two Scotland Yard trained skiers (also armed) headed for the Rüfikopf via a cable car to the mountain range above Lech and Zurs. Amazingly, by this stage the press had not caught us up. With radio contact, I set off to co-ordinate a lunch venue in Zurs.

William and Harry were quick to their beds following supper – rarely later than 8pm. Diana settled the boys with Nanny and then joined us in the bar before supper. The atmosphere was always very cordial, and the Princess was generous with her drinks to police and staff alike. The days that followed took a similar format, with lunch venues changing and different parts of the challenging Austrian Alps being skied by Diana and her party. One evening the entire group travelled by horse and sledge to the village of Klösterle – a typical Austrian log cabin restaurant. On the last evening of the holiday, Diana and Catherine Soames joined myself and some other police officers, including the Austrian Police, at the Tanburgerhoff Bar in Lech to thank us.

When we got back, Prince Charles didn't say anything but he was clearly put out that he had not introduced his sons to the sport he loved and Diana had stolen a march on him. Although a competent skier she was not in Charles's league. For her part, Diana basked in his irritation. The fact that he wanted to see the Princes William and Harry ski meant, figuratively speaking, that the mountain would have to come to Mohammed.

*＊＊

In March 1992, the following year, Charles agreed to make the effort and travel to Lech from Klosters to join his family. The Princess would have preferred him to stay away, but acutely aware that her sons would love to show off their new skills to their father, she agreed. It would be a momentous visit.

Tracking the Princess was like a military exercise to the papparazzi and a lucrative one at that; they were also extremely good at it. The fact that we had given them the slip the previous year, had annoyed them immensely . This time the Royal Rat Pack were determined they wouldn't be caught on the hop again. The British press was always pretty quick to react, too, but from my perspective they were easier to handle – the British newspaper reporters and photographers would always negotiate. For them, there was too much to lose if they overstepped the mark. But always there were a few photographers and journalists from the foreign press who simply did not care. You could make a deal with them and they would swear blind that they would honour it, but both you and they knew perfectly well that they never had any intention of doing so.

The doyen of royal watchers, James Whitaker, made his way towards me across the hard-packed snow. We had achieved 24 hours of press freedom up until this point. He looked as though he was about to explode, his complexion matching the bright red ski suit that he always wore on these occasions. Here was a man on a mission.

'How's the skiing, James – having fun?' I asked, in a bid to head him off at the pass.

'Well, as you've asked, Ken,' he replied, 'it's not all that good. I had to contend with solid ice in the morning, followed by slush after lunch. It was like skiing in a large vat of porridge.' Then, before I could even begin to feign sympathy for the lot of the royal reporter, he dropped his bombshell.

'I have some bloody serious news and I want you to be dead straight with me,' he said. His expression had become so austere that it was almost comical.

'Well, James, what on earth is it?' I said, trying not to be outdone in seriousness and sincerity. From my many dealings over the years with the Fleet Street legend, I knew that to him everything was always 'bloody serious'.

'It's the Princess's father, Ken – Earl Spencer. I have it on bloody good authority that he died last night,' he told me, before adding, 'You see my predicament, don't you? I need this confirmed before I go to press.'

If it were true, this was indeed 'bloody serious'. Worse still, James would insist on confirmation, and would make a considerable nuisance of himself until he got it. I paused for a moment, trying to maintain my composure, before offering what I hoped was a suitably evasive response.

'Well, if that really is the case, James, it's the first I've heard of it and I'm quite sure I would have been told,' I replied, trying to hide the feeling of panic creeping over me. I knew that if James's source was correct, then all hell was going to break loose. By now thoroughly anxious, I cut short our conversation, telling him that I would find out if he was right and assured him that I would get back to him as soon as possible.

With that, I returned to the hotel, where I telephoned the Princess's sister, Lady Sarah McCorquodale, in England. It was not the easiest of questions to ask a daughter and I was dreading the response. If the report was true, however, I knew that we would have to act decisively. There was a great deal at stake, and I did not know how Diana would cope. Sarah, however, assured me that although her father was not in the best of health she had seen him recently and had left him sitting up in his hospital bed; she added that he had been in quite good spirits.

Relieved, I went back to James and assured him that the news of the Earl's death had been grossly exaggerated. But he shook his head knowingly and said, 'That's amazing, Ken, it came from a bloody good source. *Bloody* good.'

Yet within a day of our conversation Johnny, eighth Earl Spencer, the Princess's beloved father and a true gentleman, would be dead. And the ski resort of Lech in the Austrian Alps, where the Prince and Princess of Wales and their two sons were holidaying together that March of 1992 would become the setting for one of the most dramatic and difficult episodes in my career with royalty.

Until the point when the Prince arrived in Lech everything had been going so well. Every morning at around nine o'clock the Princess, in company with her friends, Katie Menzies and Catherine Soames, would go to breakfast in the main restaurant of their exquisite five-star hotel, the Arlberg. The owners, the Schneider family again, treated their royal guests perfectly, with complete discretion and just the right degree of deference. After a light breakfast the party would gather in the ski room of the hotel basement and prepare to face the press. The previous evening I had met the ringleaders of the eighty or so reporters, camera crews and photographers who had descended on the resort for the Royal holiday. Without a press officer on hand, I arranged a photocall of sorts at the foot of the main ski lift. From long experience we knew that the more experienced skiers among the media pack would give chase whatever we did, but I had to try and organise something to avoid the situation getting out of control. In reality I was fighting a losing battle. Some of the foreign photographers were indeed so accomplished they could ski backwards down the piste in front of the Princess with their lenses trained on the Royal party.

Sometimes though, the press would back off and Diana would then disappear for the morning with her two girlfriends, a guide, an Austrian policeman and a trained skier from Scotland Yard before rejoining her sons for lunch in the mountains. As head of security for the trip I would remain at the hotel within radio contact. Occasionally I would join the Princess at one of her favoured haunts on the Mohnenfluh near Oberlech, a refuge about two hundred metres above the village, where the skiers would devour Austrian fare and the odd glühwein. Diana would ski for another hour or so after lunch, but by mid-afternoon the warm spring weather made conditions slushy and difficult, so she would return to the hotel for a sauna and a swim before getting ready for supper.

During my recce in 1991, I had met Cliff Richard, and the former BBC Radio 1 DJ Mike Read, with their friend, businessman Charles Haswell and his wife Susie, who had invited me to join them for dinner. They too were returning the following year that coincidentally was the same week Diana was to return. One evening Cliff and others of his party met with the Princess in the bar of the hotel. The singer suggested a musical evening to Diana. It was agreed that on the following Sunday he would sing in her suite. Circumstances would unfold that prevented it, however.

The peace was broken by the announcement that Prince Charles and his entourage would be arriving the following night, although what happened next proved in the end to be the comic relief before the storm. The Prince arrived late after snowdrifts blocked the Arlberg Pass, the only route into the village. Diana had made it clear that her husband would not be welcome in her private suite, and his personal arrangements had to be made through Hannes Schneider if he wanted rooms in the Arlberg for himself and his entourage. I arranged his accommodation after consultation with his protection officer.

Members of the Royal Family expect everything to be perfect, down to the tiniest detail, so when the Prince arrived late that night, he immediately asked for his favourite drink, a stiff dry Martini, but when he went to his room he noticed there wasn't a refrigerator. At once he called in his policeman, Inspector Tony Parker, and pointed out that despite it being the dead of night he needed a fridge and he needed it now. Enter 'Herr No Problem' Hannes, the son and heir of 'Old Man Schneider', as the Arlberg's owner was universally known.

'No refrigerator, no problem,' he replied in his slightly high-pitched, heavily accented English – even though there was not a spare one in the entire hotel. Twenty minutes later, I saw, through a window, Hannes strolling purposefully through the snow with a mini-refrigerator on his back. I have no idea where he had got it, but to the Schneider family when a prince wants a refrigerator, no matter how inconvenient, a refrigerator he gets.

The rest of the stay in Lech was not so entertaining; indeed, it turned out to be an ordeal. Once more fate intervened. As it panned out, Charles never skied in Lech that year, nor since, for on 29 March 1992 James Whitaker's grim prophecy was realised. The Princess's father, Lord Spencer, died at the Brompton Hospital in South Kensington after years of ill health.

Before her husband's arrival the Princess had been completely relaxed, as well as determined to have fun. As mentioned earlier I had even arranged for another guest at the hotel, the British pop singer Sir Cliff Richard, to give a private concert for her. Cliff, an evergreen legend, who has had No. 1 hits in Britain in each of the last five decades, knew Diana was in the hotel and thought it would be fun to perform for her. As a result, his friend, DJ Mike Read, approached me and asked if I could arrange it. I told the Princess, who agreed that it would be a great idea. In the event, the concert up in her suite never happened, for the news came through that her father had died. It was a time that was to test those around Diana and the Prince to the very limit, quite apart from the strain it placed upon the Princess herself and her two sons. For me, the tightrope that advisers have to walk between a royal couple's public and private lives was rarely so slippery as when Diana learned of her father's death.

On the afternoon of the 29th I received a telephone call from Diana's sister, Sarah. She was understandably distraught. Just twenty-four hours earlier, she and I had laughed off reports of her father's death. Now it had become a sad reality. By this time the Prince was fully installed at the Arlberg with his entourage, consisting of his private secretary, Commander Richard Aylard, and his part-time press secretary, Philip Mackie, dubbed the 'Silly Ghillie' by the media. Armed with the news, I immediately went to Aylard so that he could formally tell the Prince and ask if he wanted to break the news to his wife. I assumed that on being told, Prince Charles would want to tell the Princess, but to my surprise I was asked to see him.

It was decided by all present that as I knew Diana best, the news would be better coming from me. But I felt that it should be her husband who told her – I reasoned that the situation was difficult enough without me adding to its complications. Even so, I could not help but think these circumstances were in contrast to the touching moment in Kenya when Charles's father, Prince Philip, Duke of Edinburgh – a man so often accused of insensitivity – broke the news to the then Princess Elizabeth that her father, King George VI, had died. The two of them had wandered through the grounds as the young Queen contemplated the enormity of her loss, and how it was going to change her life forever. As Charles's aides were very anxious about the Princess's reaction, I thought that the only thing to do was to be exactly what I was – a policeman. If I could not take control in a moment of personal crisis, then who on earth could? Charles knew that his wife would be inconsolable over her father's death, and he was equally aware that he would bear the brunt of her grief and frustration. Eventually, it was agreed that I would break the news.

As I made my way to Diana's suite I could not help reflecting that this was something I really did not want to do. True, the breaking of tragic news is part of a police officer's duty, but in most cases the officer involved does not know the people he has to tell. Diana was my principal, but I had also grown to respect and admire her. This was going to be one of the worst duties I could undertake for her.

As gently as I could, I broke the news to the Princess. She was calm at first – she had not expected it and was not prepared for such bad news. But before too long her eyes filled and tears began to stream down her face.

'Oh my God, Ken… Oh my God! What am I to do?' she sobbed, over and over again.

My heart went out to her. I sat beside her on the end of her bed, feeling helpless. Then I put my arms around her, trying in vain to comfort her in her terrible distress. In that moment she looked like a lost little girl who suddenly realises she is completely alone in the world.

After a while I tentatively broached the subject of what we had to do next. As delicately as I could, I introduced the subject of the Prince. In an atmosphere you could have cut with a knife, she proceeded to make it abundantly clear that she wanted to return to her dead father and her family as soon as possible, and most definitely alone. Under no circumstances, she said, did she want the Prince to accompany her.

'I mean it, Ken. I don't want him with me. He doesn't love me – he loves that woman. Why should I help save his face? Why the bloody hell should I? It's *my* father who has gone. It's a bit bloody late for Charles to start playing the caring husband, don't you think?' she said, every word coming straight from the heart.

Foreseeing trouble, I returned to the Prince and his staff, leaving my number two, Sergeant Dave Sharp, with Diana.

By this stage in their relationship there was absolutely no dialogue between the Prince and Princess. I was therefore not so much a conduit as the last resort. To make matters worse, Diana bluntly refused to speak to Richard Aylard because he was the Prince's right-hand man, and as far as she was concerned, public enemy number one, the chief supporter in Charles's camp. Nevertheless, I passed on the bad news to Aylard. The blood seemed to drain from his already pale face as he instantly anticipated the Prince's reaction. Seconds later, Charles emerged from his suite, clearly still in shock. He was, of course, concerned for his wife, himself and his two children.

In this extremely unhappy situation I decided to take control.

'I am going to put my police officer's hat on, sir. This is a very difficult and delicate situation. How do you think we should handle it?'

But the Prince seemed by now to have come to a decision. I was left in no doubt that the task of getting the Princess back to Britain in a reasonable state and in company with her husband would be my responsibility.

Again I was asked to reason with her, on the grounds that I knew the Princess so well. There was little I could do about it, and therefore I promised to return to Diana's suite, adding that I would do my best. As I left, I turned and told the Prince that I could make no guarantees. He, meanwhile, telephoned HM The Queen, who was at Windsor Castle, to break the news that the Earl, a former equerry both to her and to her late father, King George VI, had passed away.

I was extremely apprehensive as I made my way back to Diana's suite, fully aware that there was a lot riding on this next conversation. If she decided to throw a hysterical fit and refuse her husband's request – and she was quite capable of doing so – we would be back to square one. Moreover the press, who would soon begin to mass outside the hotel, would have a field day. Lord Spencer's death was a major news story, and if the Prince and Princess did not return to Britain together then nothing, not even compassion for the grief-stricken Diana, would stop the press from going for the jugular. The truth about the Waleses would be immediately and blindingly obvious to the most naive journalist. I made my decision in the light of all this. Returning to the Princess's room, I told her bluntly that this was not a matter for debate.

'Ma'am, you have to go back with the Prince. This one is not open for discussion, you just have to go with it.'

At once her tears began to flow again. I tried to comfort her. We talked about how I had lost my father, Frank, and that, like her, I had not managed to get back in time to speak to him. Death, I assured her, was part of life. And as she continued to weep, I told her that we all have to go on for our families' sake, as well as our own.

'Ma'am, your father would not have wanted this. He was a loyal man, he would not have wanted his death turned into a media circus, would he?'

I don't know what it was that struck a chord, but something did. Her mood changed. She became calmer, and began to listen to reason.

'Okay, Ken, I'll do it. Tell him I'll do it, but it is for my father, not for him – it is out of loyalty to my father,' she told me.

Perhaps it was the word 'loyalty' that had made all the difference, but whatever it was, the Princess was back on level ground. I had done the Prince's bidding, and on the face of it, at least, a potentially damaging situation had been averted. Diplomacy, common sense and Diana's own sense of pride had won the day.

Back I went to the Prince's quarters, where I told Richard Aylard that she had relented and agreed to travel back with the Prince. There was a palpable sense of relief all round. It was only then that Aylard and the 'Silly Ghillie' headed off to the Monzabon Hotel, opposite the Arlberg, where they had asked the media to assemble for the daily briefing.

While I sat at the foot of the Princess's bed, trying to comfort her, Aylard and Mackie broke the news to the press. It was around 7pm local time, which meant that it was 6pm in London, and nobody there knew that the Princess's father had died earlier that day. At the Monzabon the press had all turned up to hear what the Royal party had been doing that day and to make sure that none of them had been injured. So when Aylard told the gathered media the news, it was greeted with a respectful silence until the veteran *Sun* photographer, Arthur Edwards, asked the crucial question: 'Richard, has this gone out on the Press Association wires?'

Both Richard Aylard and Philip Mackie looked blankly at each other for a second before replying in unison, 'No!'

At that moment all hell broke loose. There was a mass exodus of the press and photographers, as if war had been declared or the three-minute warning for a nuclear strike had been sounded. Journalists, photographers, camera crews and anchormen were literally climbing over one another as they raced for the phones so they could tell their respective editors before the first editions went to bed, or the next news bulletins went out. Some of the journalists, perhaps understandably, did not really trouble themselves too much about the other guests as they shouted their stories down the phone for the next hour or so.

The Princess refused to talk to anyone, and gave me strict instructions that no one else, particularly her husband or members of his party, would be welcome in her suite. Charles, however, appeared unmoved by his wife's directive. Instead, he went outside to play snowballs with his two sons, in the care of their detectives and nanny Olga Powell, where he gently broke the news to them that their grandfather was dead. Despite their sadness, the boys took it well. This was their first real experience of death, and the Prince, a sensitive and caring father, did his best to console them. There was nothing he could do to help the grief-stricken Princess, though.

For the next three hours I sat on the end of Diana's bed as her emotions raged. One minute she was lucid, in touch with reality, accepting of the situation. At other times she was angry at the world, shouting and screaming as the tears streamed down her face. She wanted to fly back immediately but given how late it was, a Royal Flight could not be arranged until the following morning. I could do nothing but try to calm her, telling her that it was only sensible to wait for morning.

'It makes sense, Ma'am,' I kept saying. 'Trust me on this one, it is the right thing to do.'

The Prince of Wales is undeniably a good man, and I speak as someone who has known him at close quarters. His is a sensitive, caring, even spiritual character. Furthermore, his treatment of his wife during their marriage was in some ways understandable. As much as I liked and admired her, she could be an extremely difficult woman, and it is axiomatic – indeed, almost a cliché – that when relationships or marriages crumble there are always two sides to every story.

We left Lech by car for Zurich Airport the following morning. It was a gloriously crisp day, with a beautiful clear blue sky and wonderful powder snow sprinkled on the slopes like a thick covering of icing sugar over a cake. The Prince, always a passionate skier, had never been to Lech before, and as it turned out would not return. Tony Parker, Charles's personal protection officer on this trip, was driving, with me sitting in the passenger seat alongside him. Charles sat in the back seat, next to his wife. William and Harry remained in Lech with their nanny and detectives.

The tension in the car was electric. I looked in the mirror in time to see the Princess's eyes rise heavenwards in a gesture of the purest exasperation at comments made by the Prince. There was an icy silence for the rest of the two-hour journey.

At the airport we boarded the BAe146 of the Queen's Flight that was waiting for us, while the media, who were out in force, scribbled notes and the photographers' flashguns fired. Nothing was said during the entire flight. The Princess did not want to speak to her husband and he, fearing a furious or even hysterical outburst, did not dare chance trying to start a conversation. Whatever the discomforts of the journey, however, it was soon clear that the PR spin had worked. The next day it was reported that Prince Charles was at Diana's side in her hour of need. Yet as soon as the Prince and Princess arrived at Kensington Palace they went their separate ways – he to Highgrove and she to pay her last respects to her father.

I accompanied the Princess and her sisters when they went to see their father's body at the Chapel of Rest at Kenyon's, the funeral directors in Notting Hill, London. When we arrived, Diana, who by now had become much calmer, asked me if I too wanted to pay my respects to the late Earl. I demurred, saying that I thought that this was a supremely private moment, and one that belonged to the Spencer family, and to them alone. Diana smiled, then turned and joined Lady Sarah and Lady Jane inside the funeral directors' premises.

I had met Lord Spencer on a number of occasions. He was an extremely courteous man, very much an English aristocrat of the old school. Despite claims in the media of rifts between them, he always enjoyed a close relationship with his youngest daughter, Diana. As a father he was very attentive, and was always conscious of the needs of his children. It was perhaps inevitable that there would be conflicts with his children over his second wife, Raine,

Countess Spencer, but he never let those differences come between him and Diana.

Sadly, the same could not be said of the marriage of the Prince and Princess of Wales. On the day of the Earl's funeral, two days later, the atmosphere between the Royal couple had deteriorated yet further. Diana resembled nothing so much as a volcano that might erupt at any second. If she did, I thought, we would never get her back – the full force of her fury, grief and frustration would break upon everyone around her, and no one would be able to control the effects. Certainly everyone, including the Queen, was very concerned about how the Princess would cope during the funeral. They knew she was highly strung, and were fearful of the repercussions.

That morning I drove the Princess to Althorp, the Spencers' family seat in Northamptonshire, for the funeral. The Prince also attended, against his wife's wishes, arriving by helicopter. It was an intensely sad day for her, and Diana and I did not speak much on the journey, but when she did talk, she kept returning to the same theme: 'He's going to turn my father's funeral into a charade,' she complained. 'It's so false.'

'Well, Ma'am, just don't let him,' I responded. My heart went out to her, and I felt helpless that I could do so little to ease her grief.

The Spencer family as a whole also did not want the Prince to attend, but in the event Diana's brother, Charles, the new Earl Spencer, persuaded his sister to relent. The press, however, noted that the Prince was not there to comfort Diana on the long journey to Althorp. Although her husband was at the funeral in person, it was clear from the Princess's body language that she was alone.

Lord Spencer was cremated after a quiet, private family service. Afterwards the Princess was handed the urn containing the late Earl's ashes and we returned to the Spencer family vault inside the church at Great Brington, just outside the estate walls. All the late Earl's children were there, family feuds at last forgotten as they made their final farewells. Then a great stone was lifted and I joined the Princess in the vault, surrounded by the remains of her ancestors, with a candle as our only light. There were cobwebs all around us, and the air was pervaded by a pungent dusty smell. With tears in her eyes, Diana said a prayer; then she too said her final farewell.

It seems hard to comprehend that, just over five years later, Diana herself would make her last journey too, returning to Althorp in her coffin, mourned by millions around the world.

APRIL/MAY 1992:
STUDLAND BAY,
DORSET

Diana didn't blame anyone for the restrictions being a member of the Royal Family placed on her. She craved her privacy, however, and longed 'to be normal' and to do the things so-called ordinary people took for granted. She wanted her sons to experience 'normal' travel too and asked one day if I could take them on a red London Routemaster bus. I said, with planning, anything was possible. So one day instead of driving to Smollensky's Balloon family restaurant on The Strand I agreed we could take the bus. Prince Harry in particular loved the idea. With Harry, however, nothing was straightforward. Our driver was a Pakistani and every time we set off after a stop, Harry couldn't resist tilting his head and saying loud and fast and with a slight accent, 'Bud bud ding ding!' within earshot of the other passengers and indeed the driver.

Diana was furious and immediately chastised her impish son, who I am sure was only meaning to be funny, not racist. But her admonishment had no impact – in fact it just encouraged him.

Every time the bell went at a stop, he chirped up with 'Bud bud ding ding!' until I suggested it was best we got off as we were drawing attention to ourselves. Diana apologised profusely to the driver, who was oblivious and had no idea who they were either. William, who could also be a little disingenuous, even sly, revelled in Harry's ticking off. But Harry didn't care one way or the other. (I still have a little note he wrote to me, thanking me for organising his adventure on the buses. Harry signed off with his name, followed by 'Bud bud ding ding!' He was incorrigible, but likeable all the same.)

The bus journey typified Diana's hankering for being 'normal' and she would ask me if I could, just once, allow her to take a long walk along a beach alone, without me at her side. My Scotland Yard superiors would have gone potty if they had known but I promised her that I would make it happen. Much of my childhood had been spent in Dorset on the Isle of Purbeck and I recalled the sandy beaches of Studland Bay on the approach to Poole Harbour and thought it the ideal place for her to take her cherished solo stroll. At the time Diana was receiving round-the-clock protection and as her PPO, it was my decision how many officers should be with her at any time.

'How will it work? How will you manage it?' she asked. 'What about the back-up?'

Now she was getting a little nervous, but I told her to let me resolve it. It would require each other's absolute trust. She nodded her approval.

Less than a week later, we set off early from Kensington Palace and drove to Sandbanks ferry at Poole in a saloon car. Diana was so excited. None of the other passengers on the car ferry recognised her, but then no one expected to see one of the world's most famous women on the Studland chain ferry in May. As the ferry docked, we climbed back in the car and with the Princess in the driving seat followed the vehicles heading for Studland and Swanage. About half a mile from the ferry landing point, I asked her to stop. We left the car in a parking area and walked to a wooden bridge that spanned a reed bed to the deserted beach of Shell Bay. The ferry had now departed on its return journey. Diana stared out towards the Isle of Wight before setting out on her walk to Old Harry Rocks at the western extremity of Studland Bay. A few oyster-gatherers busied themselves along the wet sand, and birds stabbed at the sand too.

I had given the Princess a two-way radio and a map I had sketched of the shoreline. I said I would meet her at the far end of the bay in a pub called the Bankes Arms. Then, a little apprehensively, she left – a tall, slim figure wearing a pair of denim jeans, a suede jacket and a scarf wrapped loosely around her face to protect her from the easterly, chilly spring wind. I watched for a while as she disappeared into the distance, alone apart from the oystercatchers, her head held high as she followed her path along the water's edge. It was a strange sensation, watching her walk away by herself, with no security detail. Strangely, I wasn't that uneasy as I knew the area well; I trusted her too. Not one of my colleagues knew of our plan – had they done so, it would have been immediately vetoed. As the Princess disappeared from view, I radioed her. Her voice was bright and lively and I instinctively knew that she was safe and revelling in her freedom.

I walked back to the car and within a matter of minutes I was turning into the car park at the Bankes Arms, a fine old pub overlooking Studland Bay. Knowing that the walk would take around forty minutes, I strolled down to the beach and sat on a wall in the bright spring sunshine. Suddenly my radio crackled into life.

'It's me, can you hear me?' she said.

'Yes. How's it going?' I responded.

'It's amazing! I can't believe it,' she said, sounding exhilarated. I paused before speaking, but she spoke first, adding mischievously, 'You could have told me about the nudist colony!' She then burst out laughing and I joined in too. I had forgotten about the nudist reserve. Whatever she had seen had made her laugh. It simply hadn't occurred to me that the nudists would venture outside on such a crisp day. I walked towards her and found her throwing sticks for a couple of dogs that had joined her on the edge of the sea.

There were no crowds, no security apart from me, no over-attentive officials, no servants... Not one person had recognised her. For once Diana felt 'normal'. During the seven years I worked alongside her, this was a phenomenal moment and one I treasured – Diana clearly did too.

Together we walked back towards the pub car park along a leafy lane and climbed into our car. Diana didn't want her freedom adventure to end, but she knew it had to. In one last bid for normality we decided to return to London via Corfe Castle, a ruined Norman fortification that had once dominated the Isle of Purbeck but had been partially destroyed during the English Civil War. We parked near the village square and walked to the castle ruins and into the National Trust shop, where the Princess bought cards and gifts. I was surprised too when she paid for them with her own cash as I, as her PPO, would normally pay and reclaim the amount.

'This is a first,' I told her.

'It's being normal, isn't it?' she replied with a smile.

MAY 1992:
EGYPT

I spotted a glint of reflected light from the building opposite. Camera lens, I thought to myself. I told the Princess and she climbed from the pool, wrapped a towel over her one-piece swimsuit and went back inside. Then I followed her, and found that from the residence we could see men on the roof of the building opposite from where the flash had come.

As the group continued to take picture after picture, even though there was now nothing of interest to photograph, Diana opened up and spoke of her feelings of total isolation.

'I want out of this once and for all,' she confided.

It wasn't Egypt she was talking about, but being a member of the Royal Family and the circus that surrounded it. I could not help but agree with her, at least where this intrusion into her privacy was concerned. I listened, but offered no advice one way or the other.

Diana had gone for a swim to clear her head in the pool at the British Ambassador's official residence in Cairo, where she was staying. She had only just arrived for the official tour of the country in May 1992 without her husband and was more stressed than I had seen her in a while. I had urged her to take a dip as swimming always helped her unwind. Climbing out of the pool, she wrapped a towel around her shoulders and said, 'If anything happens to me, you'll let people know what I was really like, won't you?'

'Are you sure, Ma'am?' I replied, trying to keep the mood light. 'You'll be taking a hell of a risk.'

Though she playfully pushed me on the shoulder as if to reprimand me for my impertinence, some serious matter was clearly preying on her mind. She dived back into the pool and started an energetic workout but after only a few minutes' crawl and backstroke and no more than ten lengths I realised we had company and were being watched.

The fact that the Princess's swim was photographed and filmed by the press irritated me. I had identified the building as a possible problem during the reconnaissance that had preceded this trip, but officials from the British Embassy had said that there was little they could do about it because some Egyptian in-house security staff were easily bribed. And that is exactly what had happened. I walked across and entered the building, playing the policeman to the limit. When I got to the roof, some of the photographers were still there with their cameras trained on the pool. An ITN cameraman, a freelance named Mike Lloyd, was also there, although he was just preparing to leave.

When I confronted them all they admitted that they had bribed the guard to let them on to the roof. Although hardly welcome, such long-lens photography was to be expected on private holidays, but most of these photographers had official accreditation passes from the Palace to cover the Royal tour – an official tour, during which they would attend scores of photo sessions – and I told them that their behaviour was a blatant intrusion into the Princess's privacy.

They agreed to leave immediately, although whether swayed by my anger or by fear of losing their accreditation, I do not know. It was more likely that they had already got the photographs that they wanted anyway.

Next morning, inevitably, the pictures appeared in most of the British newspapers, and ITN even ran the intrusive footage on the news. Diana, determined that her trip should not be trivialised, was concerned in case the pictures shown on British TV should offend Muslim sensitivities, given that they showed her in a swimsuit, and feared they might create a false impression of her attitude to her official tour, following so closely after the row over the Duchess of York's island-hopping holiday in the Far East.

Diana's press secretary, Dickie Arbiter, sprang into action, issuing briefings and threatening action against those who had snatched the pictures. He told one newspaper, 'If the first thing people see of her in Egypt is her swimming around in a pool, it puts her in a frivolous light.' It resulted in a draconian punishment for the offending journalists and photographers – against the Princess's wishes – banning them from the upcoming visit to Korea, which turned out to be the last joint tour undertaken by Charles and Diana.

In reality, Diana had far bigger concerns than some video footage and a few grainy, long-lens snapshots of her lapping a swimming pool. Andrew Morton's book, *Diana: Her True Story*, on which she had secretly collaborated, was about to be launched upon a largely unsuspecting world, and she was well aware that the mother of all rows would follow. The Princess knew that the show had to go on nevertheless. She had a private meeting with President Hosni Mubarak and she was determined not let her personal story ruin an important diplomatic mission. To that end, she set about her official duties, which included a visit to a home for blind children that moved her terribly, with astonishing energy.

Not for the first time, Fleet Street totally missed the real story and traduced the Princess, printing the swimming-pool shots rather than following her as she set about a full programme of engagements. Not only that, but they had missed another opportunity to expose the truth. The fact that while she was promoting British industry and her own brand of caring abroad, her husband was on holiday in Turkey with another man's wife was undoubtedly more in the public interest than a few cheap shots of Diana in a swimsuit. Worse still, before arriving in Egypt her flight had first landed in Turkey, where Prince Charles left the aircraft to join a party of friends that included Camilla Parker Bowles.

Diverting to Turkey to deliver her husband into his lover's arms had not only added considerable time to the Princess's journey, but had also increased the stress she was already under. Understandably, she broke down in tears as, very late at night, we approached Cairo. Somehow, though, she pulled herself together just when she needed to, vowing not to let her 'A-Team' down. Diana knew perfectly well the reason for her husband's trip to Turkey, but she was determined not to crack up while on official duty. For that she deserves enormous credit.

Although she handled the formal side of her duties with her usual charm, the Princess was in a highly emotional state and had to be handled with care. With hindsight, her tears may have had more to do with the impending publication of Andrew Morton's book than with her frustration at her husband's blatant infidelity. Yet for her, the Egypt trip delivered all that it had promised: another solo triumph. In terms of press coverage the visit was also a true Diana media spectacular, which saw her posing for photographs by the Giza Pyramids in a cream linen belted day suit (one of the stunning images is on the front cover of this book). She also stood before the Sphinx for photos and at the breathtaking Luxor Temple, known as '*ipet resyt*, the southern sanctuary', situated on the east bank of the

River Nile near Luxor (the site of the ancient city of Thebes in the time of the pharaohs). The photographers lapped it up. Unfortunately, the words that accompanied the stunning photographs when they appeared in the papers focused on the sorry state of her marriage and not the good job Diana was doing on the tour.

One of my abiding memories was our trip to the Valley of the Queens near Luxor and accompanying Diana (along with my co-author of this book, Robert Jobson, then a royal correspondent) into Queen Nefertari's excavated tomb. We all stood in awe. Nefertari Meritmut was an Egyptian queen and the first of the Great Royal Wives of Ramesses the Great, who died in 1255 BC. Nefertari's 520-square-metre tomb is the best preserved and contains the most eloquent paintings of any Egyptian burial site – the Sistine Chapel of Egyptian history, so to speak. The paintings on the tomb walls depict her journey after death to the afterlife, guided by various guardian spirits and deities, including Isis, Hathor, and Osiris. The lavishly decorated tomb, QV66, was discovered in 1904 and is one of the most spectacular in the Valley of the Queens.

Diana loved the history of Egypt and was so excited to be invited to enter the Tomb of Nefertari by French archaeologists, the first visit by any member of the public, albeit Royal public. She surprised us all by recalling the discovery of the Tomb of Tutankhamun by the renowned archaeologist Howard Carter, and imagined what it must have been like there in Egypt in 1922. How befitting then was it, that in the afternoon of her discovery of sorts, that tea was taken at the famous Old Cataract Hotel on the Nile, an imposing Victorian Palace built in 1899. Here, Howard Carter took refreshment from his discoveries. Tsar Nicholas II, Sir Winston Churchill and Margaret Thatcher all experienced the beauty and magic of this hotel near Aswan on the River Nile. Agatha Christie set portions of her novel *Death on the Nile* at the hotel after staying here.

With the utmost secrecy, Diana had sealed her own fate and

defined her future, but I am convinced that she would not have gone ahead with the deal with Andrew Morton and his publisher, Michael O'Mara, had she not truly believed that she could get away with it. In that she was right; it was only after her death that Morton revealed that she had not only secretly collaborated in the writing of *Diana: Her True Story*, but that it was she who had approached him in the first place. Many people had their suspicions about her part in the project, but she and the very few other people involved maintained their silence until the end. I was kept completely in the dark about the entire project – probably for my own good, for Diana knew that if I had found out about it, I would have been compromised.

The Princess's decision to strike a deal with the independent journalist, writer and former royal correspondent Andrew Morton through her close friend, Doctor James Colthurst, was one that she took entirely herself. She wanted to be free of her marriage and of the stifling embrace of the Palace, and she had come to believe that if Morton could pen her version of events, for all the world to read, then it would prove so damning of Prince Charles and his family that they would have no choice but to grant her, in effect, an exit visa.

It was a strategy typical of Diana, naive, perhaps even childish, but brutally direct. Andrew Morton's account proved to be a brilliant and historic document – and perhaps the longest divorce petition on record. More importantly for Diana, it achieved what it set out to do – rocking the monarchy to its foundations and freeing her from its shackles. For the first time, too, the anonymous friends so often cited in newspaper stories were named and quoted on the record in the book. What infuriated the Palace was that it was clear that, despite her protestations, they had at the very least spoken to Morton with Diana's consent and encouragement.

Diana: Her True Story broke when the first extract of the serialisation appeared in *The Sunday Times* on 7 June 1992. Then the book itself

Above: Enjoying her skiing holiday in Lech, Austria, in March 1992. Sadly, her evident happiness was about to be shattered.

© *Getty Images*

Below: The Princess leaving Lech after learning of the death of her father, Earl Spencer, 30 March 1992. Ken Wharfe sits in front of her, and Prince Charles is barely visible beside her; Diana's mood made it, by any standards, an extremely uncomfortable journey.

© *Getty Images*

Top: Visiting the Karnak Temple complex near Luxor, on the River Nile, during her solo official visit to Egypt in May 1992.

© *Getty Images*

Below left: Visiting the Alazhar Mosque in Cairo, 13 May 1992. Diana was well aware of the storm that was about to break over the imminent publication of Andrew Morton's book about her and her marriage, in which she had secretly collaborated.

© *Getty Images*

Below right: A police protection officer must be prepared, if necessary, to risk his own life for the person he guards. In Ken Wharfe's case, this included riding a camel during the Princess's official tour of Egypt ...

© *Ken Wharfe*

Above left: Diana meets local people during a field visit to Red Cross projects in the remote mountain villages of Nepal, 3 March 1993. © Getty Images

Above right: Visiting the Cairo Institute for Polio and Rehabilitation during her tour of Egypt, 11 May 1992. © Getty Images

Below: With officials during a visit to a Red Cross project in the village of Panauti, Nepal, March 1993. Despite a certain amount of ill-informed carping by some of the media, the Princess's official solo visit to Nepal was judged a great success. © Getty Images

Above left: A private photograph of Diana swimming in Nevis Island in the West Indies, during her private family holiday there in January 1993.
© *Kent Gavin*

Above right: The deal that Ken Wharfe negotiated with the assembled media, desperate for lucrative photographs of the Princess, ensured that they got their shots and thereafter Diana was left in peace. Press photographers and paparazzi on a beach after they'd been allowed on to Nevis – there is only one subject for their long lenses.
© *Kent Gavin*

Below: One of the press images that went round the world: Diana swimming in her orange bikini on Nevis, 30 January 1993.
© *Getty Images*

Above left: A policeman's lot: the ever-watchful Inspector Wharfe with the Princess in the Latin Quarter of Paris, November 1992.

© *Press Association*

Above right: Return to Lech and a skiing holiday in March 1993, a year after she had left the resort on learning of her father's death.

© *Getty Images*

Below: Diana with hers sons, Princes William and Harry, during their skiing holiday in Lech, 30 March 1993. By now she was separated from her husband, the Prince of Wales.

© *Getty Images*

Top left: Diana visits the Great Zimbabwe ruins, 1 July 1993. Her visit to Zimbabwe had the official sanction of the Queen.

© *Rob Jobson*

Top right: Visiting a Red Cross borehole project for refugees in Zimbabwe. She was visibly affected by the poverty of many of the people she encountered in Zimbawe.

© *Getty Images*

Below: 'The Princess flew deep into the African bush, to the Mazerera Red Cross feeding centre. There, standing by a huge iron cooking pot, she served the children from the ancient Karanga tribe, one by one.'

© *Getty Images*

Top: A slightly apprehensive Diana on a ride at Disney World, Florida, with William (left) and Harry (right) in the front seats, 25 August 1993. The young Princes loved their visit; Diana left Florida feeling she had 'done Disney'. © *Mike Forster/Daily Mail/REX/Shutterstock*

Below left: Although her boys loved the experience, Diana, seated at the back alongside her friend Kate Menzies, would clearly rather not look. Disney World, August 1993.

© *Mike Forster/Daily Mail/REX/Shutterstock*

Below right: At Disney World with Kate Menzies. The party left Florida for the Menzies family home at Lyford Cay in the Bahamas. © *Mike Forster/Daily Mail/REX/Shutterstock*

Her final journey: Charles, Earl Spencer, Prince William, Prince Harry and the Prince of Wales stand as the hearse leaves Westminster Abbey to take Diana, Princess of Wales to her private burial at Althorp House, the Spencer family seat in Northamptonshire, 6 September 1997.

was published, immediately becoming a major and long-running bestseller. Clearly, readers wanted to know about the Princess and thanks to Morton, they now knew a good deal more than Prince Charles, the Royal Family and the Palace had ever wanted them to know. This was not throwing down the gauntlet, it was unhorsing an opponent before he had even reached for his lance.

In the weeks that followed the Palace bluntly pointed a damning finger of blame at the Princess, but at no stage did she buckle under pressure. She stuck to her story, denying that she had co-operated with the book's writing or encouraged its author in any way. When questioned about Morton, her answer was invariably the same: 'I have never spoken to him.'

Diana was, of course, not lying. She had not given face-to-face interviews to Morton; indeed, she never met him, but had provided him with tapes of her thoughts and memories recorded in private conversations with her old friend Colthurst at Kensington Palace. The Old Etonian doctor would then deliver the tapes secretly to the author.

When questioned by her brother-in-law, Sir Robert Fellowes, the Queen's private secretary, on the question of her collaboration with Morton, the Princess again categorically denied it. This led Sir Robert to tell Her Majesty that he believed Diana was telling the truth, and that the Palace's sole remaining option, given that it was impossible to prove that the book was a work of self-interest orchestrated by the Princess herself, was to go all out and attack it, questioning Morton's accuracy and motives, and denigrating his sources. But it was too little, too late, for the book had (and still has) an authority that proved unshakeable. Some of the Prince's inner circle tried to intimate that Diana was at best hysterical, and at worst mad, but that also backfired. She was by now too popular, too visible, too beautiful – as well as too important to the media – ever to fall victim to such shabby denigration.

When it later transpired that Diana had lied to him, Fellowes offered to fall on his sword, tendering his resignation, which the Queen, who liked and respected him, refused to accept.

In Egypt, to her credit, as Diana prepared to face the tornado about to hit the monarchy, she was able to find calm in the eye of the storm. She knew that everyone who worked with her was also under strain, and she did her best to lighten the mood, insisting we take time out to 'de-stress' ourselves. On the last night of the trip she invited everyone to join her for a swim at the British Ambassador's pool because of the extreme temperatures. All of her staff were there, from baggage master Ron Lewis to her secretary, Victoria Mendham. The tour doctor, Surgeon Commander Robin Clark, Royal Navy, a congenial chap with a sweep of hair covering his balding scalp, was rather reluctant to strip off and join in the fun, preferring instead to loiter somewhat precariously at the pool's edge. For some reason he was wearing a camel suit which, in the searing heat of Cairo, must have been incredibly hot. From the pool, Diana eyed him menacingly. When we arrived in Cairo he was always complaining about the heat, which was not surprising, given that temperatures were in the mid-thirties, and he had insisted on wearing a tight-fitting wool suit. Diana even offered for him to be taken to a local suit maker for a lightweight addition to his already scant wardrobe but he had politely refused.

Diana – clearly in a very upbeat mood – kept gesturing to the doc to get his swimming trunks and come and 'cool off' in the pool.

'I didn't bring any, Ma'am,' was his reply

She left the pool and came up to me.

'Is he going to come in for a swim?' she asked, pointing to the unsuspecting doctor.

'No, I don't think he is, Ma'am,' I replied,

'Well, I think he ought to go in, in that suit.'

'I think that would be better coming from you, Ma'am,' I told her.

'If he agrees to go in in that ridiculous suit, will you help me put him in the water?' she persisted. In fact, she had no intention of asking his agreement.

'As long as I don't get sued by the Royal Navy, Ma'am, it would be a pleasure,' I said.

With that, we attacked Robin with a pincer formation and tossed him in the pool head first, his glasses flying off in the process. What we failed to appreciate, of course, was that his suit was of heavy wool, and by the morning it had shrunk dramatically. Diana, of course, offered to buy the unfortunate chap a replacement – and did so.

AUGUST 1992:
SUMMER CRUISE,
MEDITERRANEAN SEA

B uoyed by what, for the Prince of Wales, had been the success of the previous year's cruise, especially in giving the pursuing media the slip, His Royal Highness happily accepted an invitation from his friend, the billionaire John 'Spiro' Latsis, to be his guest aboard the 400-foot superyacht MY *Alexander* again. The Prince was not, it seemed, the slightest bit bothered about criticism of him in the press about accepting free trips. As far as he was concerned this was one Greek he wasn't worried about bearing gifts. Since using the Royal Yacht *Britannia* for such frivolity was out of the question, it seemed perfectly acceptable to him that he should make use of a friend's yacht. And it was quite a yacht, complete with a disco bar, 27-seater cinema, children's playroom and beauty salon. There were even a special gazebo reception area, small hospital, gymnasium, music room, heliport and an attractive pool deck with jacuzzi available on board.

Even before the Royal couple set off, inaccurate stories about this second sham 'love boat cruise' appeared in the press. The newspapers gleefully reported that the pair had been ordered to make a go of their marriage by the Queen and this was reported as a make-or-break family holiday.

The Royal Rat Pack is not for the faint-hearted. Failure was not an option and after being hoodwinked the previous year, when the same yacht had cruised from Naples around Italy and Greece, this time they were determined to track down the Royals. Kent Gavin took charge of hiring the press vessel, which he somehow convinced his colleagues from other newspapers was equipped with the latest electronic devices for finding and tracking members of the Royal Family. Compared to the *Alexander*, it was a tugboat. As it turned out, just about the only thing it was equipped with was enough drink to have kept the Royal Navy afloat in both world wars.

Moreover, with Mr Latsis's yacht, his money, and his influence in the region, even the Royal Rat Pack loaded down with cash and Fleet Street cunning was doomed to failure from the outset. In truth, we never even saw them. I heard later from Kent Gavin that two of their team did spot us, but only when we left. Nonetheless, our voyage was far from uneventful, although it was perhaps a blessing that what happened on the cruise did so well away from the intrusive gaze of the press.

Diana was in no mood to put on a show in her phoney marriage, for the Queen or anyone else. By now the plans she had made for her escape were already bearing fruit. The only voyage she wanted to make was on a straight course away from the Royal Family. Her attitude and behaviour made the trip almost impossible for those, like myself, whose job it was to look after her. A couple of weeks before we were due to sail, she suddenly refused point-blank to go, and told the Prince she would also stop their two sons from joining him on the trip. This seriously irritated Charles, not least because he was really looking forward to a private summer holiday with the boys. The Princess had successfully fired the first salvo. In fact, she had every intention of going on the cruise, but she took considerable pleasure in unsettling her husband.

By this time the Prince and Princess were barely speaking to each other, a civil nod mustered in public being about as far as relations between them went. So the prospect of a ten-day cruise was disconcerting for all concerned, including the warring couple. The guest list was much the same as the previous year: Lord and Lady Romsey again, this time with their children, the Queen's first cousin, Princess Alexandra, and her charming husband, Sir Angus Ogilvy, and ex-King Constantine and Queen Anne-Marie of Greece. Everyone on board, guests, staff or crew, knew that the Prince and Princess were at loggerheads. This was going to be a stormy voyage, even if the Aegean remained calm.

Winds gusting up to Force 9 prevented the Royals from sailing into the Aegean and instead the Royal party flew by Queen's Flight BAe 146 to Aktion, opposite Lefkada in the Ionian Sea, about two hundred miles from Athens. Initially, however, the Princess was surprisingly restrained. She and the Prince made certain that they saw very little of each other from the moment they boarded the yacht anchored at the Lefkas Canal on the evening of 6 August. If, as the press were reporting, this trip was designed to rekindle the embers of a dying marriage, it would need a miracle. Yet ironically, the Royal party charted a route that they had taken on their honeymoon aboard *Britannia* eleven years earlier, taking in the Greek islands of the Aegean and the Ionian Seas on their ten-day cruise.

Despite our fears for the cruise, Colin Trimming and I were consoled by the seemingly endless supply of caviar and vintage Dom Pérignon champagne. Although our assignment was fraught with difficulties, especially as the Princess's behaviour became increasingly erratic or irrational, there were distinct advantages to being on board the *Alexander*. The Royal couple had separate cabins, and did not venture into each other's territory. Diana suspected that throughout the cruise her husband spent hours on the satellite telephone to his mistress. Her suspicions were well founded. What she would never know, mercifully, was that five years later, after her death, Camilla Parker Bowles would join the Prince aboard the same yacht. But for now the atmosphere was extremely tense. Diana wanted nothing to do with Charles and even her sons became concerned about their mother's strange behaviour.

The captain set sail and we cruised between Ithaca and Cephalonia. We arrived the next day at Zakynthos, where we dropped anchor so the guests could enjoy some swimming in the company of sea turtles in the clear blue sea. The same day we passed the Octagonal Tower of the thirteenth-century Venetian castle of Methoni, Messenia, before heading at a leisurely pace towards the then almost deserted island of Koufonisi. The Prince of Wales was in his element, often heading to the deck to lose himself painting in watercolour. Our voyage was idyllic, every day taking in new breathtaking scenery. We anchored off Gaidouronisi ('donkey island'), known as Chrissi, a small island off the coast of Crete. It was a tiny uninhabited place, one of eighty-one uninhabited islands off Crete. A real paradise, it was surrounded by crystal-clear waters that lapped the white and golden sand beaches, which sometimes change to a rose colour, thanks to shell fragments. In the distance, cedar forests tower into the sky. It really was a little slice of heaven, but for Diana, after only four days, the voyage was becoming a living hell.

On one occasion there was a bad scare when my colleague Colin Trimming raised the alarm after a real fear that she had jumped overboard. He came to my cabin and told me that the Princess had not been seen for a couple of hours. She was not in her cabin, and no one else had the least idea where she might be. Panic set in. The Prince was informed that his wife had apparently disappeared, and I saw genuine concern on his face. Colin and I conducted a thorough search, and found nothing. I then remembered that Diana had spent some time by the lifeboats, and went to investigate. In one of them, crouched beneath the canvas cover in floods of tears, I found her. She had been sitting there alone for two hours, sobbing. I was immensely relieved – at least she was still alive.

After telling the others to call off the search, I spent the next two hours in the lifeboat locked in conversation with the Princess under the cover.

'They don't understand me. He's on the telephone to the Rottweiler, and everybody knows it. They are all in it with him. They think I'm mad and feel sorry for me, but they have no idea what I'm going through,' she sobbed.

Quite certainly she had a point. Although Diana had been unfaithful too, she at least had the decency not to flaunt her affairs right under her husband's nose. Hurt and embarrassed, she had every right to feel humiliated and betrayed.

'If he wants her here, why doesn't he fly her here and leave me alone? It's a sham, a total sham. He is only here with me because his mummy has ordered him to. He is pathetic. Pathetic!' she fumed.

She was right in that, too. It was as clear to her as it was to everyone else aboard that the Prince had no intention of even trying to make his wife feel wanted on this trip. Her reaction may have been childish, but in this instance it was entirely justified.

Having worked herself up to a fury, Diana then demanded that I arrange for her to be flown home immediately. She said that she was not prepared to stay on the yacht for one second longer than she had to and as a princess she insisted she could do what the bloody hell she liked. This was not the first time that I had had to deal with her petulance, nor would it be the last. I reminded her that I was fully aware of who she was and what authority she had. I also reminded her that I was only alongside her to protect her, not to be shouted at or ordered about like a subordinate, especially as I did not answer to her but to my seniors at Scotland Yard. Diana took the point and apologised, but still insisted that she wanted to get off what she described as a 'floating hell'.

She devised a plan whereby the captain of the *Alexander* would miss out the Turkish section of the voyage and sail directly to Cyprus, where she would get a helicopter flight to the nearest airport. From there, she said, she would board a cheap flight home, just like the thousands of holidaymakers from Britain enjoying their summer break on the Greek islands. I explained that getting a flight home at this time of year would be nearly impossible – everything would be pre-booked, with the result that it could take several days, at least, to arrange. At this she became furious again, saying that if she wanted excuses, she would go to her husband. I tried to reason with her. If she, one of the most famous and photographed women in the world, were to arrive at Larnaca Airport and sit in the departure lounge with hundreds of tourists, then it would be headline news. How on earth would she be able to explain her sudden decision to quit the family cruise? Surely, I said, appealing to her sense of reason, it would be better if she toughed it out aboard the *Alexander* for just a few more days? Then, with the final throw of the dice, I asked, 'And what about your sons?' She paid me the compliment of listening to my concerns.

Despite her occasional descents into immaturity, Diana actually had a firm grasp of the real world, even if at times she pretended not to. She knew that to make a show of defiance in front of her beloved sons would be unforgivable. She was deeply frustrated with living a lie and determined to have her freedom, but she realised to make a stand at this moment would send out the wrong signals. In the eyes of the media and the world she would be the quitter, not the wronged wife pushed almost beyond endurance. At last, to my relief, she agreed to remain aboard the yacht for the remainder of the cruise. That relief must have been written across my face. She burst out laughing, both at my look, and at our situation – a policeman and a princess crouched in conversation in a covered lifeboat.

'Come on,' she said, 'we'd better get back to the rest of them otherwise that bloody husband of mine will be cracking open the champagne, hoping that I did actually jump overboard and he can make that hideous woman his princess.'

The determined glint was back in her blue eyes. I knew, however, that we were not completely out of the woods yet. The Princess, although placated, was primed and ready to attack if her husband gave her sufficient reason. The Prince, sensibly, since otherwise he would have caught the full fury of her anger and frustration, ignored his wife's tantrum; in fact he did not even bother to speak to her that night. With several days of the holiday still to go, however, the rest of the party were living on their nerves.

It was the young Princes who, in the end, provided the link with reality that everybody aboard this floating paradise needed. Harry, ever the daredevil, started it. With the *Alexander* at anchor, the fearless boy took it into his head to leap more than thirty feet from the stern of the yacht into the sea below. Laughing as he trod water, he then dared his older brother to join him. William, who was never one to shirk a challenge, especially from Harry, followed. Both of them then tried to goad Colin Trimming into following them into the sea. It was at times like this that Colin, with magnificent timing, always managed to pull rank on me.

'In you go, Wharfie,' he ordered, absolutely deadpan. 'We can't have the second and third in line to the throne swimming around in the water without protection.'

I looked at him in disbelief. Then, realising that he was serious, I stripped to my shorts, shut my eyes and took the plunge. It was terrifying, and I had visions of smashing against the side of the yacht on the way down. As soon as I hit the water with an almighty splash, the two Princes pounced. Harry adopted his usual fighting tactic, aiming below the belt, and when I managed to wrestle him off, his brother was on my shoulders within seconds, trying to grab me round the neck and duck me under the water. Everyone watched from the deck, laughing and shouting encouragement, and a breath of normality seemed to creep back into the atmosphere aboard the *Alexander*.

Even so, the young Princes' leap caused a considerable stir. Prince Charles questioned Colin as to how they had been allowed to get away with it without being stopped. The Princess, however, thought the entire incident was extremely funny and praised her sons for their nerve in perhaps another swipe at her husband. But there were no reprisals. The Prince told the boys that they were never to do it again and it was soon forgotten. It was a welcome break from the gloomy process of keeping the Prince and Princess apart, and for that most of us were extremely grateful.

Desperate to think of ways of keeping Diana occupied, I arranged a table-tennis competition involving all the party, including the protection officers. The Princess, who could be fiercely competitive, took the tournament extremely seriously, and with a combination of a naturally good eye for the ball and a certain amount of gentle persuasion she reached the final against ex-Queen Anne-Marie of Greece. Fortunately, the elegant former queen had the good grace (as well as the good sense) to lose the match to placate her younger opponent. Everyone, particularly Prince Charles, breathed a sigh of relief when Diana emerged victorious. It put her in a good mood for the rest of the voyage, and all talk of airlifts to an airport in Cyprus evaporated.

While Diana, for perfectly understandable reasons, chose not to socialise with her husband and guests, the Prince of Wales as self-appointed captain of the ship was all for a happy crew. There were few restrictions on board, though the aft deck area was reserved for the Prince and his friends. One afternoon the sound of a piano being played could be heard. My musical interests did get the better of me and I moved closer towards the sound. I opened a door to find the

Queen's charming first cousin, Princess Alexandra, playing a selection of Gilbert and Sullivan arias from memory without manuscript.

'You sing, so Diana tells me, don't you?'

'Of a sort, Ma'am,' was my reply, not letting modesty get hold of me.

'I was planning a little concert this evening. Why don't you policemen do the policeman song from *Pirates* [*of Penzance*]?' she suggested.

It was a genuine invitation for sure, but quite how Superintendent Colin Trimming would take it, not to mention Diana, would remain to be seen.

'You will do it for us, won't you?' Princess Alexandra implored.

'It would be a shame to miss a Royal Command Performance, Ma'am – I'll speak with Superintendent Trimming,' I responded.

As luck would have it, Princess Alexandra met Colin Trimming before I did. It didn't temper his reaction when I was summoned to our area of the ship.

'Since when have you been the ship's entertainment manager?' he blasted, though with a wry smile.

It seemed not to be all doom and gloom.

The show did go ahead, with Princess Alexandra in fine form on the piano and guests joyful, courtesy of fine wines. The newly formed Protection Male Voice Ensemble appeared on the High Seas, and with some ropy high notes, in a one-off shortened performance of 'When a Foeman Bares His Steel'.

After one encore Princess Alexandra asked if we knew any Italian arias. At that point we made a quick exit stage left and quit while still ahead.

Diana had decided to absent herself from the performance but the following day, she asked me about it. With a smile on her face and a bigger one on mine, I said, 'I had no choice, Ma'am – it was by Royal command.'

Her response, given that it was from her, was surprisingly funny. She laughed out loud and said, 'Bollocks!'

From Koufonsi we cruised to Akrotiri, Cyprus and then headed to Delikada Island in Turkey, where the Prince enjoyed a river trip and some more painting, and then headed down the coast to Kekova, stopping at Fethiye and Long Beach along the way. The final stop was back at Akrotiri Base in Cyprus, where the guests disembarked and our 1,470-nautical-mile (1,690-mile, 2,720-kilometre) voyage of discovery was over. The boys, Charles and their guests had all loved

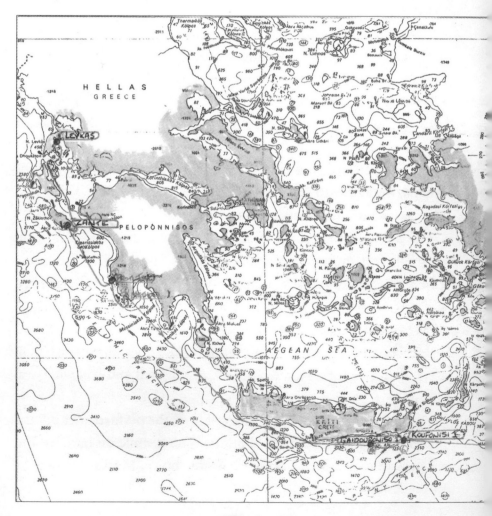

it. Sporting healthy tans, they kissed and hugged each other at the end. Then the captain handed us all a chart showing the route of our 'Mediterranean Sea – Eastern Part' voyage, which is shown below. In a nice touch, the Prince signed it at the top: 'Charles, August 1992'. Below, Diana penned her name, followed by Princess Alexandra, her husband Angus Ogilvy, Queen Anne-Marie and Lord Romsey and his wife Penelope.

There was talk of them all returning together the following year, but that was not to be.

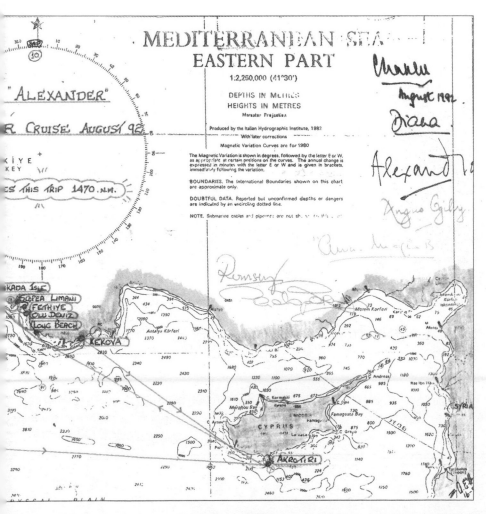

NEW YEAR 1993: NEVIS, LEEWARD ISLANDS, WI

'I can't help thinking of them [Charles and his staff] as the enemy. I know that's how they think of me – they call me that mad woman who just keeps causing trouble,' the Princess told me over one of our many lunches at the Knightsbridge restaurant San Lorenzo. In this atmosphere, working alongside her was like walking a tightrope; falling off was the easy option. So when, in early December 1992, she phoned me at my police office from Kensington Palace and implored me to help her find a Caribbean hideaway, I knew that it was imperative to act fast. Christmas at Sandringham with her estranged husband and her 'ice-veined' in-laws, she said, was simply not an option.

'Ken, I really need to get away. I cannot stand it here another day, I need some sun on my face…' There was a frantic edge to her voice over the phone. She went on to tell me that she had heard about a resort in the north of Jamaica which she thought would be the perfect escape for her and the boys.

'But nobody, I mean nobody, must know about it. You are the only one who knows my plans and I need it to stay that way.'

The line clicked and the phone went dead in my hand. This was one hell of a curveball, I thought. A few days later, on 16 December 1992, without even telling my bosses in the Royalty Protection Department the precise details of what I was doing, I boarded a flight from Gatwick under an assumed name, bound for Sangster International Airport, Montego Bay, Jamaica, on a mission.

To understand the significance that Diana attached to this holiday, it has first to be seen in context. At the end of 1992 all hell was breaking loose back home. It had become not just an *annus horribilis* for HM The Queen, but for Diana too. On 9 December, in the House of Commons, the then Prime Minister, John Major, had announced the separation of the Prince and Princess of Wales. There was, he stated, no question of a divorce, and in the event of the Prince becoming King, Diana would be Queen Consort. Even then, as people close to the Princess tried to come to terms with the enormity of what was being said, no one really believed what the Prime Minister was saying. How could King Charles reign with Queen Diana at his side if they were legally separated? It was preposterous, of course, but everyone in the hushed House accepted his words. Every member of the Royal household and staff knew the idea was ridiculous, though.

Diana did her best to put a brave face on it, largely by hiding from the harsh reality of the situation, as she had so often done before. Within a few days of the announcement the strain was beginning to tell. Decisions had to be made, and members of staff had to declare their allegiances – one wore the colours of the Prince or the Princess, not both. Unlike me, whose salary was paid for by Scotland Yard, their respective staffs had their livelihoods to think about. Not surprisingly, in all this upheaval, the Princess became increasingly agitated. She admitted to me that she felt she was becoming paranoid, but said that she could not help but feel betrayed if any member of her inner circle showed signs of siding with the Prince and his team of advisers.

After a ten-hour flight, we landed at Montego Bay and I hit the ground running – there was no time to lose. I hired a cab and headed straight for Ocho Rios on the north coast of the island to investigate the suitability of a hotel the Princess had asked me to look at. As I have said, surfing through holiday brochures was one of her favourite pastimes, a form of escapism perhaps that made her feel normal, as though she too could just jet away on an ordinary package holiday, like other people.

'Ochee', as it is known locally, was a bumpy two-hour drive in a clapped-out scarlet Ford Mustang driven by a Rastafarian chap, who seemed to be as high as a kite. From the car window, as the sun streamed in, it appeared like the backdrop for a Bond movie (and was in fact used as the backdrop to the very first James Bond film, *Dr. No*). Everything looked promising, then without warning the driver suddenly pulled into a field, got out and opened the boot of his car. Seconds later, the grinning figure appeared at my window and produced an open suitcase packed with an array of exotic substances of what he proudly told me included the best-quality cannabis on the island. I politely declined, but I'm sure if I'd told him I was a Scotland Yard policeman then he would not have acted quite so cool.

'Irie [alright], man, but you knows where to come when you do,' he said.

We carried on as if nothing had happened.

As soon as I arrived at the Ramada Beach Hotel, however, I knew that it was definitely not the right place for one of the world's most famous women to go on holiday, weeks after it had been announced to the world that she and the future King of England were splitting up. Scruffy and tired, it had clearly seen better days.

I then took a stroll along the beach. There was no privacy, security was inadequate, and to cap it all, soft drugs were openly being sold by drug dealers. Already I could visualise the headlines: 'Di and the Drug Dealer'. I made some further inquiries, but they only confirmed my first impressions.

There was nothing I could do but telephone Diana and break the news to her as gently as possible, knowing that she would be deeply disappointed. She was clearly living on the edge of her nerves and needed to escape; she was also extremely anxious that the press should not find out about her projected holiday. Then I had a brainwave. I remembered that a friend of mine, Charles Mitchell, had a stake in a small hotel on the island of Nevis (a small island at the north-western end of the Leeward chain of islands in the Caribbean), and he put me in touch with his friend, James Milnes Gaskill. There were six adult vacancies for the period Diana wanted in January.1993. When I explained that it would be difficult to get there, the Princess practically ordered me to take a private charter – the cost didn't seem to worry her.

'I'll pay for it, it doesn't matter how much it is.'

When I suggested it would be around US $2,000, she insisted she would cover it. Securing her holiday as quickly as possible was the priority.

My next call was to my boss, Superintendent Colin Trimming, back at the headquarters of the Royalty and Diplomatic Protection Department, to inform him in the most indeterminate way possible what I was up to. I then headed back to the hotel to make a few calls in the hope of finding another destination. As luck would have it, one of the people I spoke to told me about one, and it sounded perfect. For me the only problem was getting there. Given the urgency in Diana's voice, I had to find somewhere that fitted her criteria as soon as possible. Unfortunately, though, I was travelling undercover, and could not tell anyone who I was or why I was in the area.

Posing as a British businessman, I contacted the airport and eventually located two Australian local-charter pilots who were willing to fly me to Nevis. In their twin-engine, fly-by-the-seat-of-your-pants aircraft, which had clearly seen better days, we headed south in search of paradise, or the Princess's concept of it, anyway. The two pilots did not ask me what I was doing; they were simply happy to take the money.

What was to happen next was typical of what could befall someone on a 'Diana mission'. Bad weather meant that we had to divert to Puerto Rico, which is a self-governing commonwealth (rather than state) of the United States. When we touched down on the island, however, my rollercoaster ride through the Caribbean was to come to an abrupt end. While the Australian pilots were refuelling, a chisel-faced US Marine in uniform marched across the tarmac to where I was standing by the aircraft, glared at me accusingly and demanded to see my passport.

'You, sir, are on American territory. Where are your papers and what is your business here?' he boomed.

I was clearly in big trouble.

Without giving anything away about my mission I tried my best to bluff my way through. I waffled on about being a businessman (I had dropped the false name, and my passport doesn't show my profession) and needing to get to Nevis as quickly as possible. It must have sounded incredibly suspicious, and in my by now rather frazzled state I hated to think what the shaven-headed Marine thought I was up to – or into. He was not interested in that, however. What he did not like was that I had flown into an American territory on business with no visa and no papers. As far as he was concerned, I was an illegal alien and he was not about to take any nonsense from me. At that point one of the pilots tried to intervene, but succeeded in making matters worse by winding the Marine up even more.

'Why don't you loosen up, mate? It's not his fault we had to put down here and get some fuel, for Christ's sake!' the pilot drawled in an authentic Australian twang.

This proved to be the final straw. I was duly frogmarched into the airport's security office and given the grilling of my life. The easiest way out would have been to reveal who I was and what I was doing, but that would have meant that Diana's holiday plans could have leaked out, and the media would have arrived swiftly. Playing the businessman was a risk I had to take, but it was a close call. Eventually, they relented and admitted there was not much point in throwing me in the cells, even though they told me that they did not believe a word I had said. With that, I was fined $100 (£75) and ordered to leave American soil immediately.

The final indignity came when the US Marine once again demanded my passport. He flicked through it, studying every entry, which showed that on my Royal missions I had criss-crossed the globe more times than Superman. He eventually located a blank page, and then rifled through a drawer in his desk for the appropriate stamp. Then, like a particularly small-minded Dickensian clerk, he thumped it down to mark my passport with the words 'Illegal Alien'. A little crestfallen, I boarded the plane and as we taxied along the runway I could not help wondering how I could explain the incident – and the stamp in my passport – to the Commander if he pulled me up on it.

A couple of hours later we touched down at the small Newcastle aerodrome on Nevis, a tiny atoll, just six miles by eight. One of the smallest islands in the northern Leeward chain in the eastern Caribbean, it would be the backdrop to some of the most stunning photographs ever taken of the Princess. Nestled between Saint Kitts and Montserrat, it is dominated by a 3,500-foot dormant volcano, its peak shrouded with a blanket of cloud.

Unshaven and looking a little the worse for wear, I soon arrived at my sanctuary, the Montpelier Plantation Inn, which had been recommended to me. The Montpelier was well-placed, a fifteen-minute walk from Nevisian Heritage Village and St John's Figtree Church. The amazing Pinney's Beach and Nevis Botanical Gardens were just a mile away. I had called ahead to say that I was on my way, and there to greet me were the owners, an English couple, James and Celia Milnes-Gaskill, who handed me a suitably refreshing Caribbean concoction and led me to my chalet, where I was able to shower and change.

The Milnes-Gaskills had moved to Nevis in the 1960s and had begun to renovate the site, an old sugar plantation, in 1964. Over the next thirty years they had managed to develop a small but successful hotel business. The main house stood on sixteen acres surrounded by secluded gardens and stone terraces, and there were sixteen chalets dotted around the grounds. Privacy seemed to be the watchword, and I knew instantly that this was the perfect retreat for the Princess and her sons. As a Caribbean hideaway it had everything she could want, but most significantly it offered a discreet haven into which she could disappear and no one would ever know she was there. That, at least, was the hope. I admit now I might have been a little too optimistic in my prediction.

I still could not say what I was doing on Nevis, so I told the owners that I was representing a VIP, but that I could not divulge any more details other than that the person insisted upon privacy and needed total security. The Milnes-Gaskills were charming people, the embodiment of relaxed hospitality. Their business had been built on discretion and quality of service, and had thrived as a result. They therefore knew exactly what was required, and immediately set about preparing to accommodate the mystery VIP, at the same time providing me with all the information I needed. As I sat on the veranda of my chalet that evening, I could not help but feel a little pleased with myself: Mission Impossible was now Mission Accomplished. In the privacy of my chalet I had telephoned the Princess to let her know the good news. I could hear the joy in her voice over all those thousands of miles between us. The stress seemed literally to melt away.

Before I flew home I had to complete the reconnaissance to make sure that everything was in place for a secure Royal holiday. At this stage, however, I decided against discussing the operation with the local police service, believing that it would be best to do so when I arrived as the advance guard just prior to the arrival of the Princess and her party. On my return to England on 21 December, I sent Diana a brochure about the hotel and a memorandum about the holiday. She was thrilled.

'You're so wonderful,' she gushed. 'If you recommend it then I know it will be perfect.'

She would often say in her darkest moments, 'Nobody understands me,' but she knew in her heart I did my best to.

Persuading Diana had been the easiest part of the operation. I now had to write a report to my senior officer, justifying the expense for the high level of protection, and therefore the cost to Scotland Yard. My reconnaissance report to the department had recommended a total of four personal protection officers: myself, Inspector Trevor 'Heinrich' Bettles and Sergeants Dave 'Razor' Sharp and Graham 'Crackers' Craker (the nicknames were all of my making, Trevor's because I felt he bore an uncanny resemblance to the character with the same name from the popular comedy *'Allo 'Allo!*), with myself taking the operational lead for the overseas visits.

While I would have overall responsibility for twenty-four-hour policing, Trevor Bettles was responsible for William, Graham Craker would watch over Harry, and Dave Sharp would assist me in protecting the Princess and would fly with her to the island, since I would have already travelled ahead of the party to ensure that effective security was in place from the moment of their arrival. In addition, I requested that Police Constable Tony Knights should join the team as a night-corridor officer, which I felt was necessary because of the lack of any in-house night security. I also pointed out that during Diana's holiday on Necker in 1989 I had caught two locally based officers sleeping at their post at 2 a.m., and had sacked them on the spot after they had explained that they fell asleep on the job because they had to work during the day to supplement their low police income. After all, when royalty go on holiday it is not a simple case of picking up the phone to the local travel agent or searching online.

The final part of my report to my superior officers stressed that the Royal marriage separation announcement would only have intensified press interest in the holiday, and although I had planned it on a 'need-to-know' basis, it would be foolish to believe that the royal correspondents would not find out in due course and fly out to cover the Princess's holiday. I reminded the higher-ranking officers in my department who would have to sign off on the money that the Princess, as was usual, would not be taking a private or press secretary, and that I would therefore need all the help I could get to ensure that the holiday went smoothly and, above all, safely. Not only would we be her police protection team, but the only personnel there to assist her.

Once the disquiet about the high costs involved had subsided my recommendations were officially sanctioned and we were good to go. So, on 28 December, armed with a Home Office radio (my Glock self-loading pistol would come out on the plane with the police team travelling with the Princess and the rest of the party), I set off for Nevis for the second time. The Princess, with the boys, her old friend Catherine Soames and the rest of my Scotland Yard colleagues, would follow two days later.

Getting to Nevis without the press finding out that Diana and the boys were on the move was never going to be easy. All the major newspapers have paid informants at airports to alert them when a famous person is travelling, and in late 1992 they did not come more famous than Diana. I had, of course, taken the precaution of making everyone travel under assumed names, and made use of the Special Services Department of British Airways, but I knew there was still a better-than-good chance that the press would soon find out that the Princess was heading for the sun.

The Princess, her sons and the rest of the party arrived in Antigua some time after midday, local time. I had arranged an aircraft from a charter airline, Carib Air, to be waiting for them there, which, after a discreet transfer, would take them on the twenty-five-minute island hop to Nevis. Diana's face was a picture when she set foot on the island – the stress seemed to have lifted from her. She fell instantly in love with the tiny island, which the explorer Christopher Columbus had discovered five hundred years earlier.

On their arrival, Dave Sharp reassured me that everything had gone smoothly. Then came his worrying addendum: the press, he said, were definitely on the way. Indeed, some journalists had been on the same flight from the UK. The duel between Diana and the media was about to start and I would be required to step up as her champion.

Kissed by turquoise waters, lush green rainforests and dotted with coconut palms, Nevis was largely untouched by tourism, with just one main road hugging the coastline (driving is on the left, as befits the oldest British colony in the Caribbean – St Kitts and Nevis became a fully-independent country in 1983). It was peppered with nineteenth-century churches and disused sugar-cane mills, the legacy of the once-massive industry here during times of slavery. For such a small island it boasts some impressive former inhabitants: American Founding Father Alexander Hamilton was born here; British naval hero Admiral Horatio, Lord Nelson met and married his wife, Frances Nisbet, on Nevis, where she too had been born, meeting her every time he came ashore to get water from a nearby spring for his fleet. As I imparted these facts to Diana, she seemed distracted. All she and her boys wanted was to kick off their shoes and run into the surf.

As the Princess slipped away, most of the A-team of royal journalists and photographers were already out of the country, covering a New Year skiing trip that the Duchess of York and her two daughters, the Princesses Beatrice and Eugenie, had taken in Klosters. It took the press only a few hours to catch up with events, however. In the middle of the night they learned that Diana was on the move and predictably abandoned the Duchess, whose pulling power with the media was secondary to Diana's by a long way. They decamped en masse and headed for the Caribbean with their winter ski clothes, some complete with skis.

On Nevis, in the calm before the storm, Diana quickly settled into her holiday routine. With Catherine Soames and a few well-thumbed novels of the Jackie Collins type for company, she was able to relax in the sun and, wearing her bright orange bikini, splash in the surf with her sons, and generally revel in being, effectively, single again. She knew that it would not be long before the media pack arrived on the island, and as far as she was concerned, if she was to be photographed she was determined to look good. A golden tan was the first essential. After all, this would be the perfect opportunity to send back, in the form of front-page photographs, a 'glad-you're-not-here' postcard to her estranged husband as he endured the bleak winter chill.

Diana's daily routine was much the same as that of any other single woman on holiday with her children and a friend. She was never an early riser, and would emerge from her chalet with her patterned sarong wrapped around her waist for a private breakfast on the terrace at around 9.30am. She did not eat much at breakfast when on holiday – a little fruit and some juice, and occasionally a cup of tea without milk – and after that would help her boys ready themselves for a morning on the beach. They would ask the hotel to prepare a picnic, and once it was ready would climb into the pickup and head for one of the deserted beaches on the island, a short distance away. An excellent swimmer, she would always be first in the water. Although I or one of the police team would be close by in case she ran into difficulties while swimming, it was never really a serious concern, but an officer would always accompany the boys as they swam and played in the warm sea. In the evenings she would eat a light meal, the menu on offer at the Montpelier being arguably the best in the region. We tended to dine all together, sharing jokes and discussing the day's events. The boys, exhausted by their strenuous activities, would retire after the meal, leaving Diana free to chat with Catherine and me about more serious issues.

The first day on the island was media-free, but we all knew that it would not be long before they invaded our peace. Before that peace was broken, Diana relaxed. By contrast, William and Harry were always looking for different things to do on holiday while their mother was sunbathing. They loved playing in the surf with her, but she would soon return to her chosen spot to work on her tan. Restless, they decided to kidnap some of the island's indigenous population, though, mercifully, this did not involve abducting members of some lost tribe, but about a dozen giant toads. Harry was the instigator; he had spotted the creatures, which were about nine inches long, in the undergrowth and begged me to help him capture some. He and William had big plans for them. I told him to leave well alone, but he could be very persistent and eventually I relented, with the proviso that we put them back exactly where we found them. The boys became extremely excited and persuaded their mother and the Milnes-Gaskill children to join in the hunt in the vegetation around the Montpelier. The wretched toads proved to be difficult creatures to capture, but after several hilariously unsuccessful attempts we managed to ensnare about twelve of them. William and Harry tried to encourage their mother to help catch the toads, but she remained in the background, shrieking with laughter as we dived around the undergrowth in search of our prey.

'What are you going to do with them now you have caught them, boys?' Diana asked, almost dreading to think what the answer might be.

'You'll see, Mummy – just wait and see,' Harry replied mischievously.

The entire party was then instructed to rendezvous on the lush green lawn at the back of the Montpelier, where the Princes' master plan was revealed – in essence, a chance for William and Harry to make some money. After selecting the most streamlined, athletic-looking toads for themselves, the rest of us were invited to pick out runners for the 'Nevis Toad Derby', a race they had devised to be run over fifteen feet, and place our bets. Seconds later, the bewildered amphibians came under starter's orders, each held firmly on the start line by a hopeful gambler. At a shout of 'Go!' they were off, leaping the course in record time to screams of encouragement from their backers. I am not even sure that any of the toads finished the course; most, I think, simply leapt into the undergrowth, no doubt hoping never to encounter royalty again.

This was no five-star holiday with over-attentive staff, fine cuisine and a luxury shuttle bus to and from the hotel, for Nevis then was a tropical island in its most rugged sense. Our daily treks to the beach were made in the back of the Milnes-Gaskills' open Toyota truck. Diana would pack a picnic of just basic snacks and cold drinks, and then we would pile into the truck with the boys' surfboards – Mr Eames at Harrods having done his stuff – sticking out of the back. On the way to the white-sanded Indian Castle Beach or Pinney's Beach we would pass through ramshackle villages and wave at the local people going about their daily lives. Sadly, this serenity was about to be shattered.

* * *

My police contact on Nevis was a very amenable Superintendent Kelvin Foye. This was his first VIP visit to the island. Living in Charleston with his family, his local knowledge was invaluable to me. During the recce, he had highlighted a number of local sights that might be of interest to Diana. An invitation to his house was arranged, and prior to the media onslaught, we travelled in the open-top Toyota to his small home and met with his delightful family.

William and Harry wanted very much to follow a local Nevitian climb a thirty-foot palm tree, and release several green coconuts. Needless to say, their mother intervened. With a sharp machete, we all watched as the police chief cut the tops off the fresh coconuts for us all to drink the juice from within. Diana and the boys refused the rum 'top-up' but we, the protection squad – out of politeness – drank a little with our hosts. With customary chicken dishes and rice, a much-favoured meal of Prince William, this informal party was a far cry from the luxury of Royal palaces, but an occasion that lived long in Diana's memory.

Charleston, the capital of Nevis, is also internationally known for its postage stamps. Kelvin Foye suggested to the Princess that she and the boys might like to visit the centre that sold stamps – time permitting, of course. Regrettably, this never happened, but he did bring a selection to show Diana while on the famous Indian Castle Beach on the southernmost tip of the island. He presented her with several sheets of un-franked stamps depicting the beauty of the island and the face of Horatio Nelson. Diana later gave them to me, and I still have them to this day in mint condition – memories of an extraordinary visit.

I always felt it was a little absurd how, on receiving news of Diana, the Royal Rat Pack would drop everything, collect thousands of pounds in cash dispatched to the nearest airport by their newspapers, and then head off in search of her. They were essentially affable chaps, most of them, but ruthless when their quarry was in their sights; also experts in getting their own way. James Whitaker, Arthur Edwards and Kent Gavin were the leaders of the pack, but it was the quieter ones who were the most dangerous. Although royal reporters and photographers tended to work as a team (despite each being on the payroll of different news organisations), it could be a savage environment for any who defied the tribe, and God help anyone who broke their primal rules. In Klosters, as payback for having shown a certain individuality of spirit on a previous job, poor Arthur was given the slip by the rest of the group when they hit out for Nevis. So, as the rest stole into the night, heading first for London and then on to the Caribbean, Arthur, uninformed of the breaking story, was left to sleep on. He was apparently inconsolable the next morning when he made his usual diligent check call to *The Sun*'s picture desk in London, only to be told that another team had been dispatched in search of Diana hours earlier. He was ordered to stay in Switzerland to photograph the Duchess of York and her daughters.

And now the Royal Rat Pack was about to hit Nevis. Yet whatever my fears at the time, I must give credit where it's due: James Whitaker and his friend Kent Gavin were to be key figures in helping me arrange what the Princess herself described as one of the best holiday photocalls of her life, which saw some eighty journalists and photographers gathered on the public beaches of Nevis, frenziedly taking photographs or scribbling notes.

With the arrival of the press I found myself in an invidious position. With no press secretary or private staff I was left to mediate between the Princess and the worst excesses of the Fourth Estate. Diana, understandably sensitive to the criticism she would receive from the Palace Old Guard if she pandered to the press, was initially reluctant to concede a photocall, but since she had been tracked down, I told her I had to cut a deal. She asked for a couple of days' grace, but this was really so that she could perfect her tan in readiness for the bikini shots.

At first there had been a standoff when the press arrived. I made it clear that the Princess regarded their presence as a gross intrusion of her privacy and that of her young sons. A few hours later, I had a taxing few minutes with reporter James Whitaker. By an unhappy chance he stumbled across Diana and her sons swimming off a public beach. I walked up and pleaded with them to back off, but as James plunged into one of his monologues about press freedom and public interest and I started ushering them away. Michael Dunlea, a freelance photographer, fired off a few shots over my shoulder, which he was perfectly within his rights to do. It was the first minor skirmish in what would most certainly become a full-scale battle if I did not act decisively.

At that moment I knew that the press had the upper hand. With only a handful of officers, I had no realistic method of controlling nearly a hundred journalists, and because this was a private holiday, Buckingham Palace had not sent out a press secretary, so I was left with the problem. My job was security but I knew, as on Necker, that unless I took charge of the situation the Princess would be exposed to the worst kind of press intrusion, and the holiday that she so desperately needed would be ruined. For her part, Diana, while sympathetic to the problem I faced, was not prepared to bow to the pressure, even though she knew that the press had the upper hand.

'Nobody is going to stop me swimming with my sons, they will not ruin my holiday,' she said. (Subtext: not 'I, Diana, will put up with it', but 'You will prevent it happening'.) I agreed, adding that I would do everything in my power to avoid their stay on Nevis being wrecked. I therefore arranged to meet Kent Gavin in the bar of the island's Four Seasons Hotel. When we duly met a few hours later, I suggested a deal if he could guarantee that everyone present would stick to it. The alternative was that the press would be blamed for wrecking the holiday, forcing Diana and her sons to return to a bleak London winter. Kent saw the sense of this, and agreed that

Fleet Street's 'troops' and the army of freelancers would back off in exchange for a photocall the next morning featuring the Princess and her sons in the surf. The deal was done – I just hoped he could deliver his side of the bargain.

It was a crucial moment. I am not, and would never claim to be, a public-relations expert, but I had learned a lot from working with one of the world's most famous women, watching in admiration as she manipulated some of the most cynical journalists in that cynical profession until she had them eating out of her hand. I knew most of the key players among the journalists and photographers who danced attention on her, and felt that between us we could ensure that she was shown in the best possible light, and at the same time save her holiday. Besides, when the Princess insisted she wanted privacy, I knew her well enough to be able to tell when she really meant it, and when what she really meant was, 'Give them the pictures and cut a deal'.

For all her fame, Diana recognised that her success was dependent on the court of public opinion. If she did not appear in the British newspapers, then her star might wane. Being popular with the masses required hard work and dedication, and she shirked neither, but it also meant that she had to be seen as a glamorous figure as well, someone to inspire ordinary people to look beyond the mundane reality of their daily lives. She often told me that she felt a duty to the countless schoolchildren, elderly women, star-struck teenage girls and infatuated men whom she counted among her army of fans. To them she was not just a Princess, she felt, but an icon and she was determined never to let them down.

'They expect to see me. They don't want to see me looking dowdy, they want to see me out there doing my thing,' she would say.

In all the years I was at her side, Diana never did fail her public. For her, maintaining her star status was worth all the effort. She never forgot, much less avoided, her responsibility to her loyal supporters.

To have done so was simply not her style, not in her Spencer make-up. So even if she was parading on a sun-kissed beach before a horde of pressmen, she felt that she had to make an effort.

The Princess took some persuading, but once convinced, she was ready to take centre stage. After a couple of days' sunbathing, she looked magnificent on the morning of the first photocall. One memorable shot caught her as she emerged from the Caribbean surf, her bronzed skin contrasting with her orange bikini, looking absolutely sensational. Day after day she reappeared on the beach for a twenty-minute photo session, and to a man the media stuck to the deal; after each session they made themselves scarce, and the rest of the day was hers. In fact some left early so that they could send the photographs electronically back to their respective magazines and newspapers.

'It doesn't get any better than this,' Kent Gavin said to me one morning as he and some colleagues left the beach armed with rolls of lucrative film.

Back in Britain, the newspapers delightedly printed virtually every photograph and story about the Princess on Nevis that they could get. The controversial editor of *The Sun*, Kelvin MacKenzie, wrote a leader in which he praised the press arrangements. His leader even named me and questioned the need for a Palace press officer when I seemed able both to protect and promote Diana at the same time. It was not something I had either asked for, or wanted, and retribution was not long in coming. My superiors at Scotland Yard were not amused. They questioned why I was organising the press, and reminded me, unnecessarily, that I was only there to protect the Princess, not to promote myself. This was a typical reaction at the time. Scotland Yard was no doubt being pressured by the Palace, which wanted to see the Princess's profile lowered considerably so that the Prince could shine, with the result that I was caught in the crossfire.

The reprimand infuriated me – after all, keeping the press happy contributed to my charges' security – but my colleagues advised me to remain cool. At a time when journalists and photographers are often condemned for their actions (indeed, photographers were initially to be blamed for causing Diana's death), I can only emphasise that every one of those on Nevis stuck to our agreement. Not one broke ranks; they knew that the deal with the Princess was a fair one, and that the pictures they were getting frankly could not have been bettered. There was no sneaking around in bushes, no following her and her sons, no stalking her from a distance, no invasion of the Montpelier. With the exception of a few archaic-thinking members of the Royal household, who had an agenda of their own which involved trying to clip Diana's wings, and a couple of high-ranking officers at Scotland Yard, everyone was happy with the arrangement. These people were swift to criticise the deal with the press, but offered no practical advice, either to the Princess or me, about how to handle the situation. Instead, they left me to deal with the problem then complained that it was not my place to do so. Everything that Charles's protection officer, Colin Trimming, had once predicted was coming true.

Despite the unfair flak I was getting back home, the deal was working, and I knew that it would continue to do so as long as Diana was on my side. Sadly, however, I knew her well enough by now to realise that it was likely only to be a matter of time before she and I parted company too. Her erratic behaviour during her association in 1992 with the married art dealer Oliver Hoare, as well as her plans for her life in the wake of the separation, meant that she no longer wanted someone around her who constantly urged caution in her plans and actions. I had, however, always resolved that when the time came I stood a better chance in the future if I jumped before I was pushed.

After a week in the sun, the Princess, relaxed and refreshed, returned to Britain. It was 6 January 1993, the start of one of the most momentous years of her life, and one that would ultimately lead to the end of our working relationship. But at this moment that relationship was as good as it had ever been. As she stepped off the aircraft into the pale light of a wintry morning at Heathrow, Diana turned and flashed a smile at me.

'Thanks, Ken, I really needed that – you saved my life. That was the best holiday I've ever had,' she said.

'It was a pleasure, Ma'am, a real pleasure,' I replied, not without a sense of satisfaction. It was mission accomplished.

The cars were waiting to take us back to West London along the M4. As we approached Kensington I radioed ahead to the security officer at the Palace gatehouse, informing him that 'Purple Five Two' was minutes away from arriving, so we could sweep through the barrier at Kensington Palace in our burnished Jaguar without delay. Soon we were back inside Numbers 8 and 9 Kensington Palace, the Princess's official London residence. The Prince of Wales, her husband, was not waiting for her inside. He was long gone, ensconced in his country sanctuary, Highgrove House, with his mistress, Camilla Parker Bowles.

'Home sweet home,' Diana sighed ironically, but without any bitterness.

By now she was resigned to her lot in life. She had everything, yet nothing. She had once dreamed of a happy home life and a loving husband, but that dream was now long gone.

***

Those were dangerous times. The knives were being sharpened for the Princess, with powerful, shadowy figures in Palace corridors whispering disparaging remarks about her flaunting her body to the press on Nevis. By association, the knives were out for me, too. When I returned to the Palace police office I was bluntly instructed that the Department Commander wanted a full report on what had happened on Nevis, and in particular about why I had felt that I needed to take it upon myself to adopt the role of the Princess's press secretary. I complied, and explained in equally forthright terms what had happened on the ground, although I never heard what happened to the report after I had submitted it.

A few days later I received a package from the *Daily Mirror*'s Kent Gavin containing a full set of the photographs of Diana he had taken on Nevis. Inside was a note, which read: 'Many thanks for your kind assistance during the trip to Nevis. It was a difficult situation handled in a very professional manner'.

Perhaps I was in the wrong job, but at least somebody other than Diana appreciated my efforts. Yet there was no greater compliment than being afforded the Princess's trust. Diana the private person could not, and would not, live a lie. She felt that she was now ready to take centre stage in her own right, to star in her own solo show. It was of no concern to her if that meant the old stagers, the other senior members of the Royal Family, suffered by comparison with her glittering star. Indeed, to her this upstaging of the ancient regime made her solo performance all the more rewarding. Such trivialities aside, she knew that her public persona carried with it tremendous power, a power that she could harness to help change the world and the plight of its people for the better.

In any evaluation of the Princess's achievements, the part she played in focusing the public's attention on the terrible disease AIDS, promoting awareness, understanding and even compassion, must be among her greatest. With one handshake, she did more to dispel, almost overnight, the myth that the disease can be caught simply through touching a victim than a thousand press conferences given by the most eminent and convincing doctors. Diana knew her power and revelled in it, and as with leprosy, the struggle to help AIDS sufferers the world over became almost a religion to her.

She felt driven to help these people, but it was a risky crusade for it brought criticism from within the Palace.

By contrast, the Queen had an understanding of Diana, although the Princess was always very nervous of the Sovereign, who was, after all, her mother-in-law as well. At first, she told me, she had been welcomed into the family, and believed that Her Majesty was a great supporter of hers. For her part, the Queen knew that, if handled with care, the young Princess was a great asset to the Royal Family – if not the jewel in its crown, then certainly the sparkle on its diadem.

By the time I joined her team, Diana had come to be viewed by the Palace as a serious and escalating problem. In truth, she had become a thorn in the side of the Establishment. To put it simply, she outshone or overshadowed the rest of the Royals, including her husband, something that irritated Prince Charles considerably, Prince Philip being moved to state his belief that she needed to be handled with care.

EARLY MARCH 1993:
NEPAL

'Everything is hunky-dory,' the Princess said as we drove through the police barrier at Kensington Palace. She was clutching a draft outline of the programme for her forthcoming official visit to the Himalayan Kingdom of Nepal, sent to her by her private secretary, Patrick Jephson.

Diana really believed 1993 would be her year, and from the way it began she had every reason to think so. Refreshed by her Caribbean holiday and no longer shackled by the wreck of a marriage, she was in high spirits. Nor was she in any mood to mope around her Kensington Palace apartment, even though she had removed from it all traces of her former husband's existence. As for the Prince, he appeared to descend into gloom after the public declaration of his marital failure, just days after his wife returned from her holiday to rave press reviews. It seemed that there was no stopping her.

Clearly elated, Diana read part of the programme out loud, as if to convince herself it was true.

'We await details of Lynda's [Baroness Chalker, the Minister for Overseas Development, who was also going] own programme, although it is expected that several of the engagements (especially on the first and second days) will be joint.'

She paused for a few moments, as if to check that I was listening.

'See, Ken? I am getting my way – the government is backing me,' she said, and there was a genuine excitement in her voice. She had been looking at me intently from the moment I had collected her, but I was distracted, and probably rather distant. I had other matters on my mind. The negative reaction I had received from higher-ranking officers after Nevis still rankled, but more than that, it worried me. I knew that the more the Princess and the Establishment clashed, the more difficult my position would become. Oblivious to my mood, however, Diana continued. When she was on a high, nothing could get her down, and she seemed to think my quietness was due to concern for her.

'Honestly, you don't have to worry about me. I know what I'm doing. You watch – I'm going to write my own script from now on,' she smiled. I wasn't sure whether she was telling me, or reassuring herself.

'Ma'am, I have every confidence in you,' I replied diplomatically. 'You know I believe you can achieve whatever you want, as long as you truly believe what you're doing is right.' I had said it often enough before, but it was still the endorsement she was looking for.

'I promise you the next few months are going to be fun,' she added before turning her attention back to the briefing notes that Patrick Jephson had prepared so meticulously. A few minutes later she suddenly roared with laughter.

'We'll be okay – we're staying at the British Ambassador's residence. Poor Patrick and the others are staying at some place called the Yak and Yeti. Sounds awful.' (In fact, it proved to be a splendid five-star hotel, with well-appointed rooms and excellent cooking, far superior to our spartan accommodation in the diplomatic enclave.) Rightly or wrongly, Diana honestly believed she could do the official job of Princess of Wales much better on her own, no longer hampered by the constant pressure of, and press references to, her failing marriage. She was not able to see that this formal position would inevitably have to change once her union with the heir to the throne was finally dissolved. Perhaps this was a little naive of her, but it was precisely that simplicity which made her so appealing – and so successful. She truly believed that she could remain within the system, yet break away at the same time, convinced that her affinity with the ordinary man or woman on the street would always be her saviour.

In a cynical world, such optimism was refreshing. Moreover, from her point of view, the year could not have got off to a better start. The writer and journalist Anthony Holden, a respected commentator on royal matters and one of her more sympathetic chroniclers, agreed. His cover article for the January 1993 edition of *Vanity Fair* trumpeted 'Di's Palace Coup', detailing how she had succeeded in securing her solo future at the 'expense of her detractors and her depressed husband'. The article continued: 'Since the announcement of the end of her marriage on 9 December, Diana, Princess of Wales, has been visibly reborn. There is a new bounce in her step, a cheekier smile on her face, a new gleam in those flirtatious blue eyes . . .' And of the separation: 'At long last the sham was over. For Diana it was a moment of triumph. For Prince Charles it was a crushing defeat...'

The Princess was delighted when she read the article, and for a couple of days at least, it seemed that everywhere she went the magazine came too. Holden had hit the nail on the head for, invigorated, she was determined to show her estranged husband a clean pair of high heels in the battle for the hearts and minds of his future subjects.

It was now that something wholly unexpected happened which

strengthened her position still further – 'Camillagate'. At the end of January, tabloid newspapers published extracts from an illicitly recorded telephone conversation between Diana's husband and Camilla Parker Bowles, said to have taken place on 18 December 1989. It was both intimate and distasteful in its contents. Worse, with one eccentric reference during the call to wanting to become a tampon, Charles once again ceded the upper hand to the Princess, both legally and in terms of sympathy for her. The backlash was savage. Establishment figures normally loyal to future King and country were appalled, and some questioned the Prince's suitability to rule. Buckingham Palace was inundated with calls from reporters.

Driven firmly onto the back foot, all Charles Anson, the Queen's press secretary, and Sir Robert Fellowes, her private secretary, could offer was the tired and often self-defeating 'no comment' response. The Prince's camp was devastated, and Charles himself personally humiliated. Those closest to him said that they had never seen him so low as at this time. One of his team confided, 'He has hit rock bottom.' Cartoonists lampooned him in the press. One cartoon, featuring him talking dirty to his plants, particularly amused the Princess, who collapsed into fits of giggles on seeing it. More importantly, however, Diana's lawyers had solid evidence to support a cross-petition for adultery, should they need it. After all the Palace denials that had followed Andrew Morton's revelations in his book, which had effectively brought the Prince's affair with Camilla Parker Bowles to public notice, the taped conversation vindicated Morton, proving that Charles and Camilla had been lovers, if not throughout his entire marriage, then certainly from the end of 1989. (In actual fact, those on the inside knew that the love affair had been restarted earlier in the 1980s.)

There have been all kinds of views about the 'Camillagate' tape. Some commentators proffered theories that included a government plot to undermine the Prince, but I doubt that it was anything either so sophisticated or so sinister. As with 'Dianagate', when the tape was made analogue phone technology gave amateur eavesdroppers the chance to listen in. I had consistently reminded the Princess of the importance of using codenames and nicknames, and never being too specific when using a mobile phone.

The Princess, once again revelling in the role of female victim, enjoyed the moment. 'Game, set and match,' she said, clutching to her a copy of the *Daily Mirror* containing a transcript of the 'Camillagate' tape as we talked in her sitting room at Kensington Palace. Later, however, she told me that she had been genuinely shocked by some of the baser comments, particular the Prince's tampon reference. 'It's just sick,' she said repeatedly.

She was genuinely offended by the tape and was ready to inflict more pain upon her husband. In February 1993, as the Prince set off, with only a handful of press in tow, on a worthy but in media terms dull trip to peasant farms in Mexico, she was taking the plaudits as she prepared for the next step in her career as a roving international ambassador. She knew that she was winning the PR battle hands down, and she was not about to relinquish her superiority. The contrast between Charles's tour of Mexico and Diana's working visit to Nepal at the beginning of March could not have been starker.

The trip to the tiny mountain Kingdom of Nepal had been made even more attractive to Diana when the Prime Minister, John Major, confirmed that he was sending Baroness Chalker, the Minister for Overseas Development, to accompany her. The Princess was ecstatic at this very obvious declaration of official backing for her solo work. Her mercy mission to help the poor and sick in a Third World country had now been afforded diplomatic status, and she herself had become an envoy for Her Majesty's Government. No matter how hard her detractors tried to denigrate her, no one could take that away from her.

The press loved it, pointing out that this five-day visit was not to be Diana's normal hearts-and-flowers Royal tour. In another indication that Her Majesty understood Diana, the Queen was credited with upgrading the trip, and the media reported that the Princess would for the first time be holding active discussions with the Nepalese government. Even so, she wanted it to be a low-key, no-frills working visit, conscious that she needed to keep the Queen on her side. The press went further, however, claiming that the Queen was determined to ensure that the Princess, despite her separation from Charles, would not be denied the privileges befitting her status as the mother of a future British king. Naturally, Diana lapped all this up, believing every word and seemingly oblivious to the pitfalls. For the Establishment, Tory grandee Lord (Alistair) McAlpine described the government's endorsement of the planned trip as 'sheer folly' in his *Sunday Express* column. 'This is all folly of the first order,' he thundered. 'It will do no good for either the Princess, the Baroness or for that matter for the refugees. The Princess is separated from the Prince and she no longer needs to undertake public duties that will cost the taxpayer large sums.'

The piece effectively parroted the views of the Palace Old Guard, and of Charles's staunchest allies, even if they were dressed up as a nod in the direction of saving public money. Diana duly took note. She was confident and riding high on a wave of support, but she was no fool. As we drove to Gatwick for the flight to Nepal, she was in a pensive mood. For all her bravado she was genuinely nervous. This was one of the most significant moments in her career and she was understandably anxious that she might make mistakes. During the nine-hour flight she read and re-read her briefing notes, before eventually taking my advice to sleep for a while. At last we landed in Delhi, where the party was to stay overnight at the High Commissioner's residence before continuing to Nepal the following day. After the normal pleasantries and a light meal, the Princess, tired after the flight, retired to her bedroom.

Leaving the next morning, we flew into Kathmandu Airport, a death-defying experience in itself as the plane approaches between treacherous cloud-covered mountains. From that moment we stepped back in time into the magical, almost medieval kingdom that is Nepal.

The British media were on the lookout for anything that might have been deemed evidence that the Princess's visit had been downgraded. At the airport, she was greeted by Crown Prince Dipendra and garlanded by small children. The press, however, were convinced that they already had their story when the unfortunate band that welcomed her failed to play the British national anthem when she appeared. Rather than play 'God Save the Queen', an official band welcomed her with Spanish pop tunes rounded off with the 'Colonel Bogey March'. Although Crown Prince Dipendra greeted Diana she was not, the papers reported, quartered in the Royal Palace but the British Embassy, they chirped. So-called experts were quoted. 'It was a subtle way of putting the Princess in her place,' said one. 'There is nothing the Palace hates more than a "runaway royal".' What utter nonsense, I thought.

These apparent lapses – or 'gross insults' as some papers chose to call them – made front-page headlines, although it did not seem to bother the same journalists that the same thing had occurred in Egypt, Pakistan and Hungary in accordance with the protocol governing working, as distinct from 'state', visits. Any royal reporter worth his expenses would have known perfectly well that the protocol for the visit would have been agreed between the two courts, British and Nepalese, months in advance. Still, no journalist lets the truth stand in the way of a good story.

For the media, the apparent snub was enough to set the ball rolling. It did not seem to occur to them that in fact the Princess had herself requested that the working trip be treated in a low-key, informal way, but the upshot was that the Nepalese authorities were furious. The article that upset them the most, however, was one by the *Daily Telegraph* correspondent Robert Hardman (who later went on to be a celebrated royal author and documentary maker), who claimed they had laid a 'threadbare red carpet' with which to greet the Princess. One bemused official complained to me, 'Inspector, it is our very, very best red carpet, and it is brand new, it is not threadbare.' I told the insulted official not to take it to heart and he seemed placated when I assured him that the Princess had thought his red carpet was one of the best she had ever walked on.

Crown Prince Dipendra made small talk with the Princess as we drove to the Ambassador's official residence, where she retired to her room to freshen up. A short while later she called me up to her room.

'Ken, I know you want me secure, but is it necessary to put me behind bars?' she asked, pointing to the barred windows. She was joking. Then she took a deep breath. 'Well, it's make-or-break time. By the way, do you think it's wise to give the Crown Prince an engraved hip flask for a present? He looks as though he likes a drink,' she said prophetically. Eight years later the Old Etonian Crown Prince would gun down his parents and other members of his family before turning the weapon on himself in a drunken rage brought on because he had been banned from marrying his mistress. Luckily, he showed no homicidal tendencies on that trip, otherwise my Glock might have had to come out of its holster, and I'm sure my shooting the Crown Prince would have been a difficult action to explain.

Quite early on in the trip the Princess turned to me and said: 'I hope we've got Le Gadget? You know everything will go wrong without it.'

Much to her consternation, I had to admit that the said item had been left in a drawer back at Kensington Palace.

'It's no good,' she said. 'We've got to get it out here.'

Le Gadget was perhaps our finest wind-up, and an almost constant source of laughter. The small vibrator, bought as a practical joke after a staff night out in Paris during Diana's official visit there the previous November, had become her lucky mascot. I had persuaded her sister Sarah, who was acting lady-in-waiting on the trip, to hide it in Diana's handbag the following morning, which she did. The Princess only discovered it while going through her bag in between meetings with President Jacques Chirac and Paul McCartney, and found the whole episode extremely funny. From that moment on Le Gadget became her (secret) mascot for all future royal trips, and woe betide the secretary who forgot to pack it.

A telephone call was made to London and the secretary, Nicky Cockell, was asked to dispatch the vibrator by diplomatic bag to the British Embassy in Nepal. It arrived in a sealed packet, delivered on a silver tray by a Gurkha aide to the King of Nepal, just before the start of a press reception in honour of the visit that the Ambassador was holding in the grounds of his official residence. At that moment the Princess was preparing to go into the garden to meet the media who had been following her. The soldier had orders for the package to be delivered 'at once' to the Princess of Wales's equerry, Captain Ed Musto, Royal Marines, and nothing was going to deter him.

Musto, a self-effacing officer who towered over everyone present, not quite knowing what to expect, foolishly opened the packet and removed the offending item in front of everyone in the room (but, mercifully, not the press, who were starting to gather outside). There was a stunned pause (and a few bemused glances from Embassy dignitaries), until the silence was broken by Diana, who said, 'Oh, that must be for me,' and began to laugh. Musto graciously put the Gadget into his pocket and nothing more was said by the intrigued gathering of officials and dignitaries. With the delivery of our tour mascot, there could be no question about the success of the trip after that.

The following day the Princess headed for the Nepalese countryside, dominated by steep slopes and rocky paths to see, against the backdrop of the Himalayas, conditions in which most of the country's inhabitants lived. Nepal is one of the poorest countries in the world, and her objective was simple – to try to remove the threat of hunger, or even starvation, by showing the public at home the terrible plight of most Nepalis in the hope that money would pour in to the charities working to alleviate the problem. After a breathtaking flight over the foothills of the Himalayas aboard King Birendra's Chinook helicopter, we hovered over a giant open fire that was the centrepiece of a tiny, ramshackle collection of huts – the village of Majhuwa, our designated landing.

We were in a mountainous region famous as a recruiting area for the fearsome Gurkhas, the tough and valiant Nepalese hill men who have provided regiments for the British Army for over two hundred years, and who have served the British Crown with undying loyalty. The Princess's visit came at a time when the British government had proposed cutting Gurkha regiments in British service (there are Gurkha regiments in the Indian Army, as well) by 2,500 of these warriors. There was a particularly poignant moment when Diana encountered a local hero – an old Gurkha, well into his nineties, who had joined the army in 1935 – standing in his frayed demob suit, his campaign medals glistening in the sun. As the Princess walked by, he snapped to attention and gave her the smartest of salutes. What price such loyalty in the Palace, I thought sourly.

Diana was taking all the strains of the tour in her stride, unfazed by the pressure, much of it self-inflicted, in the sense that she insisted on doing as much as she possibly could. She was exhilarating to be with, but always careful to heed advice so as not to put a foot wrong.

Meanwhile, the tension between the press and the Nepalese government continued to dominate the trip, at least in the British papers. It intensified when *Sun* photographer Arthur Edwards was accused of having made a racist remark to the Nepalese Prime Minister. Arthur, whose somewhat obsequious flattery of the Princess on tour could be excruciating, sparked a diplomatic incident as Diana arrived for a state dinner at the Royal Palace. When she walked past the press pen, Arthur smiled at her and said gushingly, 'You look fantastic tonight, Ma'am.'

My colleague, Inspector Peter Brown, who was on duty as her protection officer that night, smirked at the photographer, prompting him to say, 'You don't look too bad yourself, Brownie.' Unfortunately, at that precise moment the Nepalese Prime Minister was walking past and, hearing the comment, interpreted it as a racist insult directed at him. Once inside the banqueting hall he instructed his senior aide to complain to the British Embassy about the photographer's behaviour, with the result that a bewildered – and innocent – Edwards was forced to apologise. The consolation was that his editor, Kelvin MacKenzie, thought the story was sensational and splashed it across *The Sun* newspaper's front page on the following day with the banner headline 'Sun Man in the Brown Stuff'.

Diana was beginning to stamp her mark on the trip. She had developed an excellent working relationship with Lady Chalker, whose down-to-earth approach and sense of humour matched her own. The Princess, who was in Nepal officially in her dual role as patron of the British Red Cross and the Leprosy Mission, now began making headlines for the right reasons in other newspapers. Even so, some of the tabloids continued to print trivia or dross. She made a flawless visit to the Lele Memorial Park, high in the Himalayan foothills, a gaunt, barren place that could only be approached by a winding, deeply potholed and crumbling road.

It was a testing assignment for Diana, and a sad one too. She had been asked to pay her respects to the dead of PIA Flight 268, which, the year before, had smashed into the mountainside on its approach to Kathmandu Airport, killing all 167 people on board, among them 34 mostly young Britons. When, a day earlier, I arrived on the advance reconnaissance, the coffins of the victims, which had been disinterred for reburial in the park, lay uncovered in front of the semi-circular stone memorial, which had been built on a higher plateau overlooking the crash site. I told the organiser of the visit that these poor souls must be buried before the Princess arrived. Wobbling his head from side to side, he assured me that he understood the urgency. Nevertheless, I was convinced my plea had fallen on deaf ears and that Diana would be faced with a gruesome scene when she came to the site on the next day. Over supper I raised my concerns with King Birendra's protection officer, Major Khadga Gurung, who assured me everything would be resolved by the morning. He was right, and I felt ashamed of my doubts.

Diana played her role faultlessly the next day. Dignified and determined, she was a perfect ambassador for the Queen. Unfortunately, the sunlight behind her meant that photographers took shots that showed her long legs silhouetted through her silk skirt. The following day, despite her solemnity at the ceremony, some of the newspapers ran those photographs, comparing them to the famous photo of her as a teenage nanny at the Young England Kindergarten on the eve of her engagement to Prince Charles, in which the outline of her legs had also been visible. One tasteless headline, 'Legs We Forget', she found particularly galling, especially as she had performed her duty perfectly. She became upset, convinced that the press corps was doing its best to undermine her and the visit. I told her that she had nothing to worry about, and added that her legs looked great, which drew a smile.

Later that day the Princess visited the Anandaban leprosy hospital. The small, 120-bed hospital was crammed with victims, many with stumps where hands and feet should be, who seemed to accept their terrible affliction with gentle patience and great dignity. Once more Diana's humanity dominated the visit, and it was noticeable that when she walked through a ward without the cameras on her she spent just as much time with the sufferers as she had when the press had been snapping away. She came away deeply moved, and more determined than ever to do whatever she could to help.

One of the trip's most memorable moments came on the day when we flew over the spectacular Himalayas in the King of Nepal's helicopter to visit a project to provide water for a spartan hillside village high up in eastern Nepal. At one point the Princess disappeared into a desperately run-down one-roomed shack, home to an entire Nepalese peasant family. She emerged, clearly shocked, after spending several minutes inside with the hut's simple occupants. Moved by the extent of their poverty, she set aside her own problems and put into perspective the true worth of her trip to Nepal in one crisp phrase. Sighing deeply as she left the shack, she said, 'I will never complain again.' It was a great soundbite for the media, and I'm sure that at the moment she said it she truly believed it. I knew from years of experience, however, that it was not a promise she would, or could, possibly keep. Alarmingly, it struck me that Diana appeared to be coming to believe her own propaganda.

I even managed to make headline news myself in *The Sun* newspaper: the banner headline 'RANDY PORKER RAMS A ROYAL CHOPPER' complete with a photo of me and another of a huge pig. The strapline under the photo read, 'Pork Cop ... Inspector Wharfe on Guard'. *The Sun* obviously saw the funny side, as did Diana, when two giant pigs burst into what the tabloid described as Diana's Royal 'app-oink-ment'. The Princess roared with laughter as one of the amorous pigs chased the other under the wheels of her helicopter. A huge crowd of locals hooted with laughter too when riot police made what the newspaper described as a 'pig's ear' of trying to head off the animals. As Diana boarded the chopper to leave the village of Panaiti, the 11-stone pigs started out again and chased each other under the rotor blades. I was snapped shooing away the animals before one of the wags in the photographers' pen shouted, 'Is that how the Palace deal with porkies [lies]?' I visualised the headlines before they appeared.

Nepal's King Birendra issued a statement saying he had been 'enchanted' by the Princess and 'very happy' about what he saw as the success of her tour. Despite overt attempts to scupper her solo visit Diana had won the day, and not for the first time her faceless enemies at the Palace had lost. She knew, however, that it would be only a matter of time before they secured victory against her.

* * *

After Nepal the Princess was determined to expand her schedule further, and in this respect the International Red Cross perfectly suited her interests and her ambition. There was talk of at least two more foreign trips to Third World countries that year. There followed a series of personal meetings with John Major, whom she found sympathetic and engaging – very different from his rather grey public persona. She liked and trusted him. At first, she was anxious, but once the Prime Minister had put her at ease she opened up to him. He knew, from Foreign Office feedback after overseas visits she had made, that the Princess was a real asset, and one that should be nurtured. She was elated after these meetings – at last she was being recognised for what she could do, rather than as simply the wife of the Prince of Wales.

The men in grey suits at the Palace, however, had other ideas. Just as the British government was acknowledging and acting on Diana's considerable talents, they turned on her with a pettiness that defies logic. In a ridiculous and demeaning sideswipe someone in the Palace ruled that she no longer warranted an entry in the Court Circular, a daily report that lists the official engagements and activities of the Sovereign and senior working members of the Royal Family. This was their way of telling her that her engagements were less royal – and therefore less important – than those undertaken by other members of the family. She rose above the snub with remarkably good grace. 'Silly fools,' she said dismissively on her way back from the charity première of the film *Accidental Hero* at the Odeon, Leicester Square. The occasion had been televised, she had chatted with the film's star, Dustin Hoffman, a military band had played, and the chairman of the mental health charity Mencap UK, Lord Rix, had been there to greet her.

'How much more official do they want my engagements to be?' she asked rhetorically. 'According to them, that job tonight was not an official engagement. Did you see all the people who turned up, Ken? And I suppose all the money we raised for charity was not real, either? It's just ridiculous. But at least they come to see me.'

She had a valid point. While her husband was officially receiving star royal billing, on the Court Circular at least, carrying out his official duties before a handful of loyal supporters, thousands turned up at Diana's unlisted engagements just to catch a glimpse of the Princess. Now, however, the Palace, much to her frustration, became obstructive. When she raised the idea of making a morale-boosting trip to visit British troops in Bosnia, it was blocked because Prince Charles was due to make a similar trip. She was also informed that a visit to Ireland would be inappropriate, while at the memorial service for the two children killed by the IRA's bomb blast at Warrington, Charles, not Diana, was chosen to represent the Queen. Typically, she turned the situation on its head by first calling, and then visiting the devastated parents at home.

A part of the reason for this and similar blocking moves lay with her husband's office, which, under the express direction of his private secretary, Commander Richard Aylard, was planning its own PR offensive. Aylard believed that this would redress the balance and portray the Prince in a good light, re-establishing his popularity with media and public alike. With hindsight, his decision to offer the respected broadcaster Jonathan Dimbleby 'unprecedented access' to the Prince for a warts-and-all television documentary (with a book billed as an authorised biography to follow) was at best foolhardy. In terms of the Prince's public persona it proved disastrous, and the programme (which was broadcast in June 1994) is likely to be remembered for the Prince's painful admission of adultery, and his less-than-manly complaints about the way his parents raised him.

So while Diana triumphed in 1993, basking in the media's praise and the public's adulation, Dimbleby and his television crew (with the help of Charles's entire entourage) set about the business of beginning a major PR offensive to improve the Prince's somewhat tarnished image. Dimbleby did approach Diana to ask her if she wanted to take part in the programme, ostensibly being made to mark the twenty-fifth anniversary of Charles's investiture as Prince of Wales. They lunched together and he was charmed by her, but although she was tempted, those close to her, including me, advised her to steer well clear, assuring her that it would be unlikely to bring her either credit or praise. For once, she took our advice.

LATE MARCH 1993:
LECH, AUSTRIA

At the end of March 1993 we set off once again for the ski slopes of Lech. Diana was determined that, despite all the emotional heartache of their parents' separation, William and Harry should have every chance to enjoy themselves. The holiday followed the pattern of the previous year, which had ended so dramatically with the Princess learning of her father's death. This time, of course, Prince Charles did not join the party, something that made the entire situation much less tense. It was not long, however, before the entire resort was swarming with press from all around the world. Sadly, the paparazzi were not remotely interested in Diana's wish for a peaceful holiday with her sons. To them she was a cash cow, pure and simple. As far as they were concerned she was outside Britain, on their turf, and she was fair game.

Initially, everything was going well. There was the morning photocall at the ski lift, which, although Diana did not like it, she tolerated, but what really irritated her was being followed as she walked around the small shopping area.

215

'Ken, I want you to keep them away from me,' she hissed as we walked into the Arlberg Hotel, illuminated by flashbulbs. I did my best, but there came a moment when my patience snapped. One photographer simply would not take no for an answer. He was within a few feet of the Royal party, and the Princess became very upset at what she saw as a gross intrusion. Her reaction was affecting the boys, too, and the situation was in danger of getting out of hand. The pushy photographer told me he wanted an interview with William. I told him to move. He said that this was not my country and that I had no jurisdiction as a policeman in Austria. I asked him where he was from. 'Italy,' he replied.

'Well, it's not your country either. Now just back off!' I thundered. I was rapidly losing my patience and continued to tell him in no uncertain terms to move away. He refused and, as more swarms of photographers moved in nearer, he got too close to the Princess for my liking and I took him down with one swift arm movement. Mayhem ensued, especially when another of his pals followed him down on to the snow when he attempted to punch me. William and Harry loved it.

'Do it again, Ken,' William said, beaming all over his tanned face. I shepherded them all safely inside the Arlberg and away from the problem. Outside reporters were scribbling in their notebooks, photographers were gesticulating, and one appeared to be acting out a Muhammad Ali fight. I've got some bloody explaining to do, I thought.

I re-ran the incident in my mind. There was no doubt that Diana had been upset, distressed, even. As the paparazzi moved in for the kill she had started to panic, which was why I had had to act decisively. At one point she had screamed, 'Go away! Go away!' which had astonished her boys who, until then, had found the whole thing quite amusing.

The Princess immediately retired to her suite, and her sons

followed her. I was furious. After a short phone call to Colin Trimming, I went to check on Diana. She was distraught and I told her to be calm and that everything would be fine. Leaving her again, I set off to confront some of the press pack, in the hope that I could make them see sense. I singled out a couple of senior newspaper photographers whom I knew well, the *Daily Mirror*'s Kent Gavin and Arthur Edwards of *The Sun*, and told them uncompromisingly that all bets were off. The message had to get back to the foreign media, and the paparazzi in particular, that unless they played the game I would make it almost impossible for any of them – journalists or photographers, British or foreign – to find the Royal party. There were no more such incidents, but in retrospect, the affair seems hauntingly prophetic, given what would happen to the Princess in the days leading up to her death.

Her near panic as the paparazzi closed in demonstrated that Diana was on an emotional seesaw throughout the holiday. Her feelings about Oliver Hoare had unsettled her and she was falling out with everyone, left, right and centre. Even I found it difficult to reason with her. She had always been erratic, but in the past she had invariably pulled back from the brink. What was to happen next showed just how close she had come to the edge. She leapt off it – literally – and seemed not to care about the consequences.

The first I knew about this latest drama was when the night-duty officer PC Mark Jawkowski woke me at 6 a.m. He was there to provide on-site protection to ensure that there were no intruders. There was a loud knock on the door of my room. Startled awake, I instinctively jumped from my bed, calling, 'Come in!' He entered, clearly rattled.

'Mark? What's up?' I asked as he stood nervously at the foot of my bed. Growing impatient when he didn't reply at once, I asked him again, 'Is everything okay?'

'The Princess is okay now, sir,' was his response. By now wide awake, I turned to him and said, 'Hang on, Mark, this sounds serious. Let me put a dressing gown on, then tell me exactly what's happened.'

The young officer took a deep breath and began his account in best evidence-giving manner. At about 5.30 a.m. the doorbell had sounded at the front of the Arlberg Hotel, our fortress against the press, who were scattered all around the resort in the less expensive hotels. Mark went to the door and, to his utter horror, there stood the Princess, dressed and wearing a scarf and a hat. She looked him straight in the eye, said 'Good morning' politely, and went straight to her suite.

'Christ, Mark,' I exclaimed, 'how on earth did she get out? Where is she now?'

'In her room,' he replied, sheepishly.

I calmed down. The most important point was that she was safe. Now I had to find out what she had been up to, and stop her doing it again. I made Mark a cup of tea in my room, and when he had drunk it, told him to go and get some sleep. It wasn't his fault, I assured him, and I would tackle the Princess when she awoke. As he sipped his tea, he gave me a breakdown of his precise movements for the record. This was not simply an ass-covering exercise, although God alone knows we needed one: 'Princess Evades Police Protection – Gone For Hours' was not a headline that would enhance our career prospects.

'Take me through it from the top, Mark,' I said. 'At 1am, when I retired, all doors were locked, yes?'

He nodded.

'So, when I went to bed you were in place in the lobby to deal with knocks at the door?'

He nodded again, then blurted out, 'I promise you, sir, she did not leave through the front door. I haven't a clue how the hell she got out.'

He was becoming increasingly heated. 'Sir, she couldn't have done – I had the only set of keys.'

Since there was nothing more to be learned I sent him off to bed and told him not to worry, but added a warning: 'Don't say anything to anyone about this.' Thoroughly alarmed, I dressed in an old jacket and some slacks and headed from the room. I knew there was only one way the Princess could possibly have got out – she had bloody well jumped. We were staying on the first floor of the extension to the hotel, and there was a twenty-foot drop from her balcony to the ground, but that was made less by the deeply drifted snow. I went to check. When I reached the point directly beneath her balcony I found a perfect impression of the Princess's body in the deep snow below. From the hole in the snow, footprints led away into the town of Lech itself. God, I hope the bloody paparazzi did not see this, I thought. Diana was asleep; after being out all night it was hardly surprising, but there was no point in waking her now to confront her about her leap to freedom. I decided to wait and pick my moment.

That moment came some hours later, after she had dressed and breakfasted. I found her in the sitting room of her suite, getting ready for the day ahead. After we had said our good mornings, I came straight to the point.

'Ma'am,' I said calmly, my face a blank, 'it's about last night. What on earth were you thinking?' At this she flushed scarlet. She had been discovered, and she knew that she had been completely out of order. 'I don't have a problem with you going out, Ma'am, you know that, but you have just got to tell me. What were you thinking when you jumped off the balcony? Anything could have happened,' I went on.

The Princess stayed silent. She knew she had done wrong; she knew she had been foolhardy; she knew she had put herself at risk. She also knew that she had placed me in a deeply compromising position, for if something had happened I would have had to take the blame – and live with the guilt. I then told her that I could not stand too many of these disappearances.

'You know that our relationship has to be based on mutual trust. This is a clear abuse of that.'

'Ken, I just needed some air,' she said at last, her speech higher-pitched than usual, still hot with embarrassment. She continued, 'Yes, I did jump from the balcony. I knew it was okay – it was deep, soft snow, and I knew it would be all right.'

I pointed out that anything could have happened. She could have landed on a rock and hurt herself badly. 'It was a damned stupid thing to do,' I added.

At that point I knew I had said enough. Lecturing Diana about anything was never wise, even when she knew she had done wrong. I decided to change tack.

'Do you want to tell me where you went?' I asked, knowing perfectly well that she wouldn't say.

'I know what I'm doing,' was her only response to my question.

By now I was thoroughly rattled and replied, 'No, Ma'am, I really don't think you do.'

What Diana actually did for some four or five hours that night remains a mystery, but the 'Leap of Lech' gives a clear insight into her state of mind at the time – she wanted to be free of the trappings of her position. It was an act of independence, but also one of defiance. Two years later, when I was on a private visit to Lech, Hannes Schneider, the son of the Arlberg's owner, confirmed that she had jumped from the balcony. Hannes, whom I had dubbed 'Herr No Problem', never seemed to sleep. That night, he said, a relation of his had actually seen her walk through the snow and away from the hotel after throwing herself from the balcony.

Diana's leap marked the beginning of the end of my relationship with her. It was the first of a number of key incidents that eventually led to my leaving her service. It is understandable, I suppose, that as she began to break away from her former life, and despite the many years of mutual trust and understanding between us, she began to see me, because of my position, as part of the Establishment against which she was rebelling. The leap from the balcony apart, the rift started subtly. At first she began to hide things from me, where before she had always been open with me, no matter what she had been doing. Even so, I am convinced that she was not happy with this and that deep down she knew she could trust me as she always had. But the new circle of people she had gathered around her wanted complete control of her, and the power and influence she wielded, for their own reasons. I tried to nip the problem in the bud and repeatedly confronted her about her newfound secretiveness, but she fudged the issue on every occasion.

She had no intention of answering me, and by her silence made my questions pointless. After a few days the entire Lech incident, which had made me seriously reconsider my position as her police protection officer, had seemingly been eradicated from her memory. She knew I was disappointed and she did her best to win me back by launching one of her unique charm offensives. This was a typical Diana tactic: if she had behaved badly or done something wrong and knew it, she would often simply ignore it, and pretend that it had never happened. A few years earlier I would have wiped it out of my mind too, but I was growing increasingly concerned.

JUNE 1993:
PARIS, FRANCE

Diana was in carefree mood. At last liberated from the shackles of her marriage, she was a woman determined to enjoy herself after the years of frustration. Yes, she was still technically married to Prince Charles, but she was free. As Princess of Wales, she always craved normality. She had been to Paris the previous November on her first solo trip there since her youth, but she had been on official business, surrounded by an entourage, and had created a stir wherever she went. Now she was determined to go again, incognito – or as near to that as we could manage.

'I just want to go shopping with a couple of girlfriends. I just want to be normal. Please fix it for me, Ken,' she pleaded.

I told her I would do my best, but added that I could not guarantee that she could go in and out of a great city like Paris without being detected.

'But Ken, I just want to be normal,' she said again.

Perhaps her rather obviously manipulative pleading was getting to me, for I replied, 'Don't we all, Ma'am?'

She looked daggers at me, but said nothing more.

Relenting slightly, I again promised that I would do my best, and left her to begin the process of setting the trip in hand. Her travelling companions were Lady Palumbo and Lucia Flecha de Lima. Through Hayat Palumbo, wife of the billionaire property developer Lord (Peter) Palumbo, we had use of a private jet and we flew undetected to Paris on a beautiful May afternoon. I had arranged the hire of a plain Renault Espace people-carrier at Le Bourget Airport, and in that we headed straight for Paris's high-fashion quarter, where Lady Palumbo had arranged for Diana to have a private viewing at Chanel, her favourite French couturier. She spent a couple of hours trying on the latest designs before we went on to some other boutiques in the area. The Princess and her friends spent a few thousand pounds, not very difficult to do in places like that (their purchases included an Hermès tie for me!), and we then headed for the Palumbos' award-winning house in the exclusive district of Neuilly, close to the Bois de Boulogne, where we were to stay.

So far, no one had any idea we were there, and I had taken the decision not to ask for help from local police this time for fear of leaks to the press. Next day, however, through no fault of ours, the secret trip was detected. Once again Diana ate a little, drank a little, shopped a little, and, like many other tourists, took in a few sights. Her visit, give or take the money she and her friends had at their disposal, had been as 'normal' as she could have wished. As for me, I thought we had given the press the slip completely; no one from the British media had an inkling that the Princess was even in Paris.

Diana, who loved to think that she had hoodwinked the media, was like a bird released from its cage. She was almost skipping along as we approached the chic Marius et Jeanette restaurant. As I followed our party in, my heart sank. There, sitting on his scooter outside the restaurant, was one man and his lens – Jean-Paul Dousset, who at that time worked with the notorious paparazzo

Daniel Angeli. The year before, they had together exposed the Duchess of York's love affair with John Bryan with those infamous toe-sucking photographs, shot from cover with a telephoto lens. Luckily, Diana did not spot him and so remained oblivious to the fact that her secret trip was suddenly a secret no longer. As his shutter clicked and clicked, I racked my brains to work out how we had been found out. Then I realised that we hadn't. For in the corner of the restaurant sat the actor Gérard Depardieu, one of France's most celebrated sex symbols, and the reason why Dousset had been waiting outside. The photographer had struck double luck, and doubtless could scarcely believe it.

Depardieu recognised the Princess at once, and like the perfect French gentleman he is, came over immediately to stand by her table, talking of her great beauty and what a privilege it was for France, for Paris and for him personally that she should be there. She was putty in his hands. And we were all putty in the hands of the freelance photographer outside, who must already have been working out exactly how much he was going to make by selling a set of pictures of one of the world's most famous women at a secret assignation with France's sexiest movie star.

I decided to act immediately. Without saying anything to Diana other than a mumbled apology, I slipped out and confronted Dousset. He looked surprised, but was perfectly courteous. We talked around matters for a few moments and then, knowing that he was not a security threat, I offered him a deal. If he kept a discreet distance so that the Princess did not know he was watching her, I would not interfere with his job. In return, he would not release the pictures until we were safely out of France, so that she would not be mobbed and thus have her short break ruined, and her security put at increased risk. He agreed, and was as good as his word.

For the rest of the day Jean-Paul trailed us, but always at a distance and never too close to alert the Princess. True to our deal, he dispatched his pictures only after we had left Paris (and I have to say that his covert photography was very professional). I was happy too. Through my secret deal – for I never told the Princess – I had kept the number of paparazzi to the smallest number possible – one – and Diana was able to enjoy a trouble-free break. Obviously, she would not be too happy when she found out that photographs had been taken, but I reasoned that by the time she discovered what had happened she would be safely back at Kensington Palace, refreshed from her brief interlude in Paris, and my job would have been done.

JULY 1993:
ZIMBABWE

A signed memorandum from Sir Robert Fellowes arrived on Diana's desk, giving her official sanction for the next stage of her solo international career – a trip to Zimbabwe. The last line read simply, 'Her Majesty would be quite content with such a visit taking place.' The Princess was delighted. She knew that the Palace's hands were tied, for if they thwarted her she would leak the story to a friendly journalist, leaving them looking, at best, petty, and at worst, spiteful and vindictive. The Queen, however, wanted a favour in return.

Her Majesty instructed Diana and Charles to put on a public show of unity to honour World War II veterans, to which the Princess agreed with alacrity. Outwardly, as she and her husband arrived together at Liverpool's Anglican Cathedral to mark the fiftieth anniversary of the Allied victory in the Battle of the Atlantic, Diana was in an excellent mood. Prince Charles, at first a little apprehensive, found his estranged wife charming company and soon relaxed. Watching them smiling and laughing together in the blustery wind and rain, some onlookers found it difficult to understand why they had separated, and a number of misguided reporters even wondered in print whether their appearance together marked the start of a reconciliation. Nor could Diana resist the chance to show her husband what he was missing. One veteran of the battle, George Stansfield, dared to put this to the Prince. 'You both look wonderful. It is so nice to see you together again,' he said.

Charles made one of his flippant, off-the-cuff replies, which seemed to me to speak volumes about the true nature of his relationship with Diana. 'It's all done with mirrors,' he said, without looking up at his wife, who was standing a few feet away. His response was perfectly truthful. Deep animosity and mistrust governed their relationship, and on that day they were simply following the Queen's orders in a public show that, like a trick with mirrors, was really only an illusion. Diana put on a perfect performance for the crowds, but she did so for her mother-in-law, thus letting the Queen know that if the Princess got what she wanted, she was happy to repay the favour.

On the surface, 1993 was still going well for Diana, but she was brought down to earth by the news of the death of my colleague and friend, and her former police protection officer, Chief Inspector Graham Smith. She broke down in tears when I told her the news even though it had not been unexpected. A few days earlier, at Diana's insistence, and with the approval of the sister at the Brompton Hospital, we smuggled the desperately ill Graham from the Royal Marsden Hospital and took him for dinner at Diana's favourite restaurant, San Lorenzo. This unusual night out was, however, some time in the planning. Graham was well respected by everyone and Diana thought he would cherish a very private meeting with a few close professional friends. The select few included Diana's mother Frances Shand Kydd, the Queen's Flight captain, David Greenway, Diana's equerry, Wing Commander David Barton, and the entire protection team. The week before, together with Robert Pritchard, who taught music at William's pre-preparatory school, we had composed a musical medley titled 'The Smudger and Supergran' (Graham and Frances's respective nicknames).

The late and wonderful Mara Bernie, owner of San Lorenzo, arranged for a baby grand piano to be placed upstairs in the restaurant, with Robert agreeing to play and provide the music. I can still remember the many expressions on Graham's face and the fun and laughter, tinged with sadness, on that evening Diana had planned. Skeletally thin, Graham was hardly recognisable, but he still maintained his sense of humour to the end, and we all spent hours talking over old times. All of us knew that it would be our last meeting, but nothing was said and it proved to be an evening of joy. At the funeral the Princess was distraught. She hugged Graham's widow, Eunice, and consoled his children, Emma and Alexander. He was only in his mid-fifties when the disease struck him down.

A few weeks later, Diana was back on her official duty abroad, her personal campaign trail, more determined than ever to make her mark. It was a scorching July day when we touched down in Harare, the capital of Zimbabwe, and she embarked on what I believe to be the highest point of her Royal career. Before agreeing to go she had not only sought clearance from HM The Queen, but also from Princess Anne. Until then she had shied away from African tours because, in royal terms, the continent was regarded as Anne's territory. Although both the Palace and the British High Commission in Harare had ruled that this was to be a low-key visit, it was in effect a major set-piece tour that followed the pattern of all previous official visits made by the Waleses prior to the separation. The only difference was that Prince Charles was not included, and thus Diana had the speaking part.

After claims that her trips were a waste of taxpayers' money, Diana had decided to fly out Economy class, although British Airways did ensure that she was 'in the bubble' (on the upper deck of the 747) and that she had three seats to herself so that she could stretch out and sleep. With her private secretary Patrick Jephson, her sister, Lady Sarah McCorquodale, as lady-in-waiting, Geoff Crawford, who had replaced Dickie Arbiter as her press secretary, and me heading up security, Diana had what she called her 'A-team' to support her. In her desire to become a roving ambassador, she was helped by the fact that many heads of state in foreign countries were only too delighted to accommodate her. Indeed, Robert Mugabe, President of Zimbabwe, was completely smitten.

Mugabe had not addressed a press conference to the Western media for years, but after spending half an hour with Diana seemed positively anxious to share the experience with the travelling British press corps. 'She brings a little light into your life, naturally you feel elated,' he told the astonished journalists who had gathered outside Government House. The Princess later confided to me that she had found him a 'frightening little man' who had not stopped sweating throughout their meeting, adding with a mischievous smile, in typical Diana fashion, 'It was rather hot.'

The Princess had been steered away from political controversy by Foreign Office advisers, particularly the issue of land acquisition that was to erupt so bloodily a few years later. Instead she focused on the work of three charities, the International Red Cross, Help the Aged and the Leprosy Mission, of all of which she was patron. She even avoided the controversial subject of AIDS.

Initially, when the trip began the press were more interested in the Spencer sisters' reaction to the recent marriage of their former stepmother, Raine, Countess Spencer, to a French count, Jean-François Pineton de Chambrun. 'As far as I am concerned that woman is ex. She is no longer my stepmother,' Diana said, and then proceeded to giggle with her sister Sarah over newspaper photographs of Raine in her wedding dress. This bitter feud with Raine would end before Diana's death and the two women would become close, united by their mutual love of, and respect for, Diana's late father, Johnny Spencer.

That aside, the Princess's excitement about the job in hand rubbed off on the rest of the team. She led by example, and our sense of kinship and our morale were high. In many respects she was the perfect ambassador for her causes, prepared to endure all that the Third World had to offer, focused on what she was there to achieve. Nevertheless, she did have her off moments, although they were usually over fairly quickly.

One evening, during a particularly overcrowded reception in Harare, she became increasingly frustrated, as it seemed that the entire population of Zimbabwe had turned up to shake her hand. It irritated her, too, that the Rat Pack had managed to buy tickets for the event, and in particular that her sister, Lady Sarah, was having a sneaky cigarette with them. By the time I freed her from the mêlée she was fuming, particularly at the unfortunate Patrick Jephson, who bore the brunt of her anger. 'I'm very unhappy,' she told him, loudly enough for the High Commissioner and his wife to hear. And with that she retired.

Patrick was upset. Had all his planning gone awry? What would the Princess's mood be like in the morning? Listening to him airing his concerns, I decided that the poor man needed a drink. There was another big day ahead of us all tomorrow, and he needed to wind down if he was going to get a wink of sleep. Diana, as Patrick had predicted, was in a foul mood with all of us, including Lady Sarah, the following day. During these moments of schoolgirl petulance there was nothing one could do but meet her head-on. That evening, at my suggestion, after the official engagements for the day were over and the Princess had gone to bed, the entire Royal party gathered downstairs in the High Commission around the grand piano. After I had led an enthusiastic sing-song, Diana descended the stairs, ostensibly to complain about the noise.

In reality she was feeling left out. Within a few minutes she was joining in with the rest of us, and the tension that had threatened to spoil the tour immediately disappeared.

My enduring memory of the visit is an almost biblical scene. The Princess flew deep into the African bush, to the Mazerera Red Cross feeding centre. There, standing by a huge iron cooking pot, she served the children from the ancient Karanga tribe, one by one. I watched one hungry little boy hold up his bowl to this beautiful lady. Four-year-old Tsungai Hove had walked seven miles through the heat and dust to the feeding centre. As his turn came to collect his only daily meal he boldly pushed the bowl towards her like an African Oliver Twist. Diana looked down and smiled at him, and the shy smile he gave her in return was almost heart-rending. She relished the part she was playing, ladling huge portions of bean stew from the cooking pot into the bowls of the patient children. The press lapped up the photo opportunity and one British newspaper ran the headline the next day, 'Dinner Lady – Diana Serves Up Royal Treat for Hungry Children'.

Yet the experience had troubled the Princess. She was close to tears as we flew back to Harare because she knew that she was returning to comfort and plenty, while these poor, hungry children faced a trek of many miles back to their mud-hut homes in the drought-ridden countryside.

Those who believe that Diana's work was nothing more than a series of photo opportunities in glamorous locations around the world should have seen this drained, exhausted woman sitting in the back of a helicopter that day and heard her speak of the heartbreaking scenes she had just witnessed.

AUGUST 1993:
DISNEY WORLD, FLORIDA,
USA AND LYFORD CAY,
NEW PROVIDENCE
ISLAND, BAHAMAS

My recce of Walt Disney World a few weeks earlier had been inestimable. I advised Diana in my briefing memo that the fact that Disney is spread over 43 square miles was to our advantage in our habitual battle to outwit the media because, unlike any other theme park, it has a VIP package which uses reserved routes to rides and attractions along a predetermined course. A network of restricted paths and 392,040 square feet of tunnels, not accessible to the public, enabled special guests literally to pop up at the front of queues and go straight on to a ride without anyone elsewhere in the park knowing which attraction they were on.

Conscious of Diana's fear of being criticised for using her royal status to secure star treatment, my memo, dated 2 August 1993, reassured her because I had recommended the VIP package for security reasons: 'At this time of the year up to 1 million people could be using the complex. Many rides and attractions will have queues of 2 to 3 hours' waiting. The VIP method is not queue-jumping, and will not be seen by others so to be.' The note was returned with a huge tick from her pen through that section.

But something was nagging me about this trip. It came at a time when the Princess, understandably, wanted to rid herself of the trappings of royalty. As a result, she was inevitably beginning to regard her police protection as another constant reminder that although she was now distanced from the Royal Family because of her separation from Prince Charles, she was still enveloped by the system. The trip also took place at a critical point in her uncompromising propaganda war against her husband. With her usual sure instinct for these things, she knew that photographs of her and the boys enjoying the sort of holiday experienced by millions of ordinary people would be seen as a refreshing change, while Charles would once again be unfairly portrayed as a dreary, out-of-touch and, above all, absent father. It was too good a photo opportunity for Diana to pass over.

From the moment Sid Bass, a senior Disney executive, had invited Diana and the boys, assuring them of a minimum of fuss, I had felt that she was acting strangely about this trip. I sensed that she was not being completely straight with me. As I have said, it is standard protection practice, and essential for security, to carry out a reconnaissance ahead of any visit, official or private, planned by members of the Royal Family. As well as the two-day stopover at Disney's Florida complex in Orlando, she proposed to spend the rest of the week at the family holiday home of her friend Kate Menzies at Lyford Cay in the Bahamas, a short flight from Florida. As I was preparing to leave on the reconnaissance, however, the Princess told me out of the blue that she did not think that it was necessary. I was a little taken aback – she knew the rules as well as I did.

'I really don't think there is any need for you to go and check this one. You must stop wasting the taxpayers' money,' she said.

I looked at her quizzically, before answering, 'Ma'am, with the greatest respect, you know the police procedures. The security arrangements for any visit made by you and your sons is my call.' Then I added, only half-jokingly, 'And since when have you been worried about spending taxpayers' money?'

In retrospect, this was perhaps a little blunt, or even disrespectful, but we were going through one of our difficult periods, and I was not in the mood to be told how to do my job.

Diana did not challenge my decision again. I explained that the Menzies's own villa was not really big enough to accommodate the police team too. It would have been a tight squeeze anyway as it was small by comparison to the others nearby, many of which were empty as it was low season. Fortunately, a very helpful woman at the Lyford Cay residential offices had found me a property owned by a Canadian called Tom Wyman, who was prepared to rent his house, with its exclusive beach frontage (and which just happened to be about twice the size of Diana's holiday accommodation), to us for the reduced off-season price of £3,000 ($5,300) for the week.

'Do you know how much it cost, and who is footing the bill? Ken, this cannot be right,' Diana raged. 'Who is paying for this?'

Equally angry, I hit back. 'Where do you think the money is coming from, Ma'am? The Metropolitan Police Force, of course.'

'So I was right. The taxpayer is paying for you again. It's all too much.'

'With the greatest respect, Ma'am, we have already covered this,' I replied, doing my best not to lose my temper. In fact I was so perturbed that I asked her directly if she was keeping something from me. Again she refused to talk about it, but intuition told me that something was up. Although she wanted her sons to have a good holiday, I suspected that she was planning to use this trip with them to hit back at the Prince as the state of their relationship continued to deteriorate, fuelled by a concerted PR offensive in the press. That was beyond my remit, however, and there was in any case very little

I could do to stop her pursuing that ultimately self-destructive war except – as usual – advise caution.

On the advance security review at Orlando one of my first tasks was to address senior Disney security managers, so that between us we could ensure that Diana and her sons would be safe during their stay. Most of the professionals employed by Disney to police their resort were former state security officers or FBI agents. They were great guys – utterly professional, and convinced that if they could deal with the visit of a US President and Michael Jackson, then looking after 'Lady Di', as they called her, would be 'a piece of cake'. I was not so sure, however.

Diana's uncharacteristic attitude to the reconnaissance puzzled me, and I still had that nagging feeling of doubt about her motives. Although she had assured me that, apart from her and the boys, and Kate Menzies, only I knew about the private holiday, I had a hunch that she had released the information about her trip to the British press via a sympathetic reporter. I therefore asked one of Disney's senior security chiefs if it would be possible to run a name check through the company's computer. Within seconds the name Richard Kay flashed up on the screen.

The *Daily Mail* journalist was booked to arrive at the Grand Floridian hotel on exactly the same day as Diana; even more significantly, the booking had been made on the very day that the Princess had told me of her wish to go to Florida. My hunch had proved correct, and I now understood why Diana had been acting so strangely. It was clear that she had personally tipped Kay off, and I was reasonably certain that he would have passed on the information, at her behest, to the rest of the Royal Rat Pack. She had wanted to stop my advance security check because she was worried that I might discover what she was planning. She had been right to be concerned, but at least I now knew what I was dealing with. Despite my disappointment at this underhand behaviour I still had a job to do.

Upon arrival we were met by an army of Disney characters: Mickey Mouse, Pluto, and Sleeping Beauty. Prince Harry, excitable at the best of times, was off the scale, in his element. The wonderful Disney executive Jayne Lee Kear, the chief protocol officer who planned all the visits of VIPs, was determined to make this a visit the Royal children would never forget. Jayne (who sadly passed away in 2010) was a true pro, on top of every detail. She arranged that upon arrival Diana, Harry and William would be secreted away for a magical evening 'Float Boat ride' on the lake adjacent to our hotel. I asked her if the actress playing the character Sleeping Beauty could accompany us and a besotted Harry, aged eight, sat holding her hand for almost the entire evening – he certainly knew how to play Prince Charming, even then. We tied up on a nearby island and watched the magnificent fireworks – far away from the madness and crowds of Disney – and Diana described the evening as truly 'magical'.

On our first full day the Princes experienced the Disney secret tunnels. Harry loved the idea that he was getting special 'secret' treatment. The tunnels, known as the 'Disney utilidor system', were in fact, I found out later, not actually underground. The 'basement' level of the park is actually at ground level, and the part of the park visitors experience is the second floor. Cast members access the utilidor system via staircases positioned at key areas in the park. This in itself was an adventure, with Harry insistent that we hit the Space Mountain ride first. Our assigned US State Department agent was the irrepressible Dave Benson, who was the usual jovial character and guaranteed Harry as many rides as he wanted on Space Mountain. We walked straight on to the boarding platform of Space Mountain, the ultimate queue-jump of the number one attraction for thrill-seekers, with an average queuing time of around forty-five minutes. Clearly advance signals had been sent, and Harry clambered into the leading capsule, only to be hauled out by William, who wanted to be in the front. A battle royal ensued between the then second and third in line to the throne until Diana intervened and threatened a return to the hotel and scrapping all rides for the day unless they stopped fighting.

With Sergeant Dave Sharp and I each with one of the boys, our journey into space began. Diana roared with laughter throughout the entire 'flight' through fright. Harry loved it, though William was keen to abandon the capsule after the first flight. After the first flight Diana decided not to return but Harry was a glutton for punishment and booked a second, third, and fourth flight until dragged off forcibly by Diana and me. We had lunch at the Brown Derby to witness the gargantuan portions of food before we headed off for more rides. This time it was William's turn to pick the next ride. A keen swimmer, he ruled that we should head for the wave machine. This was a potential nightmare for security. I instructed Dave Sharp and Dave Benson to don their swimming trunks. For the next thirty minutes William and Harry were continuously being washed ashore, followed by Sharp and Benson – Diana and I from our vantage point watched them play.

Each day took a similar format, to include – in no specific order – the log flume again. The sheer fun of this meant return rides, with access to it from service access points denied to the general public. We were very lucky and Diana kept reminding her sons of their good fortune. One evening, again organised by Disney's Jayne Lee Kear, we went to *The Hoop-Dee-Doo Musical Revue* – a Wild West audience-participation show at Fort Wilderness, reached via a float boat from another nearby island. We arrived and sat in a packed auditorium, a huge barn fitted out for stage and musical numbers; there were even buckets of food for the table to share. The room went dark and the announcer told us to 'Giddy-up, pardner, and get ready for a rootin' tootin' good time!' The show began with a man on stage with a lasso asking for an assistant. William, not to be outshone by his brother, and without permission from his mother, ran forward

– a complete surprise, totally unrehearsed – and clambered on stage to a loud applause. There, standing at one end of the stage, he was repeatedly lassoed.

Inevitably, Harry wanted some of the action but was grabbed by his mother. William returned with the lasso, and of course Harry wanted it. In order to maintain peace, Dave Sharp was dispatched to find another. With an endless supply of ice-cold fizzy drinks and buckets of deep-fried chicken, this was a great night. After it, dressed in full Western attire, we walked to our awaiting boat to take us back to the hotel.

'Indiana Jones and the Temple of Doom' was the perfect set location for William and Harry the next day. Armed with lassos they were again given 'access all areas' and played the part of Indiana Jones, and set the rolling stone free.

Every day was Christmas Day – another set that only Disney could recreate. 'The Runaway Train' and the waterslide were repeat rides for the not faint-hearted Princes; Diana was content with one ride and off, though her enthusiasm seemed never to diminish.

Each morning I met with Diana in her suite to discuss the day's events. While the Princes were running on adrenalin, she had 'done Disney!' although she was still in good humour. She enquired about my American colleague Dave Benson, as said, a long-time US State Department official who had accompanied King of Pop Michael Jackson on his visit to Disney. 'Would he join us for a coffee?' – 'Sure,' I replied, and called Benson via my radio.

Within minutes he arrived at her suite, where William and Harry were yet again in a scrap, fighting with life-size Disney creature toys. Benson arrived eating a huge double hamburger, with all the gooey trimmings. Diana greeted him at the door with an outstretched hand. Benson, with burger in mouth, and somewhat embarrassed, took one last bite in a panic, and offered his right hand. The last bite, however, catapulted the mayonnaise filling and ketchup three feet into Diana's apartment to land on the pure white, deep-pile carpet by her feet.

Diana arched her back, and gave one of her unique laughs. She thought this was very funny. 'No one has ever knowingly spat a burger at me before, Mr Benson,' she told him. William and Harry, upon hearing the laughter, ran from within the apartment and found the whole incident hilarious – they didn't care about the damage, but decided that they too wanted one of the gooey burgers.

Benson, embarrassed, excused himself and asked to use the house phone. Within moments the hotel fixer appeared with a box of tools, cutting and removing the ketchup-stained carpet piece, and gluing a new one in place – all within the space of five minutes of Benson's burger hitting the deck. Diana loved the incident and talked about it for weeks.

With breakfasts taken in the hotel restaurant, William and Harry remained transfixed on the size of portions other guests ate.

'What's that bread with holes in it, Mummy? Can we have some?'

'No, it's a waffle with honey,' came Diana's response. She was definitely over Disney by now.

'But Papa says honey is good for you,' William responded, knowing he was chancing it.

'Shut up, William! Papa would go ballistic if he saw this,' Diana replied.

***

Next day, confident that everything was under control at Walt Disney World, I flew to Nassau in the Bahamas to reconnoitre the second phase of the proposed holiday. Sergeant Glen Roy of the Bahamas Police Department, who drove me to Lyford Cay to check the arrangements at Casuarina Beach, the house belonging to the Menzies family, where the Princess and her party were to stay, met me there. It turned out to be set in a development that afforded a great deal of privacy, being part of a huge luxury complex, privately policed and spotlessly maintained. The house itself had a magnificent swimming pool, the beach was less than fifty yards away and there was an added bonus at that time of the year, for despite the temperatures nudging 35°C (95°F), this was low season, with very few people around.

Diana would be accompanied by her girlfriends, Kate Menzies and Catherine Soames, and otherwise by only one member of staff, the boys' nanny, Olga Powell. William and Harry would have friends with them. William's pal was Andrew Charlton and Harry had Catherine Soames's son, also called Harry, as a playmate. My team consisted of Trevor Bettles, 'Jack' Tarr, Dave Sharp and night-duty officer PC Knights.

Deep down, I was still unhappy about Diana's decision to tip off the media about the visit. Yet much to her private irritation, the VIP system at Disney of driving along the restricted routes, or walking along the labyrinth of underground walkways, meant that for most of the time we were out of sight. So far not one photograph had appeared in the press. Some journalists had even resorted to placing an advertisement in the local newspaper, asking any tourist who had taken a photograph of the Princess and her sons to call them.

So far so good – except that, mysteriously, the press kept arriving in roughly the right place, albeit usually a few minutes too late. But whatever the Princess's motives (which, to be fair, were above all else to ensure that her sons had a terrific holiday), William and Harry were in their element. This in turn could be relied upon to make their mother happy. I returned to my suite that evening convinced that the tide was turning, and that in a few days Diana would be her usual fun-loving self.

My hopes that the Princess's mood would improve were to be dashed, however, when she appeared the next morning in the foulest of moods. Not even her sons' happiness could shake her out of it. She had taken another call from her lawyer, which had driven home to her the fact that, even in the Florida sunshine, she could not escape the pressures arising from her separation from Prince Charles. From her fulminating it was clear that she wanted to strike back at her husband, but I sensed that the security operation had been too good and she had failed in the PR coup she had tried secretly to orchestrate.

Catherine Soames and Kate Menzies were on this trip. My heart sank even further when, prior to our departure for Nassau that day, I received information that the media were aware of our destination. At the very least it meant that I had drastically to rethink my security plans. I immediately redeployed Dave Sharp to travel ahead of us and establish a daily patrol around Lyford Cay, which proved a politic move. Dave, with the help of a private security company employed by the property owners, detained two men who claimed to be 'looking for the Royal party', having read about the Princess's impending arrival in a local newspaper. I also increased the night mobile patrols by the Bahamas Police, and had them maintain a daily shore-side patrol to prevent unauthorised landings. Despite the arrest of the two trespassers, I was confident that the Princess would be safe, and told her so.

When Diana complained about the cramped arrangements at Nassau, despite the fact I had fully briefed her before her arrival after I checked it out on the recce, I explained again that I had rented another house nearby to afford her and her friends greater privacy. I had engaged night patrols too and a local police presence outside. Lastly, I explained that while this was not a perfect security arrangement, I was prepared to compromise, and for this she seemed genuinely grateful. My best-laid plans backfired, however. The inevitable subject of cost came up – I urged her not to discuss the burden on the British taxpayer, discussions that were often on the agenda, but ones she was inevitably unable to justify since her expenses for dresses ahead of official foreign visits were huge.

Arriving in Nassau we had a short car journey from the airport to Lyford Cay. It was a beautiful day, with everyone happy at the prospect of yet another luxury holiday location. The house of Menzies was most welcoming, with the boys stripped of their clothing and into swimming trunks and the pool. I gave Diana a map of our house, which was less than a quarter of a mile away. Cycles were available for the boys and they were soon keen to see where we were. The boys' playtime in the pool proved short-lived, and immediately they scrambled on to the bikes and came with us to the house designated for security, which had a white sand beach frontage. William and Harry rode straight to the beach, and then began a close inspection of the interior. Having made their assessments, with my colleague Trevor Bettles they rode back to the Menzies's house.

Within thirty minutes Diana arrived by bike.

'William says your house is bigger than ours,' she announced, a little disgruntled.

'That's true, Ma'am,' I replied, 'for the reasons I explained to you earlier,' I added, standing my ground.

She surveyed the house and was clearly miffed that her police details had better accommodation, but said nothing.

During the time at Lyford Cay I would visit Diana three times a day. Apart from the poolside, there was little other activity. We had excellent radio communication, and discreet patrols. Thankfully, Lyford Cay was almost deserted, as it was low season, a fact that helped us enormously. But after two days the press finally arrived, anchored two hundred yards from the beachfront of our house. They assumed that the Princess was there – justifiably, because William and Harry spent most of their day with us, something that annoyed Diana. We fed the press the line that she was with us, but preferred to use the pool out of sight and that a press call was unlikely. Diana really didn't know how to handle this one – I couldn't be criticised for not revealing her location because occasionally we, the police, were accused of informing some media outlets. Meanwhile her relationship with Catherine Soames and Katie Menzies was also showing signs of strain – Diana was clearly preoccupied with her future. It was difficult to explain the continued wish of her two sons to be with us constantly, and her foul mood led to her criticising me personally, and also my team.

I had been on duty for fourteen days without a break, and in the circumstances I thought it best to step back from the situation and hope that this would lessen the tension. Seething myself, I left before I said something I might have regretted. The dialogue between us was waning fast. For me, it had reached a point where talking to the Princess was really a question of stating the bare essentials, and stopping at that. Strange as it may seem now, I think that part of the problem was that the press had not tracked her down (for which I was to some extent responsible); she was spoiling for a high-profile confrontation with them, but perhaps more significantly she was also desperate for the publicity.

On one occasion when the press were bobbing about aimlessly offshore in their chartered boat, hoping to get a photograph of Diana or the Princes, she actually walked outside the house and began striding up and down the beach looking out to sea. Unfortunately, the press had focused on our large 'police house', and because I was sitting outside it with Dave Sharp, they assumed that it must be where the Princess was staying. Even more unfortunately, the two boys then came over and rushed on to the beach and into the water for a swim, which was all the confirmation the media needed. Pictures of our 'police house' were published in all the British national newspapers with captions saying that it was Diana's 'holiday home in paradise' (something which, inevitably, led to me having to justify the cost to senior management in my department).

Out on their boat the hacks took a few pictures of the boys. I contacted the local police chief and took a launch out to the press boat, the aptly named *No Limit*, to ask them to move away and leave Diana and her party in peace. It was a very light-hearted affair. After a few jokey comments I said that since they had got their photographs, they could move on, and perhaps go fishing. They agreed. I made one mistake, however, while talking to Arthur Edwards, *The Sun*'s royal photographer. After years of following Diana around the world Arthur, a perceptive man, knew instinctively that something was wrong, probably from my demeanour.

'How's Ma'am?' he asked.

It was wrong of me to do so, but I was still frustrated at Diana's behaviour towards me. In reply, I shrugged my shoulders and gave a rueful grin, as though to suggest that she needed a good talking-to. It was harmless enough, but it was a moment that came back to haunt me. After Diana returned to Britain, she got wind of what had happened and suggested that I had spoken indiscreetly to a member of the press. Naturally, this led to another sticky conversation between the Princess and me.

By the end of the holiday storm clouds were gathering both literally and metaphorically. The Princess had not had a good time, and she was at odds with everyone. It was clear that she was finding the pressure arising from her separation and her new life difficult to cope with, even on holiday with friends. She was behaving increasingly erratically, and before we left for the flight back to Britain she made one last concerted effort to be photographed, which for security reasons I thwarted. She was not pleased.

'I'll do what I want. I think it's so unfair that I can't do what I want, I just want to be normal. God, nobody ever understands me!' she wailed, like a petulant child.

After years of operating on her wavelength, I was now beginning to think that perhaps she had a point and that no one did understand her – not even the Princess herself. I no longer felt I could offer her the level of protection on which my department prided itself. I had long begun to suspect her motives, and felt that I no longer understood what her objective was – I seriously doubted whether she knew, either. There was no question now that it was only a matter of time before we parted company.

Sad as I was at the thought of leaving her service after nearly eight years, if the Princess no longer felt that she could be completely open and honest with me in my professional capacity, I could not offer her the level of protection on which my department rightly insists. I think that Diana also had mixed feelings about the course she was following, but deep down she believed that if she was to break free of the trappings of royalty that so irked and hampered her, then she would have to rescind her police protection.

It was to prove a high-risk strategy.

SEPTEMBER 1997:
HER FINAL JOURNEY

A solemn calm fell over Central London on 6 September 1997 as millions took to the streets to pay their respects, lining the route along which the Princess's coffin would be borne, on a gun carriage, from Kensington Palace to Westminster Abbey. After thirty-six years, her Camelot was in ruins and the magic, I was sure, would never return.

As the pallbearers – Welsh Guardsmen, as was fitting – struggled with her lead-lined coffin, it seemed almost inconceivable that the radiant young woman who had once charmed the world was lying silently within it, completely at peace for perhaps the only time in her all too short life. It was a brilliant life, brutally snuffed out by a combination of high spirits, stupidity and human error. That her death had been avoidable made me angry, yet it also numbed me inside, as it had most of the rest of the world.

The organ resounded to William Harris's *Prelude*; the bells rang out hollowly as the great and the good – from princes and prime ministers to so-called 'ordinary' people – arrived to pay their last respects to an extraordinary person. Princes William and Harry, whom I had once guarded before I became Diana's own personal protection officer, showed courage beyond their years. Now, with their mother gone, they faced the greatest test of their lives. In their dark suits, focused in their grief, they walked behind her coffin. On the flag-draped coffin a handwritten card lay among a cloud of lilies. On it, the single word 'Mummy' seemed to say everything.

Ahead of the funeral I had stolen a solitary moment with the Princess, saying my own silent farewell to her as she lay in the Chapel Royal, St James's Palace. It was cold. She lay at one end of the chapel in her coffin, her personal standard – the standard of the Princess of Wales – draped over it. I murmured a prayer, and talked out loud about some of the things we had done, some of the amazing places we had visited and extraordinary people we had spent time with. I remembered our last meeting. For once she did not answer me, so often with laughter bubbling near the surface. I shed no tears, nor do I think she would have expected me to, but like millions around the world I was moved by the loss of someone who had, as she had so earnestly wished, 'made a difference'.

As I walked to the Abbey from Buckingham Palace on the day of the funeral to assist with the security operation, my final engagement with the Princess – with the roads closed, there was no other way of getting there – the scent of flowers was heavy on the air. Diana's coffin had been moved from the Chapel Royal, where she had lain, to Kensington Palace at some time the previous evening. Everywhere her famous face peered out from the thousands of newspaper and magazine special editions being sold on the streets to mark the historic event.

The nation had come to a complete halt as television coverage poured into millions of homes; around the world, more than 2 billion people sat and watched an event that many had believed they themselves would not live to see. At variance with the sombre mood, the mourners, many in jeans and T-shirts, were bathed in warm sunshine. The muffled sound of the bells of Westminster Abbey, which tolled throughout the procession, carried mournfully over the near-silent capital.

The Duke of Edinburgh, and Diana's brother Earl Spencer joined the Prince of Wales, along with his two sons, as they walked the procession route behind the coffin. Behind them were 500 selected mourners; charity workers, nurses, artists, people from all walks of life representing organisations or causes that the Princess had held dear to her heart. The tension was palpable. As the gun-carriage passed on to the Mall, past Buckingham Palace, the Queen, who had been publicly attacked for her cool response since the death of the Princess, led other members of the Royal Family, who, standing in front of the Palace, all bowed as it passed. Above them, from the flagstaff on the Palace roof, the Union Flag fluttered at half-mast. The Queen had finally relented, after yet more criticism in the days before the funeral, and given the order for the flag to be flown thus. It was the first time in history that it had done so for the death of anyone other than a monarch.

There were 1,900 invited guests within the spectacular Gothic interior of the Abbey. The sun streamed through its great windows. At just after ten o'clock the VIPs began to arrive. Shepherding them to their seats was like a military exercise, and my team had to be alert, not least because some of the world's leading terrorist targets were gathered within this august medieval structure. America's First Lady, Hillary Clinton – whose husband, President Bill Clinton, was one of countless world leaders who, only hours after her death, had publicly praised Diana and her life's work – examined the tributes of flowers near the entrance as she walked past. Two former prime ministers, Baroness Thatcher and John Major, joined Prime Minister Tony Blair and his wife, Cherie, on the long walk from the West Door to their seats in the Abbey.

Mohamed Al-Fayed entered shortly after the Spencer family. My heart went out to them all, especially Diana's mother, Frances Shand Kydd. Within the next few minutes the Royal Family arrived. Lastly, at 10.50am, came the Queen, the Queen Mother and Prince Edward. In deep silence they took their places near the altar, directly across the aisle from the Spencer family. Then, as the bells of Big Ben tolled eleven, the procession reached the West Door. Eight Welsh Guardsmen, faces taut with strain, carried the quarter-ton coffin on their shoulders as they slow-marched the length of the nave. A profound hush fell over the Abbey. Prince Harry broke down when the coffin passed. As the tears flowed down his small face, his father pulled him closer and his brother William laid a comforting hand on his shoulder.

The bitterness between the House of Spencer and the House of Windsor that had come to the fore in the days since the Princess's fatal accident in Paris had given the national press something to write about, in a vain bid to try to divert the public's attention away from the media's involvement in the killing of their Princess. Yet such accusations were as pointless as they were wrong. The paparazzi may irritate like flies, but they don't kill. Diana's death, I kept thinking, was senseless. (As the world knows, in the early hours of 31 August 1997, a black Mercedes carrying the Princess and Dodi Al-Fayed had crashed at high speed in the Alma Tunnel in Paris, killing the driver, Henri Paul – a Fayed employee – and Dodi and Diana; only their bodyguard, Trevor Rees-Jones, survived, though terribly injured.)

The 'Libera Me' from Verdi's *Requiem* – reminding me of our magical evening with Pavarotti in Verona – shook my resolve; not the soon-to-be-knighted Elton John's specially written adaptation of 'Candle In The Wind', with its tear-jerking first line, 'Goodbye, England's rose', not even Diana's favourite hymn, 'I Vow To Thee, My Country', which had been sung at her wedding. It was Verdi. Contrary to popular opinion, the Princess had loved classical music, a passion we both shared. As the 'Libera Mc' pierced the air and our souls, I felt the emotion of that piece engulf the Abbey, moving every one of the throng of mourners. Prince Charles looked as though he was being torn apart as the music swelled and dwindled, and finally died away.

Then, just as the congregation was united in grief, Lord Spencer unleashed an entirely unexpected verbal assault, his words thrusting like a rapier into the Prince's heart. No one, other than Charles Spencer, knew what was coming as he composed himself before delivering a five-minute eulogy that electrified the world. It was a piece of pure theatre, but it was also from the heart.

He took no prisoners. Earl Spencer lashed out at the Royal Family for their behaviour towards his beloved sister, and savaged the press for hounding her to her death. Throughout the mauling the Queen bowed her head as her godson fired salvo after salvo, talking directly to his dead sister. 'There is a temptation to rush to canonise your memory. There is no need to do so: you stand tall enough as a human being of unique qualities not to need to be seen as a saint,' he said. Nor, he added, was there any need for royal titles – a barbed reference to the Queen's petty decision to remove from the Princess the courtesy title of 'Her Royal Highness' as one of the conditions of her lucrative £17 million ($25.5 million) divorce deal. He said bluntly that his sister had possessed 'natural nobility', adding, cuttingly, that she transcended class and had proved in the last year of her life that 'she needed no royal title to continue to generate her particular brand of magic'. Never before, in forty-five years on the throne of Britain, had Queen Elizabeth II been publicly and savagely admonished by one of her subjects. Yet, ever the professional, she did not flinch.

What happened next was extraordinary, and something that only those inside the Abbey that day will ever fully appreciate. Lord Spencer's loving yet devastating address was followed by a stunned silence. Then a sound like a distant shower of rain swept into the Abbey, seeping in through the walls, rolling on and on. It poured towards us like a wave, gradually reaching a crescendo. At first I was not sure what it was; indeed, with security on my mind, I was momentarily troubled by it. It took me a couple of seconds to realise that it was the sound of people clapping. The massive crowds outside had heard Spencer's address on the loudspeakers and had reacted with impromptu applause; as the sound filtered in, the vast majority of the people inside the Abbey joined in. People don't clap at funerals but Diana was as different in death as she had been in life, and they did at hers. The Earl had spoken the plain truth as he saw it, and the people respected him for his courage as well as for the tribute he had paid his sister. William and Harry joined in the applause; so too, generously, did Prince Charles. The Queen, the Duke of Edinburgh, and the Queen Mother sat unmoving in stony-faced silence.

The service ended with the contemporary British composer Sir John Tavener's 'Alleluia'. I found it uplifting and at that moment my numbness lifted. Yes, our Princess was gone, but I knew that her spirit of compassion would live on and that her life's work would not be forgotten.

Outside in the sunshine were millions of people, apparently united in grief. Though it may seem harsh or cynical, I felt that there was something spurious about the mass mourning that followed her death and attended her funeral. True, most people had loved her, but they had not known her. They loved the media image; they loved the glamour, the humanity, the sympathetic tears, but they had little idea of the real Diana. Truly they loved her because of what they had read or seen or heard about her. What they were mourning was an image moulded by the media and by the Princess herself from her years in the public eye. Now the press was being vilified. Yet surely, if the newspapers and photographers were to blame, in part, for her death, then the people must also share some of that blame? After all, they had bought the newspapers, pored over the magazines, read the books, and sat glued to the television and radio coverage.

By another irony, some of them were clutching special Diana editions as they abused photographers who had gathered to record the funeral. As I looked at the hordes of people who had stood for hours to share this day and express their sorrow, I felt vaguely disturbed by it all. Despite her ego, her concern for her image, Diana would not really have wanted this.

Everywhere there were flowers, from single buds picked that morning to enormous bouquets – 'floral tributes', as florists (and undertakers) call them. She liked flowers; she would have liked the people's thoughtful tributes. At Kensington Palace, where I had spent so many happy years, there had been a sea of flowers. They had begun arriving on the morning of the day she died, and now there was a field of them – literally, tons of flowers – outside the gates. The smell of them was almost overpowering. Luckily, someone had the good sense to have them removed before they began to fade and rot, but still they kept coming.

Once the service was over, Diana began her final journey. Her coffin was placed in a black hearse and driven the 75 miles north of London to Althorp, where she was to be buried in the presence of her family at the Spencer family ancestral estate. The limousine drove slowly through London with streets lined with people, each wanting to say a final goodbye. They threw flowers on the roof, on the bonnet, on the bumper. Sometimes the driver had to turn on the windscreen wipers in order to see the way ahead. When the hearse joined the motorway north more police outriders joined it. On the opposite side of the motorway the cars stopped and drivers got out, bowed their heads or waved at Diana one last time.

The Princess should have been laid to rest in the Spencer family tomb in the church of St Mary the Virgin that serves the village of Great Brington, but in order to prevent it becoming a place of pilgrimage the Spencer family chose a small wooded island on the estate lake to be Diana's final resting place. Flowers were heaped at the black, ironwork lattice of Althorp's main gates and stacked along the stone estate walls for a hundred yards in each direction. The hearse arrived, flanked by police outriders. There was a loud applause from those waiting as the escort circled and then swept back towards London while the hearse continued alone. As the gates closed behind her for a final time, still watched by billions around the world on television, Diana disappeared into the distance: she was home at last. At dusk, she was buried in a private ceremony on an island in the Oval, the beautiful ornamental lake in the park to the northwest of Althorp House surrounded by an arboretum, which includes oaks planted by Diana herself, her two sons and other members of the Royal Family. The tranquil setting for Diana's final resting place is overlooked by a temple brought there in the mid-nineteenth century by the fifth Earl Spencer from the gardens of Admiralty House in London. Prince Charles, the Princes William and Harry, Diana's brother, Charles, Earl Spencer, and sisters, Lady Sarah McCorquodale and Lady Jane Fellowes, her mother, Frances Shand Kydd (Diana's best friend), and a clergyman were the only ones present. In her hands Diana clasped a rosary, which she had once received as a gift from Mother Teresa.

England's rose was finally at peace.

She may have passed, but she certainly made the world sit up and take notice in the time she had on earth. Diana was a magical person, a woman of great character, strength, generosity and determination, but she had needed to be channelled, her qualities guided in the right direction. Her self-pity and sometimes explosive mood swings needed to be tempered.

***

During Diana's life I had met on numerous occasions her brother Charles. In my view he was forever protecting her best interests, and has been in some sections of the press very wrongly represented on matters that involved his sister. I had been present on Necker Island when he accompanied her there with his other sister, Jane, and his mother, Frances. It was an extremely happy and loving time for them all. The very negative media reporting about his reluctance to give Diana a place to live on the Althorp Estate was simply not true. Unreasonable police recommendations on the height of the perimeter wall were the real reason Diana herself pulled out so as not to inconvenience her brother. She visited him many times at his house on the estate, 'The Falconry', before he moved into the main house.

In 2001 Earl Spencer, with whom I had kept in contact after Diana's death, invited me to lunch at Althorp. Afterwards, we walked to the lake and looked out to the island where the Princess is buried. It is a truism to say that someone's death tends to make us view that person through rose-tinted glasses. Certainly I remembered Diana like that for a while, and so too, I'm sure, did almost everybody. But she was certainly no saint, as her brother had publicly insisted. She would have laughed her infectious laugh out loud at the very thought of it.

Charles Spencer had said in his eulogy that Diana was every inch a real woman, not some iconised image. True, she loved her image, and even hated it when she was not in the newspapers, or when a picture showed what she thought of as her bad side. In fact, she was as vain as are most of us, someone who really cared about what she looked like, and how she appeared to other people. She could laugh at herself, though, something that perhaps showed that, at heart, she had as much humility as vanity. Which is why, in the end, she would not have wanted millions of people – especially the 'ordinary people' with whom she empathised so much – to mourn for her.

Diana's life was all too short. She had, however, made the very best of her time on this planet. She devoted much of her energy to the care of the sick and to children, and her genuine warmth and kindness found many outlets. She travelled hundreds of thousands of miles enhancing the lives of all those who came into contact with her. She was someone who flew in the face of convention; someone whose very presence could light up a room filled with people close to death; someone who just by touching a man dying of AIDS could completely change our attitude to that terrible disease. Diana was never one to go by the rule book, always leading from the heart, rarely the head. She tackled suffering head-on. It was something she drummed into her sons, too. She wanted them to connect with people, to appreciate their insecurities and personal distress. The work they are doing now in the charitable sector is a credit to her – they are part of her lasting legacy.

But Diana was much more than a charitable entrepreneur or a celebrity. She was loved because she gave her love unconditionally; she was warm, not distant, and embraced those so many others had shunned. She was a true free spirit who did what her heart told her to do.

Now, on that tiny island, Diana lies silent and at peace. Her life's journey ended needlessly, her infectious laughter silenced for ever. I shared so much with her and travelled so far around the world with her during the years when I served her. In an age when so-called stars seemed to become more ordinary, Diana shone. Life goes on, I thought, as I looked across to her island grave. I was certain, however, it would never again sparkle so brightly. In quiet moments on our travels together Diana would often say, 'Life is just a journey.' Hers, however, was a remarkable one, and I am truly honoured to have travelled at least part of the way with her.